Sommaire

articles

Recensions

JAPANESE ECONOMIC PHILOSOPHY: AN INTRODUCTION

GILLES CAMPAGNOLO*

How economic philosophy developed in Eastern Asia is an issue that the *Revue de philosophie économique/Review of Economic Philosophy* has set to tackle. We open the debate with this first thematic issue on Japanese economic philosophy. A second volume will address China and neighboring areas.

International readers have scarcely heard of non-Western – in the present case, Eastern Asian – economic philosophy. We aim to bring to the fore the theoretical output of Eastern Asian economic philosophers. They often publish in their own language: for instance, authors featured in this issue usually publish in Japanese. Some do in English or French as well. Yet, when it is so, the articles in another language often display (at least slightly) different ideas. As a consequence, a (large) part of their works remains out of reach for the global audience in the discipline. Only Westerners who read Eastern languages have access and few do. Programs dedicated to "Japanese studies" throughout the world seldom bear upon topics such as those

* Gilles Campagnolo is a full research professor at the French National Center for Scientific Research (CNRS) in philosophy and economics (CNRS, Aix-Marseille University, EHESS, Centrale Marseille, Aix-Marseille School of Economics) and the co-Chief Editor (with E. Picavet) of the *Review of Economic Philosophy*. He specializes in economic philosophy. He is an expert on European and Eastern Asian traditions, specifically liberalism. He was visiting professor and/or a "specially appointed professor" in China and in Japan (at the International research center for Japanese Studies "*Nichibunken*", Kyoto, at Hokkaido University, Sapporo, at Rikkyo University, Tokyo, at Shandong University, China, notamment). From 2013 to 2017, he coordinated the International Research Scientific Exchange Scheme "LIBEAC" for the European Union. Since 2019, he is PI and Coordinator for the International Research Network "Justice and Interest", comprising groups from the London School of Economics and the universities in Louvain/Leuwen (Belgium), Rotterdam, Helsinki and Lausanne.

Gilles. Campagnolo@univ-amu.fr

in economic philosophy, while the discipline would benefit from the wealth of diverse cultural backgrounds.

The aim of the *Revue de philosophie économique/Review of Economic Philosophy* in these two volumes is thus to remediate this situation. We will stress two aspects in our undertaking. On the one hand, we will highlight Eastern Asian economic philosophy in the historical perspective of its various local traditions. In this issue, for example, readers will discover who the founders of economic philosophy in Japan were through the words of their most contemporary representative, Yûichi Shionoya, recently deceased and whose texts we were granted permission to publish here.

On the other hand, the authors featured in this volume are most likely little known to our readership, and thus it is the ambition of the *Revue de philosophie économique/Review of Economic Philosophy* to make them known to the community of economic philosophers. We will feature present-day authors and publications related to economic philosophy. The wealth of articles in this issue displays these two goals.[1]

The region now called "Eastern Asia was formerly often called "the Far East", at a time when very different international relationships prevailed. The name, itself, was then tainted by different periods of discovery and a spirit reminiscent of past epochs when the study of Asian cultures was mostly the fruit of (sometimes adventurous) work carried out by missionaries, diplomats or scholars, most of whom were "specialists" of some Asian language or art (beginning with the martial arts). Their endeavors forged Asian studies *per se.*

1. The *Revue de philosophie économique/Review of Economic Philosophy* opens its columns to academic contributions well beyond "the West", in line with programs developed by the co-directors of the journal. In particular, the present undertaking was given momentum by EU network "LIBEAC": the work leading to this invention has received funding from the European Union Seventh Framework Programme (*FP7/2007-2013*) under *grant agreement* n° PIRSES-GA-2012-317767. Gilles Campagnolo created and coordinated LIBEAC (Liberalism In Between Europe And China) from 2013 to 2017, notably cooperating with Beijing University, Tsinghua University (Beijing), Hokkaido University (Sapporo), among others. Approximately 60 scholars benefitted from this international research staff exchange scheme. The present paper expresses the views of the author, who wishes to thank members of the network for their rich interaction. For more information, see the website: www.libeac.org.

The publication project started with the idea of only one thematic issue entitled "Economic Philosophy in Eastern Asia" for the *Revue de philosophie économique/Review of Economic Philosophy*, in addition to the collective volumes, such as *Liberalism and Chinese Economic Development: Perspectives from Europe and Asia* (Campagnolo 2016a). Due to the number of submitted papers that got positive reviews, we then opted for a two-volume set.

Some were inspired by a sense of attraction or admiration, others by fear or repulsion, while some were awed by a mix of all these feelings.

Although what still distinguishes present-day "areal studies" has evolved, the cultural traditions and linguistic, historical, and intellectual frameworks remain. Scholars of the past built such frameworks. Scholars of nowadays who deal with Japan are *not* all specialists of Japanese studies. They mostly contribute to their own field (here philosophy, economics and economic philosophy) and may meet issues related with Japan. This introduction, I hope, will help to shed some light on such disciplines with respect to Japan.

First (and for the sake of simplicity), the unity of the geographic area studied is the result of the (major) use of (originally) Chinese characters in the countries studied, with some extension.[2] For instance, "economics" presented here is called *jingjixue* in Chinese, *keizaigaku* in Japanese, and in both cases is written 経済学. The characters that were put together for "philosophy" are 哲学 (Japanese: *tetsu-gaku*, Chinese: *zhexue*) and "economic philosophy" is expressed as 経済哲学 (Japanese: *keizaï tetsu-gaku*, Chinese: 经济哲学 *jingji-zhexue*).[3]

The use of ideograms as a criterion for designating a geographic area naturally derived from this script, which carries a deep meaning anchored in cultural frames of thought. In a sense this created major difficulties for the Japanese, after they later met Western languages. As the Japanese sociologist Masao Maruyama, notes :

> [...] A Japanese native speaker who studied a little English, German or French while at University will find it easier to read, and will feel more acquainted with the philosophical works written in European languages than with Edo-style treatises by Confucian masters of those times, written in Sino-Japanese script [*kanbun*]. That makes

2. In the case of Korea, this is obviously a different script, namely *hanggul*, yet ideograms are still in use for names and understood by scholars. Korea is evidently part of the area heavily influenced by Chinese culture, like some other regions: see the "Introduction" to the second thematic issue on "Eastern Asian economic philosophy".

3. See the next section for the history of these terms.

See the last part of this introduction concerning transliteration used throughout the volume(s): for Chinese characters used in China, the so-called "*pin yin*" transcription is used, while older transcriptions are mentioned for names. Regarding the transcription of ideograms used in Japanese, the standard is the so-called "modified Hepburn" system: as a consequence, the reading of transliterated Japanese is somehow self-evident in English. French-language readers, please refer to the Appendix at the end of this introduction for more details.

> for a major difference between the Japanese and the French erudite audience.[4] (Maruyama 1996, XIV; our translation).

This assessment gets full illustration in the "documentary section" of the present issue. There, we introduce the author, Yûichi Shionoya (1932-2015), one of the most eminent scholars of economic philosophy in Japan over the last decades. We dedicate a special section to him, with an introduction (in French). An obituary (in English) has been provided in homage by Bertram Schefold (Professor Emeritus, University of Frankfurt/Main), a dear German colleague of the late Shionoya. This section then boasts two texts by Shionoya that are actually translated for the first time into a Western language.[5]

One text bears on the Interwar founders of economic philosophy in Japan, namely Kiichirô Sôda (1881-1927) and Kôzô Sugimura (1895-1948).[6] The other text is based on the metaphor cherished by Shionoya that economics is a stream whose banks should be of particular interest to professional economists. Both texts are taken from the book that Shionoya dedicated to economics and ethics, which also includes a discussion of the philosophy of the Welfare-state (published by Tokyo University Press in 2002).

The many essays that precede the documentary section in this volume display the development of economic philosophy in Japan, which we can classify into two categories: one favors a historical perspective while the other discusses contemporary issues.

From a historical perspective, this issue lists a story of some misadventures (and sometimes downright errors) in the reception of the works by Adam Smith in Japan (Masataka Muramatsu), a narrative of a paradigmatic author fallen into disrepute for share in nationalist

4. The *kanbun* script is the exclusive use of Chinese characters in Japanese while usually the Japanese language also makes use of two syllabaries (called *hiragana* and *katakana*). This "Sino-Japanese script" requires special training for Japanese and is usually related to texts older than the 19th century. *Kanbun* basics are still taught in Japanese high-schools today, somehow like Latin in the West (albeit learning *kanbun* is most often compulsory, thus keeping the link with old traditions in a world of otherwise "hyper-modernity").

5. We thank for the authorization generously granted for translation into French, the Tokyo University Press and the heirs of Yûichi Shionoya.

6. Note that the order of first (given) name and last (family) name are reversed in Japanese and in Western languages. For simplicity's sake, we restore the Western order everywhere, such that, for instance, the family names of these two economists are Sôda and Sugimura. Any deviations from this format are noted by the contributors to this volume, and sometimes capitals may be used for clarity to avoid any ambiguity.

economic policies, Yasuma Takata (presented by Shigeru Kitajima and Hiroki Yokota) and an account of more recent reception of libertarian thought in Japan (Akio Fukuhara).

Contributing to this issue, and alike Schefold and Shionoya an internationally famous scholar, Kiichirô Yagi shows how, in the late 1920s and early 1930s, the philosopher Kiyoshi Miki related hermeneutics and anthropology in search for a philosophy of history influenced by Marxism and economic thought altogether. Indeed, in his research, Miki included concern for socio-economic phenomena through Marxist views notably – but it is the spirit of the times (*Zeitgeist*) as well that lives through the text provided by Yagi. This is the chance of an overview of the atmosphere that prevailed in a period that Shionoya studied as well when deciphering the *economic philosophy* forged by Sôda and Sugimura, when economic philosophy first rose in Japan.

On the contemporary side, in this issue, economic philosophy settles into modern-day debates over hot-button issues, such as taxation on the one hand (Susumu Morimura discusses in a note conditions under which to debate about "just taxation") and, on the other hand, economic freedom and socio-economics (Tsutomu Hashimoto), while the account of libertarianism mentioned above implies discussing schemes of basic income for today and for tomorrow (Fukuhara), including debating with Morimura's views as expressed beyond his note on "just taxation" in this volume.

In all the essays, philosophy and economics are interwoven with sociological or cultural concerns. Each author, in his or her own way thus makes a contribution to "Japanese economic philosophy", reviving a tradition inaugurated long ago, as Shionoya reminds us.

Within this framework, this introduction aims to provide Western readers with the minimal notions necessary for understanding matters in Japanese economic philosophy. The following pages assume that the reader is new to debates in (and on) Japanese philosophy.

The common thread throughout is not only convergence, but also the divergences with regard to how philosophical issues may (very) diversely be interpreted in the West and in Japan. We shall not survey the literature dedicated to that vast topic.[7]

7. The interested English reader may refer to (Piovesana 1997), (Blocker and Starling 2001), (Porter and Ross 2003) and, for more recent literature, to (Heisig and Uehara 2008) and

In the present journal, the main focus is on "economic philosophy". Hence, it is necessary to recall the origin of the import of Western-style economics into Japan, and this shall serve as our starting point. Readers should also keep in mind that the impact of Western cultures – and, to begin with, the import of Western languages – has created the conditions for a fast-paced modernization process, where traditions seem sometimes to have become remote from contemporary issues even for the Japanese, as Maruyama rightly wrote in the passage quoted above. Western readers may feel even more at odds with a different world where the ideas originated in their own world, the West, have been adopted and adapted in ways unfamiliar to them. The next sections aim at giving a broad outline of the intellectual history of economic philosophy in Japan, and thus at illuminating the path for the readers.

WESTERN PHILOSOPHY REACHES THE SHORES OF JAPAN

We shall first clarify the framework wherein "modern", or "Western-style", philosophy and economics were adopted and/or adapted to local needs after reaching the shores of Japan.

Japan was the first country to become modernized in Eastern Asia, and even, more generally, outside of the Western world.[8] This was due to so-called "*Meiji* enlightenment",[9] a revolution from 1868 on. In reality, this phenomenon had started some 15 years earlier, while the so-called "*bakufu* (幕府) Shogunate" regime of the Tokugawa family lived its last two decades under pressures from Western powers to open its harbors to trade and diplomatic representation; the regime had virtually closed access to the empire of Japan after taking power

(Heisig, Kasulis and Maraldo 2011), (Hori and Curley 2008) as well as texts compiled in vol. 3 Part 2 of (de Barry, Gluck and Arthur 2001-2006). French readers, notice that publishing house Vrin (Sorbonne) issued a volume entitled "Textes clés de philosophie japonaise" (2013) wherein texts deal with Japanese general philosophy (metaphysics, phenomenology), though the volume lacks practical philosophy (political, moral and economic): see (Dalissier, Nagai and Sugimura 2013).

8. Besides any other consideration of texts submitted from Eastern Asia within deadlines by potential contributors to the *Review of Economic Philosophy*, this historical precedence suffices to legitimate the choice of the *Review* to dedicate this first issue to the Japanese case.

9. 明治 (in Japanese: *meiji*) means "Enlightenment" in the sense of the French, or the Scottish period of scientific and political history of the 18th century.

in 1603. The (almost) full closure (*sakoku* 鎖国 in Japanese) lasted for some 250 years, keeping a lasting peace (天下泰平 *tenka taihei*).[10] After that, one may speak of 150 years of "Modernization", to use a simple term for a complex phenomenon, or 160 years since doors opened: for instance, the first reciprocal diplomatic representations between France and Japan dated from 1858.[11]

In a nutshell, the Japanese sought to learn all from the Europeans new ideas and techniques, as well as government and investment strategies, and the Europeans obliged by conveying indispensable underlying values. While European powers ruled most parts of the world, the Japanese pulled the rug out from under their feet, so to speak, by adopting and adapting the same efficient methods and values in their own name. Countries that aimed to escape European power were left with no other choice but to follow this very same European model. The Japanese thus preserved their independence by bringing about major changes at home, from their political regime (by achieving the *Meiji* restoration of imperial power) to everyday lifestyles and their entry into industry and mass-production. Japan was successful in those reforms. Taking an accelerated remedial crash-course in modernization, Japan became the first and most prominent non-European power for one century by all standards. Japan would, in turn, impact neighboring non-European parts of the world, where it would, for better or worse, learn to rival with Western powers, playing strong cards and tough games, including rising nationalism and World War II – horrors which were both committed and suffered by Japan.

Forces at work to spread modern ideas on production included liberalism and its adverse currents of thought (Marxism, various kinds of socialism and anarchism, *etc.*); capitalist industrialization and militarization were also on the rise. All in all, Japan trod its modernization path, leaving behind the technical features of its traditional society: this process was labelled "Westernization" since it was grounded on doctrines originated in Europe. Moreover, the

10. The symbolic end of that period was marked in 1853 by the presence of the armada of "black ships" under the command of US commodore Matthew Perry in the Bay of Tokyo (then called "Edo").

11. Hence, the sesquicentennial was celebrated in France in 2018 with a twofold interpretation: either as the 150th anniversary since Meiji began, or as the 160 years of Franco-Japanese diplomatic relations. A full-fledged campaign of artistic and cultural events labelled "*Japonismes*" aimed to bring Japan closer to the French.

"Western" view of the world spilled over from the empire of the Rising Sun to other areas of Eastern Asia: Japan often served as a gate for Western ideas to enter the Middle Kingdom of China, whose intellectuals and revolutionaries often began their discovery of the world and newer ideas in the natural and social sciences, in the arts and in modern politics, on Japanese shores (Kobe or Nagasaki, to mention only the two harbors already open to them under the pre-*Meiji* Tokugawa regime).

The query whether Japan was still Oriental, or not yet Western raised many doubts about Japanese identity. Blocker and Starling state strikingly that the Japanese offered no reluctance to the introduction of new Western ideas, in the sense that they did *not* seek to maintain some previously existing "Oriental self" (in sum, they saw no "self" to maintain). So they did not see themselves as Oriental. Yet, since the idea of the significance of the proper self is a very European marker, they were not Western either. In the end, they were neither one nor the other: "in other words, Japan is nothing" (Blocker and Starling 2001, 192).

Before truly coming in contact with the new subject matters of Western academic disciplines and their specific conceptual vocabulary, the Japanese had simply no name for them. A quantity of words had to be coined. Firstly, names to designate subject-matters as such: for instance, the names "philosophy" and "economics" seen in modern, "Western-style" guise. Ideas were already imported by the Japanese before the official end of the *bakufu* in 1868. A tradition of the controlled import of knowledge of so-called "Dutch studies" (蘭学 *rangaku*) was cultivated. During the 1850s, Japanese scholars started to realize that the English language (and not Dutch) was most commonly used among Westerners to understand one another. It was insufficient to translate works from Dutch into Japanese. It was also insufficient to deal about techniques (medicine or strategy) for transmitting in-depth Western knowledge. English, German, French languages were now paid attention. It became necessary to label in Japanese the "new sciences" to help their compatriots understand the fundamental ideas thus discovered. Modernization was not only about importing techniques, but about more fundamental notions, even about views of the world.

An illustrative example is provided by one major character of Japanese modernization, Ôgai Mori (1862-1922). An army surgeon, Mori studied four years in Germany. His father was a medical doctor who had studied Dutch medicine, while his grandfather practiced Chinese medicine. Mori himself served at war, for instance against Russia (1905). He translated many works from the German: Clausewitz's classical *Vom Kriege* (*On War*), medical treatises and philosophical works.[12] He was kin to Amane Nishi, of the prior generation, whom we now mention since Nishi coined the Japanese word for "philosophy".

If one may generally speak of "philosophy" as a *Weltanschauung* that conveys civilizational traits (be they Japanese, here, Indian or Chinese, French or German elsewhere), this is not enough to embody the "scientific" point of view that European philosophy tends to promote, from Descartes to Auguste Comte, from John Locke to Herbert Spencer, to quote only two names that would become very popular in Japan. In this sense, "philosophy", based on the ancient Greek notion of *logos*, or a reasoned discourse, is a methodology based on systematic criticism to raise notional problems, which evolved into an academic discipline. Thus, "philosophy" in a restricted, delineated perspective is but one "way of thinking", but it is also the reflexive attitude that distinguishes it from other such ways and provides it with its efficiency. In that sense, as Chômin Nakae[13] famously and provocatively put it in 1901: "From Antiquity to our days, there has never been any philosophy in Japan".[14]

Nakae attempted at naming the latter new discipline based on a scientific approach with the word "*rigaku* 理学", which makes good sense given that *ri* (理) means "principle", coming from a long

12. For example, among many texts: Max Schasler, *Kritische Geschichte der Aesthetk. Grundlegung für die Aesthetik als Philosophie der Schönen und der Kunst. I: von Plato bis zum 19. Jahrhundert*, Berlin, Nicolaische Verlagsbuchhandlung, 1872). Mori also translated Shakespeare (from a German version). He changed the style and rhythm of the phrase in Japanese literature.

13. Well-known under this pen-name, his real name was Tokusuke Nakae (1847-1901). In his crusade for justice, he chose to change his first name to *Chômin*, which means "the people", to become Nakae Chômin (in Japanese order where name comes first, just like one usually speaks in Japan of Mori Ôgai and Nishi Amane).

14. Quoted from (Blocker and Starling 2001, 1). In China, the same question was raised as Western philosophy was introduced largely following a Japanese *detour*. It was formulated: "was there ever genuine Chinese thought of a kind equivalent to that in the West?"

tradition anchored in Chinese thought. Nakae articulates his "doctrine of principle" in his work titled *A Philosophical Quest* (理学鈎玄 *Rigaku Kôgen*). It is probably less well-known than his *Dialogue between Three Drunkards* or *One Year and a Half* and its sequel: *One Year and a Half. A Sequel*, the most cited works when his philosophy is debated. In his *Quest*, Nakae never forgets to interweave wit and a joyful attitude towards life – maybe taken from his interest in French philosophy and mindset?[15] He describes how reflection occurred gradually in the minds of men, and not at all from the start, when they only "ate what they could gather and drank from rain with their bare hands, like wild beasts".[16] The word *rigaku* 理学 was not adopted, however.

Actually, as I already hinted at, one word was already coined earlier on, by another thinker of this period of modernization, Amane Nishi.[17] Nishi conscientiously imported the ideas of Auguste Comte and John Stuart Mill into Japan. He knew about other currents of thought and voluntarily favored their "positivistic" attitude. As a consequence, the Japanese first knew of Western philosophy through these views and not through earlier metaphysics. Things happened as if the Japanese would start learning of Western thought with what Comte regarded as the "last" stage of the development of thought (the first one being the stage of religion, the second that of metaphysics and the last one being "positivism" Comte put forth).

Nishi coined the term "philosophy" (哲学 *tetsu-gaku*) in 1862. He was under the inspiration of his studies in the Netherland. His interests lay in psychological studies, the philosophy of French positivism – as just indicated, he saw in it a development of Cartesian views by Comte and modern European thought through the lens of Mill's ideas. For Nishi, there was the chance to provide a new classification of all sciences to be characterized for modernization that Japan had so much use for. Nishi had a pro-active mind and very practical in that

15. That may to some extent have included the famously-known French joyful attitude towards life (known as *joie de vivre*), see (Dufourmont 2009).

16. The development that leads to later civilization and the ability to reflect requires spare time, which beasts do not know of. The idea most probably originated from reading the book *La philosophie* by French anthropologist André Lefebvre (1884), as Haruo Miyamura points out about *Rigaku Kôgen* (Miyamura 1989, 152-158). Nakae learnt French first in Nagasaki (under the missionary *Frère Petitjean*) and then in Tokyo with the official interpreter of the Imperial court. Later, Nakae went to France (1872-1874) and met with French Republicans.

17. The name of Amane Nishi (1829-1897) is definitely the main name associated with the voluntary systematic introduction of Western philosophy in Japan.

sense for a philosopher – actually he would end his career as very high official of the regime. Nishi's *Hyaku-ichi Shinshuu* (*One Hundred and One New Theories*, 1862) represents precisely the attempt to introduce positivistic views with the new discipline under a new name.

Briefly, the story of Nishi's education and travels to the West goes as follows. After learning Dutch and English, Nishi was sent to the Netherlands among the first nine young Japanese students sent to Europe by the Japanese government in 1862. The trip was first scheduled to America, but as the American Civil War just started, the plan was changed and the trip was re-oriented towards Europe. The study-squad, so to speak, was made of five military men, two medical doctors and two researchers of the recently founded "Institute of research on foreign books" (*bansho shirabesho*). Nishi was one of those last two young men.[18] During his stay, the Japanese government requested that he would study in Leyde under the professor of economics, Simon Vissering. The discipline of economics had thus, from the start, been identified by the *shogunate* government as one source of knowledge important for modernizing Japan. This is documented since Nishi sent letters to the Rectorate of the University with explicit requests to be authorized to follow lectures, on the one hand, in law (natural, international, constitutional), economics and statistics, politics and diplomacy, and philosophy, on the other hand. This coupling of the humanities and the social sciences was present from the start of Japanese modernization. Nishi himself explained:

> [...] I would also wish to study what you [*tr.* at the University] call philosophy. I think that what Descartes, Locke, Hegel, Kant and others have told and put forth in the past, none of that pertains to religious thought that is forbidden by our law [*tr.* in Japan]. Although philosophy may indeed be extremely difficult to learn, I am convinced that it is absolutely indispensable to study it in order to develop and cultivate our country [*tr.* Japan]. This is why, despite all foreseeable hardships, I wish to learn it, at least partially as much as possible.[19]

Nakae and Nishi had, interestingly, diametrically opposite perspectives in many ways, not the least politically. Nakae would

18. That was in itself an achievement. In the next generation, Mori (mentioned above) failed to pass the examination to benefit from that same grant. Mori enjoyed one from the land-army (*rikugun*) to study strategy and medicine in Germany. As mentioned, Mori was to bring much from his trip to the Japanese mindset.

19. This quote from Nishi is taken from (Takashi Koizumi 1989, 43-4, our translation).

come to be called "the Rousseau of the Orient", not only for his translations of the French thinker, but also for his praise of popular sovereignty and his support of incipient socialism in Japan; he was eventually exiled from the capital city for his militant activities. Nishi, on the other hand, did not only coin the term that remained in use for philosophy, but was also an active and fully engaged participant in modernizing his country. As we already mentioned, he ended his career as a very high dignitary of the imperial state.

Together, Nakae and Nishi illustrate the paths that incipient Japanese philosophy could and would take. Nakae's wording prevailed in another case, that of esthetics, where the word he coined remains to this day (美学 *bigaku*) in the way he presented it in his work of 1883–1884 based on a translation of *L'Esthétique* by the French thinker and Republican militant Eugène Véron. Nakae possibly had the chance to meet Véron in the city of Lyons, where they both dwelt at the same time, and where Nakae acquainted himself with Republican circles during those first years of the Third French Republic when Nakae was in France (January 1872–May 1874).

Mentioning all this influence from France, it may appear to the reader that French thought operated much of the change brought by Japanese early philosophers. That would not be false, albeit excessive. Chance also played its role, like when the country chosen for the Nishi-mission was changed to the Netherlands from the United States, where it was first scheduled to take place (and became impossible because of the Civil war).

One should also stress the major philosophical influence of Great Britain as well, especially the social evolutionism of Spencer, and later progressive views illustrated by Bertrand Russell. There were many more thinkers, especially on the Continent, whose ideas were imported to Japan, whether they supported vitalist views, like those of the Frenchman Henri Bergson, or *Lebensphilosophie*, by the German Nobel-Prize winner (in literature) Rudolf Eucken. Many other schools of thought were imported into Japan, such as Neo-Kantian schools of Rickert, Natorp or Cohen (developed in South-Western Germany and in Marburg), Neo-Hegelian or phenomenological (Husserl, Heidegger) schools of thought. The latter inspired the first so-called "genuinely national" Japanese philosophy led by Kitarô Nishida with the so-called "Kyôto School" (*Kyôto-gakuha*). This is not the place to expound on these points: we shall focus rather on economic philosophy and, for that purpose, on how economics, in turn, reached Japan and how "economic philosophy" emerged *stricto sensu* and *expressis verbis.*

"WESTERN" ECONOMICS REACHES THE SHORES OF JAPAN

The "Western" science of economics reached Japan from the very first moment of encounter between the Japanese envoys and their European professors: the above-mentioned lectures by Vissering that Nishi attended in Leyde are proof enough. Soon, many other channels were opened and the trend flourished once Japan entered the *Meiji* period; liberal ideas brought about the rise of circles like the *Meijiroku shakai* (the society of members of the Year 6 of the *Meiji* era, that is to say 1874, also known under the short acronym of 明六者 *Meirokusha*).[20] Innumerable works were translated, and the reception of the ideas of Smith became commonplace among Japanese economists, while textbooks became widespread, like the one written by John Elliott Cairnes. Obviously, the effort by Japanese authorities was enormous for building up not only the economy, but also the field of economics. This produced a demand for economic studies that would, in turn, bring awareness that this development raised many concerns. The government's efforts to spread economic ideas finally resulted in the emergence of "economic philosophy" as a field *per se.* How should that wording be understood then, and first of all, called by the Japanese? That is partly what this thematic issue explores.

At the onset of this process, the word coined for the discipline of economics was highly influenced by British and German perspectives, the countries from which the Japanese had imported the discipline. Like philosophy and the natural sciences, there were different attempts to name the discipline – in physics for example, the term 格物学 (*kakubutsugaku*) was put forth by Nishi, but it is the later-coined 物理学 (*butsurigaku*) that prevailed and that is still in use today. "Western"

20. The journal of the movement, titled 明六雑誌 *Meiroku Zasshi* (the *Journal of the Sixth Year of Meiji*) published the works of these intellectuals – among many others, for instance, the *Treatise on the Intellect* 知説 *Chisetsu* by Amane Nishi, whom we shall further present below.

economics also got its name and the science thus labelled accompanied the rise of Japanese economics, building one of the main industrial powers of the world: the Japanese coined the word *keizaigaku* with the characters 経済学. The term results from combining 経 and 済 (学 simply means "study" or academic discipline), short-hand for a longer four-character proverb 経世済民 (*keiseizaimin*), which combines the two mottos "govern the country" (国を治める *kuni wo osameru*) and "protect the people" (人民を済 *jinmin wo sukuu*). Its introduction into the curricula of Japanese universities was a deliberate process, supported by authorities (as for instance Soyeda 1893 documented), and the term newly coined came to *exclusively* mean *Western* economics.

The word "economic philosophy" appeared half a century or so later. During the time that had elapsed, a new era followed that of the *Meiji*: the short-lived *Taishô* era (1912–1926). Japan had become the main power of Eastern Asia. The *Meiji* government, for example, defeated China in 1895, thus winning its first war ever against China (if one does not count the resistance against the twice-attempted Mongol–Chinese invasion in the 17th century).[21] Japan used modern weapons, technology and strategy. In neighboring areas, Japan invaded and colonized Korea in 1910, and extended its maritime power by swallowing up Taiwan, (then known as Formose). Japan built a fast-expanding empire. Among the winners of World War I, Japan was rewarded with its first stronghold on continental China by taking over the formerly German-influenced Shandong peninsula around Qingdao.[22]

The time when the Japanese stayed within its borders and traded only with Chinese and Dutch merchants in the restricted areas of Kobe and Nagasaki was long gone. Naval dockyards for civil and military ships had been built (by the French in Yokohama, for instance), and Tokyo became heretofore (since moving from Kyoto in 1868) a major capital on the world map, even in the eyes of Western governments. Before World War I, the Japanese conservatives often favored Germany or Austria, feeling closer to their conservative imperial views than

21. The 1895 Japanese victory initiated the period called the "Chinese break-up", representing the last decades of the Manchu dynasty in China.

22. The Germans had settled there in 1897, forcing the Chinese into a Treaty, developed a harbor and mining, and also set up a beer industry there, the *Tsing-Tao* beer; it has been internationally well-known ever since, partly thanks to the Japanese brewery industry that made it its own for a third of a century.

the republican France (which had, moreover, supported the earlier defeated *bakufu* until the last fight). Japanese Liberals would favor the UK and the US. Their top academic institutions were copied, and new institutions were built to bring power and glory to the rising sun.

Japanese intellectuals imported a vast quantity of knowledge from their travels during the period from the 1850s until the 1920s. From Europe, they brought back scholarship gathered from Britain and continental Europe or America, either directly or indirectly, since Japanese translations that introduced modern thought (in Japan as well as in the rest of Eastern Asia, beginning with China) were often re-translations from an English version of a Continental work; these were called *compendia*, digests or rewritings, and so on.

Questions such as how "Western" economics was introduced into Japan, how the currents of thought of Marxism played a major role, or how what the Japanese called "modern economics" (*kindai keizaï gaku* 近代経済学) developed, from the 1930s and especially after World War II to our days, all deserve their own history. Such history, however, has been written, so we shall not repeat it here.[23]

Textbooks are a useful tool for examining such history, as they provide a sampling of all currents of thought, from liberalism to collectivism. The most widespread textbook of Classical political economy, by J. E. Cairnes, was mentioned above. Marxism also impregnated a large part of the Japanese academic world, however it never seriously expanded, in contrast with China.[24] Translations sometimes started from mere transcriptions of texts in English, with Japanese scholars in European universities copying excerpts later

23. For an overview, see, for instance, (Sugiyama 1994) or (Morris-Suzuki 1989) a widely-used basic history of Japanese economic thought. See also the many monographs or collective volumes by Japanese historians of economic thought, who often deal with their topic in addressing in-depth one facet only among the many hinted at in this introduction. The reader will find many titles in English in series dedicated to the history of economic thought by specialized publishing houses.

24. That is why the role of Marxism in economic philosophy in Eastern Asia shall find a larger place in the second issue of the *Review of Economic Philosophy* dedicated to economic philosophy in Eastern Asia. This is not to say that its influence in Japan deserves less to be stressed, including internationally famous economists like Michiyo Morishima, or philosophers like Kiyoshi Miki, to whom Kiichirô Yagi dedicates his essay in this volume. However the *Review* divides subject matters as best possible. Similarly, the role of Hayek in Eastern Asia is illustrated in the later coming volume with a text about "Hayek in Korea" while the reader is reminded here to consult our text "Hayek in Japan" in volume 17/1 of the *Review of Economic Philosophy* (Campagnolo 2016b).

to be translated. The archives centers that we have visited in many university libraries of Japan keep these deeply moving examples of keen scholarship and major painstaking work accomplished by Japanese scholarly envoys.

Texts translated into Japanese from English were themselves sometimes already translations from another European language, such as German or French. The Japanese scholars in economics often learned German instead of English, a tendency that would later depend as well on political ties with the various powers. They also often kept to one foreign language, which had the disadvantage of narrowing their horizons, as well as cutting themselves off from a useful way of checking the value of the translations they used.

Admittedly, given the long chain of translations and interpretations, much of the original meaning was lost in translation. Losses and/or changes in content were thus an inevitable price to pay for the massive adaptation of such ideas into the local language. Moreover, adaptation to the Japanese conceptual framework also considerably modified content, sometimes to the point of leaving almost nothing from the original untouched. Western readers are often surprised by what actually reached the final Japanese reader (of that period in time, naturally), albeit an erudite scholar.

Let us pause here to recall that the ideas put forth since the European Renaissance, and even from the Ancient times of Rome and Ancient Greece, were swallowed up by the Japanese over a couple of decades, at most a half century (the period 1860s-1920s). How could such a concentrated overload of ideas not result in a mix resembling something like a "tomato purée", to use a culinary analogy? We must also remind the reader of the Japanese framework in which such imported ideas had to be made to fit. Let us, first of all, recall that economic concerns were formerly regarded as low-class in *samuraï* Japan. To work as a merchant was indeed higher than working as a peasant (leaving aside the stratum of social outcasts, the so-called *burakumin*), but buying and selling, in general, was inferior to any other kind of social activity.

Since the 17th century, however, a whole body of genuine Japanese economic knowledge had been built out of interest for the increasing number and power of those sellers. Indeed, the Japanese had worked out some forms of contracting and buying and selling that paralleled a few Western traits of nascent capitalism.[25] Such times are recorded, for instance, in the *stories of merchants*, like those narrated by the great writer Ihara Saikaku. His narratives are testimony of that development in the Western area of Japan – the Kansaï region – including Matsuzaka, Kobe and Osaka, wherefrom major Japanese companies would later emerge. The vast body of such literature, neither necessarily related to eventful narratives nor to abstract knowledge, emanated in Japan from the rising merchant class (while in China, such literature more often originated from the imperial state power of the moment). The new discipline imported from the West was as opposite in abstract and universal characteristics as were the Japanese and Chinese "economic" writings dating back to before the existence of Western economics.[26]

This is not to say that Japanese early *ethos* would fully parallel the European development of capitalism based on free enterprise. For instance, Morishima stated:

> A remarkably idiosyncratic *ethos* prevails in Japanese society, and as a result of these ethical feelings Japanese capitalism has to a considerable extent deviated from the typical free enterprise system. The question is [...] why the possessors of this kind of non-Western attitude came to gain such control over the industrial techniques produced by the West. (Morishima 1984, VIII)

Part of the answer lies in the religious behavior that played a role along the centuries as Max Weber notoriously pointed. Some facets of Christianity could be paralleled by Buddhism, on the one hand, Confucianism and Taoism imported from China approximately simultaneously in the 6th to the 8th century, on the other hand. The principle of "virtue" (that has to be followed), displayed in

25. Some historians (and a mathematician economist who tackled the issue from sheer interest: Morishima 1984) see the following feature as decisive: in the Middle Ages, both Europe and Japan were ruled by feudal structures. There, faithfulness to one's word was a most revered value between competing lords, who built domains upon that basis. So-called "free cities" were also major players in the birth of an early capitalism in both regions of the world (in a striking parallel between Italian seaports and Western Japan cities like Matsuzaka, Osaka, and so on); early entrepreneurs and bankers built structures that would later be ready to serve modern industry. That theory is often supported by stressing a specific Japanese *ethos* in the face of China, where an altogether different historical form of development prevailed characterized by long periods of authoritarian imperial rule, followed by shorter periods of great turmoil, leaving no hope but in a new despot. See also (Powelson 1997).

26. The term 政治 (Japanse *seiji*, Chinese *Zhengzhi*) changed meaning is still in use today to say "politics" at large.

the character 理 (Chin. *li* and Japanese *ri*), was fundamental – and would pervade thought, especially in its reflexive attitude towards economics (we shall come back to this later). But there was also clearly a nationalistic stand, as well as an anti-intellectual mark in Japan's evolution. It is not *coincidental* that a culture of immanent views lying far from any Western-style "abstract" reasoning would appear as the general background upon which the reception of Western ideas and, among others, economic ideas would have to prevail in Japan. But practical structures (banking, entrepreneurship) indeed existed in early-modern Japan.[27] As a structured feature, practical goals would always prevail, even when respect was paid (at least, at face-value) to imported theories.

As far as economic doctrines are concerned, there are many strong illustrations of Japan submitting its foreign imports through a tedious process of sifting and refining. Much like its imports from earlier epochs – writing from China, pottery from Korea, and so on – the modern sciences that Japan imported from the West were adapted to fit its own local use. But could that not be said about most countries? And is that not true of most major civilizations?

What makes the Japanese case very specially characteristic and distinct from others in that regard is still probably related to the following paradox: while the Japanese imported almost everything from other cultures, they are also proverbially known for their unique specificities. Centuries of the closure of its bordures help to explain that they developed "national", almost "family-like", attitudes and behaviors specifically of their own. There may be more to it. In a sense, the void space that not only techniques, but concepts, knowledge, ideas etc. came to fill from the outside were engulfed in the Japanese civilizational "space" as if that space was void, and meant to be filled.

The purpose of adapting foreign ideas is deliberate, hence the need to reserve a space to "welcome" these ideas, in order to "digest" them, so to speak. The Japanese civilization thus developed thanks to an inner ability to clear enough room to adopt and adapt not only the techniques, but also the spirit of other cultures, *without* "truly" incorporating them. The whole issue is what "truly" may here mean.

27. When meeting the modern West in the form of, say in 1853, the "black ships" of commodore Perry, Japan already had ready "sophisticated banking and exchange practices, commercial law, and bureaucracies capable of handling advanced economic policy" (Powelson 1997, 2).

What is clear though is that neither the Chinese formerly, nor the Westerners, may easily recognize the features coming from their own respective worlds in Japanese guise. In other words, the Japanese "newer" version of imported views is tailored to the needs of the Japanese (and gains interest mostly, if not exclusively, in that regard). It serves no other functioning structure (be it Buddhism and neo-Confucianism from China or liberalism, Marxism and nationalism from Europe). Japanese are masters in the refined use of all sorts of doctrines and ideas, but they do not ever commit themselves to any.[28]

JAPANESE ECONOMICS RISES WITH THE JAPANESE ECONOMY AND "ECONOMIC PHILOSOPHY" EMERGES

The slight digression that concludes the previous section was made in order to explain in this section the deep change that took place within the framework of Japanese academic institutions, first in the 1870s and then in the 1920s.

With positivism brought by Nishi, liberalism and utilitarianism were at a par since he imported the views of Mill as well as those by Comte. Nishi was not alone: the generation that brought into Japan such ideas was nicknamed the "*Enlightenment thinkers*" (啓蒙家 *keimôka*). They soon split between the latter and another trend, much less liberal in thinking yet eager as well for modernization, but advocating protectionist views that are part and parcel of German imported influences.

To put it in a nutshell, theories were always regarded as tools by those in power, which meant that the tools had to be sharp to cut through old customs. Imported methods could be made subservient to the rise of the nation's economy as well as military power, for instance, this paving the way for the later rise of nationalism. Signs of approval of the import of foreign views are thus at the same time,

28. To illustrate that point with daily life images: envoys and entrepreneurs of the Meiji epoch, much like those of today, can at will adopt Western clothing or recite Buddhist sutras, but put back on their kimonos at the end of the day They see absolutely no contradiction between acting in these different ways as long as they are beneficial, or may only potentially be, or appear to be beneficial: since they may work, let them be tried, a pragmatic stance that impregnates the so-called "Japanese mind".

tokens of an open-minded spirit of the time, of interest in earnest for a new scientific faith, as well as of a pragmatic wish for practical use and the nation's service.

A major push in all these directions at the same time was given by Yukichi Fukuzawa Yukichi in his *Call to Study* (Japanese 「学問のすすめ」 *Gakumon no Susume*) as early as 1876.[29] Japanese intellectuals acted as catalysers, helping to establish the first universities, starting with "Keio college", which Fukuzawa founded in Tokyo. This was soon imitated, and the *Meiji* Emperor established the University of Tokyo, followed by the famous "seven Imperial universities" across the country. Private universities and colleges founded by foreign missionaries were also granted permission by the Emperor; some remain to this day the major learning institutions of Japan.

Intellectuals– much like their famous ancestors of the Japanese study-abroad movement Nakae and Nishi – followed in cohorts and, decade after decade, systematized connections with the West. In this perspective, the eclecticism of "Western recruits" among the great thinkers has been remarkably varied. We have quoted a few names, but specialists were also "imported" to Japan as professors of imperial universities, such as Ernest Fenollosa at Tokyo University[30] or William Smith Clarke at Hokkaido Imperial University, at Sapporo, the capital of the late-colonized and developed Northern island of Hokkaido whose landscapes unmistakably evoke the American Middle West.[31]

In the 1920s, the Faculty of Economics became independent from the Faculty of Law and Politics at Tokyo University and at Kyoto University, which had been their harbor for almost half a century. That trend was only natural, reproducing what had happened two or three decades earlier in Germany and France, and would become an institutional pattern for many developed countries: there would be independent faculties for law on the one hand, and for economics on the other hand – while those faculties naturally continue to interact in order to raise the future elites in the top universities, the independence gained by economics was crucial for the development of that discipline

29. On Yukichi Fukuzawa (1835–1901), the reader may consult (Kumagai 1998).

30. Ernest Fenollosa (1853-1908) was a professor of philosophy and political economy at the (then Imperial) university of Tokyo.

31. William Smith Clark (1826-1886) was an American scientist recruited to build up the Agricultural College that was to become Hokkaido University, upon the model of what he had done in the United States.

in Japan (like everywhere else), bringing it full academic recognition for the first time – in other words, a grand academic revolution for Japan.

This modification to the academic landscape of Japan is still felt today. The decision was also strategic, since the governmental hoped to find solutions against economic evil (poverty and unemployment) at a time when the effects of military demand from previous decades (including World War I) was temporarily lacking. This situation caused unemployment. In the eyes of many, it also displayed how the economy and the military were linked (which comes as no surprise in many modernizing countries).

In 1923, this independence between faculties coincided with the 200th anniversary of the birth of Adam Smith. Both events were celebrated and greatly deepened Japanese research on Smith: on the one hand, Smith became a new symbol of support for liberal economics; on the other, it gave the Japanese the chance to study the thinker, introduced during the first years of the *Meiji* regime, for what he was: a major *philosopher*. His science of jurisprudence and moral philosophy were as pertinent as ever in the eyes of the new scholars interested in his works. At the same time, Japanese thinkers prided themselves on spreading the difficult words of German philosophy, especially those of the Neo-Kantian schools of thought. Nishi's hopes of bringing Western philosophy to Japan, as quoted above, were thus not in vain.

Moreover, with Japan's turn towards nationalism, famously known as *tenkô* in Japanese, the "conversion", many intellectuals turned to nationalistic views. In the 1930s, a genuinely national philosophy would develop in that spirit, notably but not only within the so-called "Kyoto School of philosophy" 京都学派 *Kyôtogakuha*. Such a nationalistic philosophy would have less to do with economics than other critical currents of thought, and more to do with a transcultural understanding of individualism (Altobrando 2016). Such views were alternative to what the most liberal among the Japanese would hope for, however. Nationalistic tendencies brought thinkers like Yasuma Takata to illustrate views related to economics.

While socialist thinkers were isolated or "converted", a real trend of alternative thought emerged with ideas brought to the fore by two professors from Hitotsubashi University, namely Kiichirô Sôda and

Kôzô Sugimura. Both unfortunately were to die young. Yet, they set forth the idea of "economic philosophy" in Japan. These founders were economists, both inspired by German neo-Kantian schools. One may say that their most important contribution was founding the field of "economic philosophy" in Japan and that their readers and followers made a heyday of its first period of existence and success of the new discipline.

Like the founders of new disciplines before them, Sôda and Sugimura coined new words: with the characters for economics and for "philosophy", the field of "economic philosophy" resulted as 経済哲学 (Japanese: *keizaï tetsu-gaku*). Another word that Sugimura attempted to promote under the influence of German Neo-Kantian axiological theory resulted in 経済倫理学 (*keizaï rinrigaku*), evoking "economic ethics". One may find these words as entries in dictionaries of economics of the 1920s. The first word remains in Japanese vocabulary (*keizaï tetsu-gaku*). As we already pointed, this volume welcomes the essay by Yagi who renders an expressive account of the atmosphere of the first rise of "economic philosophy" in Japan through the figure of the philosopher Miki. And the first translation in a Western language of texts by the late Shionoya recalls the role of Sôda and Sugimura, unfairly forgotten, and does justice to them.

One should note that, while Japanese dictionaries of economics of the 1930s included the entry "economic philosophy", as well as the names of its founders, Sôda and Sugimura, those after WW II do not often record them. One reason is due to the impact of what became known as "modern economics" (*kindai keizaï gaku* 近代経済学), a complex, even bizarre mix, of very diverse theories as long as all included mathematical economics and econometrics. In the spirit developed by the journal *Econometrica*, the science of economics became "mathematized". But that was not all there was in "modern economics", of course. But in Japan, all that could be seen as the alternative to Marxism was gathered under this one name. Notice that there were also Marxian attempts at modelling prices and mathematized Marxism counted internationally famous Japanese scholars like Michio Morishima (who had been the student of Yasuma Takata). The non-Marxist approach was a mix of Keynesianism macroeconomics and microeconomic modelling where the underlying feeling was that mathematical economics should bring out the similarities of all these "new" currents. In any case, times were changing and philosophy was blindly rebuked. The most striking sign of its loss was the allegiance to plain instrumentalism in the style of Friedman's 1953 essay, a minimal economic methodology that bore upon positivist views already outdated in the eyes of professional philosophers. The gap between economists and philosophers was widening.

In our times, in the 21st century, the perspective drawn by Sôda and Sugimura is still capable of sparking a revival of economic philosophy according to Shionoya. The prospects may look good since the guidelines were set and times of crisis in economics call for a revitalized interest in conceptual thinking. We refer the reader to Shionoya's texts, providing here the following quote:

> Let us notice that Kantian constructivism, as Rawls developed it, appeared in the United States without any relationship to the German tradition that had existed after Kant himself. We therefore conclude that the in-depth work that Sôda and Sugimura had thought of were absolutely original contributions to social post-Kantian philosophy -which we have largely demonstrated in the previous pages. This deserves all the more our attention in an ethical framework since it is the 'perfectionist' views that Sôda formed in a systematic theory of values that join in a prevailing value within the frame of the world of culture. The task to relate an ethics of 'justice' with an ethics of 'virtue' from a Kantian basis, this indeed was a major project, that one may still consider as paradigmatic nowadays. It is in this way that economic philosophy was thus born in Japan, after being impregnated with Neo-Kantian thinkers, and it certainly has not come to an end, like a flower that would fruitlessly fade into the air. Quite the contrary, since the undertaking [of these two Japanese economists] allowed to display the whole potential of their basic scheme in the Kantian perspective, they still appears nowadays capable of development. This is why we may indeed set the ideas by Sôda and Sugimura at the very origins of Japanese economic philosophy, as we are convinced that their plans are deemed to succeed and develop further in the present and future.[32]

This was written after 2000, and it set a task for this 21st century.

In any case, in Japan like in the West, the crises that economic theories fail to mend are cause that more and more academics debate

32. See the final page of the text on Sôda and Sugimura by Shionoya in this volume. Our translation in English from the French translation (checked against the original Japanese).

models that were once taken for granted, and that reflexive attitude is what economic philosophy promotes. Times are indeed changing, hopefully towards a more favorable stance on "economic philosophy". If one follows the hope that Shionoya formulated, this special issue is one sign that a "revival of economic philosophy" is occurring in Japan.

This also suggests that this presentation shall not end without questioning what the stakes for economic philosophy in the present context may be. Europeans and the Japanese seem to have serious reasons to share some values. The difference with the times of Nakae and Nishi is that nowadays exchange is mutual: envoys go both ways and Japan is not merely importing values and ideas from the West, but exporting some to the West.

THE STAKES TODAY : ECONOMIC PHILOSOPHY AND LIBERAL NORMS BETWEEN EUROPE AND JAPAN

In previous encounters between East and West, so to speak, some strange behaviors could be observed – such as Westerners adopting some customs, and even at times clothing outdated for the local Japanese, who in turn were keen to "Westernize" their lifestyles. On the side of Westerners, sometimes they were in admiration of their Japanese counterparts (to the point of being naïve), while other times they were paternalistic (sympathetic, at best) or downright racist (in the worst case).

Such attitudes cannot, however, be upheld any longer. They were partly endorsed by naïve newcomers to Eastern Asia, but also by scholars of two categories: either favorably biased admirers or arrogant paternalists. In the 21st century, these categories of Westerners will vanish among erudite scholars, if not fully among the increasing number of tourists visiting Japan. We, scholars, now connect as equals, and this is one outcome that the rising economic power in Eastern Asia has achieved. The times of Nakae and Nishi are long gone for our Japanese counterparts as well. Self-confidence is now widely shared; rather, what remains of boldness or shyness depends more directly on individual characteristics rather than on cultural traits or specificities. What is coming, and what must come, is a new type of scholar, who fits the global need for education and knowledge: on both sides, such scholars are "masters of their trade" and teach their disciplines as specialists of philosophy, law, sociology or economics, rather than of some under-determined "Asian studies".

In this issue of the *Revue de philosophie économique/Review of Economic Philosophy*, the contributors debate with their counterparts on even ground in a world of global knowledge. The word *keizaï tetsu-gaku* remains clear in Japanese vocabulary today, even though its contents must be re-explained in a contemporary context, much like Sôda and Sugimura had to do. In a sense, half a century of "modern economics", following the end of WW II, had the paradoxical effect of science regressing in its understanding of some fundamental notions.

Today, it is therefore necessary to re-introduce a few conceptual issues, which would not have received attention outside of a context of crisis. The stakes of economic philosophy are that we must deal once again with the consequences of not only a financial crisis, but also a crisis of social, moral, political and economic values. Post-WW II history made Japan the main ally of the US in the Asia-Pacific region. Japan pledged allegiance to the United States and has bases to this day harboring the 7th Fleet of the US Navy: this has not (yet) been put into question (except locally, like in Okinawa with special difficult relationships).

However, the general framework is no longer post-Cold War, but post-post-Cold war (that is post-US hyper-hegemony), due to marked changes in US foreign policy, as well as to increasing challenges posed by China and so-called BRICS countries. This has unleashed trends that question liberal values anchored in European traditions and adopted, to a large extent, as a consequence of the century and a half of import/adoption/adaptation of European economics and philosophy by the Japanese, as briefly evoked in this introduction.

As an illustration, let us mention that relations between the European Union and Japan have reached a promising point as the EU and Japanese authorities concluded in July 2018 the world's largest Free Trade Agreement. This is worth keeping in mind while reading a journal issue such as the one the reader presently holds in hand. Is this agreement a turning point? That is for future history to say. Clearly, this Agreement aims to defend liberal ideas, while anti-liberalism is on the rise, as some contributors of this issue stress. The role of economic and socio-political norms must be highlighted with regard to what

Europeans and the Japanese share, given their history of interaction, as summarized in the previous sections of this introduction.

If the lessons of adoption/adaptation of Western, European-originated ideas in Japan are the active framework within which common views for the present world are rising, then we may ponder such queries as the following: is economic pressure still the main driving force for the import of foreign ideas? Could the exchange become reciprocal, particularly as ideas born in Japan find a way to renovating older patterns, for instance so-called "liberal" patterns? How can some signs of economic crisis that regularly surge in liberal capitalism be confronted? Answers to recurrent crises require focusing on economic development, with a comparative analysis of the different contexts in which it is displayed in Eastern Asia: what are the different ways to interpret Japanese, Korean and Chinese modernization, and which elements embedded in those cultures shall we retain (Campagnolo 2016a)? To give an example, the influence of the legal framework on mid- and long-term trade is of interest to law and economics and to the history of economic thought, but also to economic philosophy (Debin and van Zanden 2011).

The EU–Japan agreement is presently nothing less than the world's largest Free Trade Agreement. It is called an Economic Partnership Agreement (EPA) and is accompanied by a Strategic Partnership Agreement (SPA), legally binding, which mandates political and security cooperation. The conclusion of these agreements is timely, coming as they do in the shadow of a crisis of liberalism, punctuated by the rise of China and the US presidency of Donald Trump. At a strategic global level, the conclusion of these two agreements may raise the question of whether the EU and Japan can effectively exert joint global leadership to help maintain a liberal international order.

For instance, Japanese Prime Minister Shinzô Abe promotes "Pro-active Pacifism" and "Values Diplomacy" in foreign policy, critiquing previous policy that he claims as merely professed peace while doing little to promote it. This "Values Diplomacy" asserts that Japan will promote the values of liberal democracy, human rights, and the rule of law. Given that the EU is also actively promoting such values, these Abe administration policies apparently promise greater EU–Japan political and security cooperation. Whether the Abe administration's implementation of these two new policies really portends greater cooperation, or whether they are merely tactical responses to China's rise that offer little potential for expanding EU–Japan cooperation, such are the issues that political scientists and statesmen themselves must assess.[33]

One task of economic philosophy in practice may clearly be to help define and question the fundamentals of international relationships based upon such norms and values. Our journal is concerned with a longer perspective however, which started, as mentioned above, in the 19th-century disciplines such as the German philosophy of the German modernization era (the so-called *Gründerjahre*), French sociology (in the style of Auguste Comte or Émile Durkheim) and British "Manchesterianism", among other currents of thought.

The Japanese modernization process acts as a sifting and sieving mechanism. It thus was first in the nineteenth century to raise debates in Eastern Asia with symmetric conceptual traits to those within European systems. It still does. This resulted, and still results in comparisons between, on the one hand, Japan adopting some kind of "community style liberalism", somehow embedded in Japanese group culture and illustrated in the local practices of the Welfare state later, and on the other hand, a European concept of "*Sozialmarktwirtschaft*" originated in a more Continental European view, as its German-oriented name suggests enough.[34] If modernization in Eastern Asia, and specifically in Japan, was never merely a copy of European powers and doctrines, Europe nevertheless set the tone with its "culture of growth" based on innovation in science and governance.[35]

Typical traits are conveyed in modernizing countries according to their own "civilizational style", and this is what so-called "Modernization Theory" has endeavored to study. Where such studies meet the framework of economic philosophy, they shall also

33. This is what, among many others, Paul Midford, a Professor and Director of the Japan Program at the Norwegian University of Science and Technology (NTNU) in Trondheim, investigates. Let us mention his presentation "The EU-Japan Partnership in the Shadow of China: The Crisis of Liberalism", given on February 5, 2019, at the International Center for Asian Studies (Temple University, Japan Campus, Tokyo).

34. This topic deserves more space than can be granted here. Regarding the building of an "economic nation" in Germany upon the basis of the criticisms of political economy, see (Campagnolo 2010) for instance, amidst an immense body of literature.

35. See the eponymous volume by Joel Mokyr (2017): the *Review of Economic Philosophy* schedules a book-review in an upcoming issue as a French translation is scheduled by Paris publishing house Gallimard.

be useful[36] to readers of the present thematic issue. Individualistic theories may diverge deeply from an anthropological, or civilizational, point of view, but there exist genuine Eastern Asian types of such individualistic approaches beyond the *cliché* of "group culture" already mentioned. In that sense, are individualization and liberalization on a par? This is one question for economic philosophy as well (see Campagnolo 2016a, part II, 109-86).

Economic philosophy comes in to challenge commonplace views and debate representations, to question what civilizations share with respect to rationalism, individualism and liberalism (pros and cons), values and norms. The Europeans set forth these norms and values, which the Japanese picked up as they modernized. What both sides seem to need now is to reassess them together. Comparative studies of economic and philosophical doctrines and their reception/transfer illustrate this perspective, which is for economic philosophy to contemplate. The present issue is one such example for readers to enjoy.

REFERENCES

Altobrando, A. 2016. "The Essence of Individuality in Kitarô Nishida's works : a Contribution from Eastern Asia to a transcultural Understanding of the Meaning of Individualism." In *Liberalism and Chinese Economic Development*, G. Campagnolo (ed.), 111-30. Abingdon and New York : Routledge.

Blocker, G. H. and C. L. Starling. 2001. *Japanese Philosophy*. Albany : State University of New York Press.

Campagnolo, G. 2010. *Criticisms of Classical political economy. Menger, Austrian Economics and the German Historical School.* Abingdon and New York : Routledge.

— (ed.) 2016a. *Liberalism and Chinese Economic Development : Perspectives from Europe and Asia.* Abingdon and New York : Routledge.

– 2016b. "Hayek au Japon : la réception d'une pensée néolibérale", *Revue de philosophie économique/ Review of Economic Philosophy* 17(1) : 171-208.

Dalissier, M., S. Nagai et Y. Sugimura. 2013. *Textes clés de philosophie japonaise : le néant, le monde et le corps.* Paris : Vrin.

De Barry, T., C. Gluck, T. Gluck, and E. Arthur. 2001-2006. *Sources of Japanese Tradition*, vol. III : *From 1600 to 2000, part 2 (1868 to 2000)*, New York : Columbia University Press.

Dufourmont, E. 2009. "The Spirit of Nakae Chômin and the 'Philosophy of Joy'." In *Whither Japanese Philosophy?*. Tokyo : University of Tokyo Center for Philosophy booklets.

36. For a survey of this literature, see (Gharbi 2016).

FUKUZAWA, Y. 1876. 「学問のすすめ」 *Gakumon no Susume* [*A Call to Study*]. First edition self-publication, no mention of place (in Japanese) ; In 「福沢全集」 *Fukuzawa Yukichi Zenshû* [*Complete Works by Fukuzawa Yukichi*], vol. 2. Tokyo : Jiji-Shimpo-sha. 1898.

GHARBI, J.-S. 2016. "Modernization Theory, Chinese Modernization and Social Ethics." In *Liberalism and Chinese Economic Development*, G. Campagnolo (ed.), 86-106. Abingdon and New York : Routledge.

GORDON, A. 2003. *A Modern History of Japan. From Tokugawa Times to the Present.* Oxford : Oxford University Press.

HAN, S.-J. and Y.-H. SHIM. 2016. "Dual Individualization in East Asia : Individualization in Society and in the Family." In *Liberalism and Chinese Economic Development : Perspectives from Europe and Asia*, G. Campagnolo G., 147-66. Abingdon and New York : Routledge.

HEISIG, J. W. and M. UEHARA (eds.) 2008. *Frontiers of Japanese Philosophy. III : Origins and Possibilities.* Nagoya : Nanzan Institute for Religion and Culture.

HEISIG, J. W., T. P. KASULIS and J. C. MARALDO. 2011. *Japanese Philosophy : A Sourcebook.* Honolulu : University of Hawaï Press.

HORI, V. S. and M. CURLEY (eds.) 2008. *Frontiers of Japanese Philosophy II. Neglected Themes and Hidden Variations.* Nagoya : Nanzan Institute for Religion and Culture.

IKEO, A. 2001. "History of Japanese Economic Thought : the Present and the Future." *Annals of the Society for the History of Economic Thought* 39 : 94-102.

KOIZUMI, T. 1989. *Nishi Amane to Ôbei shisô to no desai* [*Nishi Amane meets Western Thought*]. Tokyo : Mitsumine Shuppan (in Japanese).

KUMAGAI, J. 1998. "Enlightenment and Economic Thought in Meiji Japan : Yukichi Fukuzawa and Ukichi Taguchi". In *Economic Thought and Modernization in Japan*, S. Sugihara, T. Tanaka (eds), 23-41. Cheltenham : Edward Elgar Publishing.

LEFEBVRE, A. 1884. *La philosophie*, Paris : Reinwald.

MA, D. and J. LUITEN VAN ZANDEN (eds.) 2011. *Law and Long-Term Economic Change. A Eurasian Perspective.* Stanford : Standford University Press.

MIYAMURA, H. 1989. *Rigaku Chômin* [*"Chômin" the Philosopher*]. Tokyo : Misuzu shôbô (in Japanese)

MOKYR, J. 2016. *A Culture of Growth. The Origins of the Modern Economy.* Princeton : Princeton University Press.

MORISHIMA, M. 1984. *Why has Japan Succeeded? Western Technology and the Japanese Ethos.* Cambridge : Cambridge University Press (1st ed. 1982).

MORRIS-SUZUKI, T. 1989. *A History of Japanese Economic Thought.* Abingdon and New York : Routledge.

NAKAE, C. 1983-1986. *Nakae Chômin Zenshû* [*The Complete Works of Nakae Chomin*]. Tokyo : Iwanami Shoten (in Japanese) including : *Rigaku Kôgen* [*A. Philosophical Quest*], vol. 7 ; *Ichinen Yûhan* [*One Year and a Half*], vol. 10 : 125-200 ; *Zoku Ichinen Yûhan* [*One Year and a Half. A Sequel*)] vol. 10 : 221-92.

– 1984. *A Discourse by Three Dunkards on Government* [*Sansuijin keirin mondo*], Eng. tr. by Nobuko Tsukui and Jeffrey Hammond, Boston : Weatherhill.

NISHI, A. 1862. 「百一新論」 *Hyaku-ichi Shinshuu* [*One Hundred and One New Theories*]. Tokyo : self-publication (in Japanese).

PIOVESANA, G. K. 2013. *Recent Japanese Philosophical Thought (1862-1996). A Survey.* Abingdon and New York : Routledge.

PORTER, Th. M. and D. ROSS (eds.) 2003. *The Social sciences in Japan.* Cambridge : Cambridge University Press.

Powelson, J. P. 1997. *Centuries of Economic Endeavour. Parallel Paths in Japan and Europe and their Contrast with the Third World.* Ann Arbor : University of Michigan Press.
Schefold, B. 2016. "Asian Classics – Japan." In *Great economic Thinkers from Antiquity to the Historical School*, 369-93. Abingdon and New York : Routledge.
Soyeda, J. 1893. "The Study of Political Economy in Japan." *Economic Journal* 3(10) : 334-9.
Sugiyama, C. 1994. *Origins of Economic Thought in Modern Japan.* Abingdon and New York : Routlege.

appendice : indications sur la translittération de la langue japonaise pour les francophones

Un appendice similaire concernant la langue chinoise et les particularités de sa translittération *pin-yin* sera fourni dans le numéro thématique de la revue « Philosophie économique en Asie orientale (2) ». Ce qui suit concerne le japonais.

Pour la translittération des mots japonais en caractères latins, que le texte donné soit à lire en français ou en anglais, nous adoptons le système le plus répandu, dit « Hepburn modifié ». Sa prononciation est assez intuitive pour les anglophones, mais pour les lecteurs francophones, les quelques indications suivantes sont utiles :

– *e* se lit « é » ;
– *i* se lit « ï » ;
– *u* se lit « ou » ;
– la prononciation sépare toutes les syllabes et en particulier toutes les voyelles (ainsi « Inoue » se lit « i », « no », « ou », « é » : « i-no-ou-é », et ainsi de suite) ;
– *g* est toujours occlusif (c'est-à-dire « dur » : *ge* = *gué* ; *gi* = *gui*) ;
– les voyelles portant un accent circonflexe sont allongées ;
– *ch* se lit « tch » et *sh* rend le son « ch » ;
– *r* et *l* se confondent en une sonorité unique, notée par la lettre « r » ;
– tous les « h » avant voyelle sont aspirés.

L'ordre du nom et du prénom est inversé en japonais par rapport aux langues occidentales, mais nous rétablissons pour la présentation au lecteur en langue française ou anglaise l'ordre qui lui est familier (sauf précision du cas contraire ; pour éviter tout doute, le nom de famille est à certains endroits différencié par l'utilisation de majuscules).

Les titres des ouvrages publiés en anglais sont toujours cités dans cette langue, mais les titres des ouvrages en japonais sont traduits par les contributeurs en anglais ou en français, selon la langue du texte proposé dans la revue.

Il faut souligner l'impact de la langue sur la manière de philosopher japonaise, au point que celle-là pourrait pratiquement conditionner celle-ci, en raison de sa complexité et de la difficulté d'y transmettre les catégories et les manières de raisonner des langues occidentales. Inversement, le processus de modernisation et d'apprentissage des savoirs occidentaux a entraîné une acclimatation au sein des disciplines académiques qui rend presque leurs préoccupations étrangères à la tradition autochtone (nous renvoyons le lecteur à la citation de Maruyama plus haut, dans l'introduction).

SUFFICIENTARIAN-LIBERTARIANISM AND BASIC INCOME

AKIO FUKUHARA*

Résumé
Le présent essai soutient une position qui s'inscrit dans le courant dit « libertarien » tout en explorant les implications de la politique qui prône un revenu de base et suscite présentement un débat vivace à travers le monde, y compris au Japon. Il existe diverses formes d'éthique libertarienne. Ici, dans la lignée de Nozick, la « propriété de soi » et la clause lockéenne sont reconnus comme deux rouages essentiels de l'argumentation qui conduit à leur ajustement en vue d'une éthique spécifique. Nous examinons comment Nozick défend la « propriété de soi » : son argumentation respecte la séparabilité des personnalités et elle accorde une grande importance à l'élaboration libre par chacun d'un mode de vie lui convenant. Une fois révisées la nature du droit dit « d'appropriation » et de la clause dite « lockéenne », nous réinterprétons cette position centrale des libertariens en considérant la position fondamentale de Nozick comme prenant appui sur une conception égalitariste de la notion de dispositions suffisantes. Les avantages de cette position sont dus non seulement à l'adéquation entre la théorie et un principe de distribution, mais encore à l'image de l'individu doté d'une propriété de soi réaffirmée, dans la vision libertarienne que Nozick déploie. Cette approche fournit les bases de la morale d'une activité libre exercée sur les marchés : ce point est essentiel pour les auteurs libertariens, qui refusent toute aliénation de la propriété privée et toute redistribution. Une version simplifiée du revenu de base une fois définie en l'adaptant à des cadres variés, dont le cadre japonais nous mène à conclure que le revenu de base, quoique séduisant, est partiellement conforme aux thèses libertariennes et qu'une version minimale serait à retenir.
Mots clefs : clause lockéenne, éthique libertarienne, Nozick (Robert), revenu de base, thèse des dispositions suffisantes (*sufficientarianism*).

* Akio Fukuhara is a researcher presently benefitting from a Grant by the Japanese Society for the Promotion of Science and located at the University of Hitotsubashi (Kunitachi, Tokyo).

Abstract :
This article defends the position of a certain type of libertarianism and explores the policy implications of basic income that are actively being discussed across the world, including in Japan. There are several types of libertarianism. In the genealogy of Nozick, self-ownership and the Lockean proviso are two cogs and wheels of such arguments. Libertarianism can take shape only as other argument supports the other. From this point of view, this paper examines in detail how Nozick has tried to defend self-ownership. His argument respects the separateness of persons in a certain way and attaches the importance to make it possible for people to freely design their own lives and live a meaningful life by themselves. In addition, after reviewing the nature of historical entitlement theory and the Lockean proviso, I will take up the interpretation of the Lockean proviso, which is a central theme in recent libertarianism. In this paper, I mainly consider the baseline of Nozick, sufficientarian interpretation and egalitarian interpretation. There are advantages to such a sufficientarian interpretation, derived not only from the adequacy of the theory as a distributive principle itself but also from the fact that (Nozickian) libertarianism bears a specific image (a person with self-ownership). Furthermore, this sufficientarian understanding provides a moral basis for free economic activity on markets, which libertarians regard as important, and it is different from divesting legitimate private property and redistributing it that libertarians reject. I define a simple and general basic income for theoritical purposes and for Japan. This paper ultimately concludes that basic income does not completely morally conform to the conception of sufficientarian libertarianism, despite its appeal, and I will defend a system such as guaranteed minimum income, though some difficult issues remain.
Keywords: Basic income, Libertarianism, Lockean proviso, Nozick (Robert), Sufficientarianism.

JEL Codes: H21, H24, N35, P17

1. FOREWORD

What is the main claim of libertarianism or classical liberalism? Several answers to this question are conceivable. One would be to reduce the size of the government. Effort to reduce government interference for citizens seem to advocate such positions, whether the subject of such limitations relate to interference or finances. Moreover, in a more philosophical context, it is said to be a position to defend the right to secure individual freedom, such as self-ownership. The trend of the recent philosophical debate in the UK and the US pertains to this argument. However, to some of those who pose this argument as the basis for discussion, as in another part – in the Lockean proviso – it is more positive in redistribution and more economical in terms of equality rather than freedom. In this way, the position of libertarianism and classical liberalism seems to be twisting at a political level and philosophical level (Van der Vossen and Vallentyne 2018). However, in my view, the argument of aiming to balance the concept of self-ownership that is colored by the glorious libertarianism of Robert Nozick and some kind of equality of goods is not fundamentally trying to discourage the value of freedom while wearing a libertarian mask. Rather, seeds defending this position are embedded in the argument of Nozick. All arguments that follow this genealogy aim to adequately defend valuable personal freedom in each way. In this sense, while using the terms rights and entitlement, these arguments can be said to be "individualistic liberalism" centered on individual freedom.

On the other hand, when looking at the reality of Japan, hope for economic growth, increased living standards, and greater tax revenue has diminished; thus, it is becoming increasingly unbelievable for a financial margin to operate an ideal welfare state. Although this is a problem for not only Japan but also developed countries in general, the declining birthrate and increasing aging and the stagnation of economic growth have placed pressure on the model to support everything including the old age generation by active generations. While suppression of bloating social security expenditure is an urgent issue, it is difficult to undertake major changes of demanding social security for the life of the elderly in the present democratic system due to the population constitution. In this sense, it is natural for the political interest of young people to be low, where their voting rate remains a low standard. In addition, it is ironic that young people who will obviously incur a heavier burden from now on to day "let's go to vote!"

While such low growth and the need to suppress social security expenses constitute a self-evident premise, the idea that has been advocated by various writers (intellectuals, scholars, business person) is basic income (BI), even if it has some pros and cons. While not knowing exactly what it means to use BI, some political parties and politicians have also mentioned being for/against BI. Recent discussions on BI are based on the prediction that many unemployed people will be generated by AI. In this article, I would like to ask whether the proposal of BI is justified by libertarianism or classical liberalism – whatever the reason for supporting it.

What I want to mention in advance here is that this paper does not inquire whether BI is feasible or possible in reality. In other words, I do not delve into problems such as whether we can actually secure a financial base to cover the BI using Japanese tax revenue or what kind of tax system should be adopted. This stems from the fact that I am a legal philosopher and do not have sufficient knowledge, such as knowledge on economics or fiscal finance, to discuss such aspects. Many of the discussions on BI in Japan also concern the following issues: how much is the benefit amount, how can we finance the revenue, is it feasible, will people lose an incentive to work, what will happen in a society in which BI has been realized, and how can we realize BI in real politics. However, with only a few exceptions, few arguments explore the moral legitimacy of BI. Even in such cases, there are mostly those introducing the discussion of BI by Philippe Van Parijs or that are motivated by the usefulness of social movements.[1] In this paper, I would like to discuss how distributive policies including BI can be evaluated from the Nozickian argument. First, I explain the libertarianism of Nozick and confirm that consideration for distribution exists in his argument. Next, I examine interpretations of the Lockean proviso, which is in the center of the distribution problem of libertarianism, and dismiss some influential interpretations and defend a sufficientarian interpretation. Finally, I would like to consider briefly whether the principle that I defend advocates for BI.

2. DISTRIBUTIVE PRINCIPLES OF SELF-OWNERSHIP LIBERTARIANISM

I would like[2] to argue about libertarianism that defends self-ownership in this chapter. Of course, I understand that there are consequential arguments, not just those based on rights, among the

1. Saito (2010) summarizes the van Parijs's argument and the discussion of BI in Japan.
2. Most of the arguments in this chapter are based on Fukuhara (2017).

libertarian and classical liberal arguments.[3] However, here I do not use consequential arguments, such as the economic efficiency or maximization of well-being. I would like to consider whether people have a right to receive any distribution even on the basis of self-ownership. Many of the protection arguments of BI treat it as a right; thus, I think that it is meaningful to consider BI from the viewpoint of the existence of the right to receive distributions. Below, I would like to introduce a method of combining self-ownership and the Lockean proviso, which is a representative discussion method of a self-ownership type of libertarianism.

2.1. *Self-ownership*

Currently, most of libertarian theories are based on self-ownership. It is said that it is in its origin and is mentioned as follows in the argument of Locke. "Though the earth and all inferior creatures be common to all men, yet every man has a "property" in his own "person". This nobody has any right to but himself. The "labour" of his body and the "work" of his hands, we may say, are properly his" (Locke 1690/1988, Essay 2, Ch. V, Sec. 27, 287-8). Rewriting this phrase more analytically would be the next passage by G. A. Cohen expressed in criticism against Nozick. "[E]ach person is the morally rightful owner of his own person and powers, and consequently, that each is free (morally speaking) to use those powers as he wishes, provided that he does not deploy them aggressively against others." (Cohen 1995, 67). Libertarians derive general freedom of action – free speech, economic freedom, and so on – from such rights. Many libertarians regard self-ownership as a given initial right, and they often go immediately to an argument on private property, world ownership, or resource distribution (Vallentyne 2009; Wendt 2018). Therefore, most of the attention in the discussion of the theory of libertarianism is directed to the problem of economic freedom and distributive justice – that is, the interpretation of the Lockean proviso.

3. For example, Askew (1994) distinguishes libertarianism by the scale of the government and justification grounds. According to Askew, the justification of libertarianism is made by either natural rights, consequentialism, or contract theory. Zwolinski (2011) Ch. 2 also refers to consequential libertarianism. On the other hand, the general condition for being called a libertarian in analytical philosophy today concerns the adoption of self-ownership. See Vallentyne and van der Vossen (2014).

However, here, I would like to note that Nozick's argument that most libertarians focus on is not necessarily the case. At the beginning of *Anarchy, State and Utopia*, Nozick started his argument with a spectacular libertarian declaration, as indicated below.

> Individuals have rights, and there are things no person or group may do to them (without violating their rights). So strong and far-reaching are these rights that they raise the question of what, if anything, the state and its officials may do. How much room do individual rights leave for the state? (Nozick 1974, IX).

On the other hand, in a few pages after this declaration, he argues,

> This book does not present a precise theory of the moral basis of individual rights [...] Much of what I say rests upon or uses general features that I believe such theories would have were they worked out (Nozick 1974, XIV).

It is difficult to pass through this confession. Certainly, it may be intuitively convincing that individuals have rights and that they exist in the form of self-ownership (side-constraints, in Nozick's term). However, I believe that we need to understand the nature of self-ownership in a bit more detail. Indeed, people with self-ownership will be a necessary element in fixing criterion of distributive justice. We will consider the distributive principle only for people with self-ownership.

Despite confidence we may have in Nozick's approach, he himself did not provide us with an analytically precise justification for the foundation of self-ownership as he confessed. On the other hand, we have the following fragmented hints. "Side constraints upon action reflect the underlying Kantian principle that individuals are ends and not merely means; they may not be sacrificed or used for the achieving of other ends without their consent. Individuals are inviolable." (Nozick 1974, 30-1). "To use a person in this way [for others or society] does not sufficiently respect and take account of the fact that he is a separate person, that his is the only life he has" (Nozick 1974, 33). These descriptions clearly show that Nozick regarded self-ownership not as a given initial right deriving from intuitive persuasion but as a right deriving from the interpretation of Kant's declaration or moral interpretation of separateness of persons (Zwolinski 2008). In other words, self-ownership is not an independent and non-based moral principle; rather, it is a moral principle about the treatment of persons deriving from adequate respect for persons.

On the other hand, we should also be aware that self-ownership derived in this way is not a right that arises because of animals who are "*homo-sapiens*". If we derive any moral importance on the grounds that human beings are just homo-sapiens, such un-universalizeable argument cannot escape the fallacy of so-called "egoism of species". There is also a self-enslave contract as a characteristic example showing the difference in treatment between humans as a species and persons. If self-ownership means "each person is the morally rightful owner of his own person and powers", there is the question whether you can make yourself a slave of your own will. This self-enslave contract often seems to be a tragedy that self-ownership reaches from other standpoints, and some defenders of self-ownership try to show that such a contract is not established (Morimura 2001, 61-2). On the other hand, more than a few libertarians regard that the establishment of a self-enslave contract is not a tragedy that should be avoided but rather proof that is consistent with respect for individual freedom; thus, self-ownership can well protect freedom (Nozick 1974, 331; Steiner 1994, 232, n. 5; Vallentyne 2011a, 163).

Although I would fall into the latter group, the issue to address here is the following: if "self-enslavement contracts" are possible, humans can become the property of some others, and one's ownership can be transferred to others. At this time, there are humans who lost their self-ownership. Since self-enslavement is not a contract for one to quit being a human as a species, self-ownership is obviously not derived from being human. What you can find from this point is that self-ownership has an aspect as a moral status that can be acquired/lost and that the grounds are not merely human as a species. In other words, it is not a fact that one is a human being, but the specific form of treatment of something morally important, which a person has, supports the status of self-ownership.

Nozick asked straightforwardly:

> In virtue of precisely what characteristics of persons are there moral constraints on how they may treat each other or be treated? [...] why these characteristic connect with these constrains." (Nozick 1974, 48).

Nozick regards self-consciousness, free will, rationality, and so on, which are not appropriate rationale (Nozick 1974, 48). "If being is capable of choosing autonomously among alternatives, is there some reason to let it do so?" (Nozick 1974, 48). Even if you have the ability or talents like rationality and you can choose something yourself, what does it mean by itself? Or why such a choice should be respected? It cannot be answered to these questions, from "able to choose." Here, Nozick turns his attention to the way of human life. He found a characteristic aspect in human life;

> [A] being able to formulate long-term plans for its life, able to consider and decide on the basis of abstract principles or considerations it formulates to itself and hence not merely the plaything of immediate stimuli, a being that limits its own behavior in accordance with some principles or picture it has of what an appropriate life is for itself and others, and so on. (Nozick 1974, 49)

These is the overall conception related to human life that cannot be fully reduced to something like free will or rationality:

> What is the moral importance of this additional ability to form a picture of one's whole life [...] and to act in terms of some overall conception of the life one wishes to lead? Why not interfere with someone else's shaping of his own life? (Nozick 1974, 50).

The answer by Nozick is: the *meaning of life*. He thus writes:

> A person's shaping his life in accordance with some overall plan is his way of giving meaning to his life; only a being with the capacity to so shape his life can have or strive for meaningful life. (Nozick 1974, 50).

The concept of meaning or meaningfulness that appears here does not reduce to well-being. It does not mean that well-being is obtained only when people make their lives meaningful through a certain overall conception ability. Rather, paternalism that intervenes in an individual's free decision is convincing because it professes to increase the well-being of the recipient. Even if other people can manage the life of someone better than themselves through the contribution in promoting their well-being, if you find a difference in people living their lives *by their own hands*, the meaning of life is clearly something different from the promotion of well-being. If we can find value in the separateness of persons, the significance of giving meaning to life by our own hands is remarkable. In other words, respecting the separateness of persons, for libertarianism, means that, at least, each person makes life meaningful by living one's own life.

Thus far, the reason for having this, perhaps dubious, argument here will become clear later, but the conclusion is simple. Libertarianism regards each person as a morally legitimate owner of one's body and ability, and this self-ownership is derived not from being human but from the moral principle as a Kantian principle or respect for the separateness of persons. The core of this principle for libertarianism lies in giving meaning to life. In the following, I will call a person with self-ownership with such background a "self-author." I have discussed the nature of self-ownership thus far; then, I would like to move to the argument of the Lockean proviso – the central problem of distributive principles.

2.2. *Historical entitlement theory and the range of the Lockean proviso*

In the first place, it may seem strange to discuss the distribution principle in libertarianism. Is it not for libertarianism to call out the result caused by the market principle through free economic activities (if called) distribution situation? However, if you go through a self-ownership-based path, it will become clear that there are conditions for which we regard the principle we call free economic activity in the market as legitimate.

Let us have a look back at the historical entitlement theory. Nozick advocates the following principle of the distribution situation of goods (Nozick 1974, 151).

1. A person who acquires a holding in accordance with the principle of justice in acquisition is entitled to that holdings
2. A person who acquires a holding in accordance with the principle of justice in transfer, from someone else entitled to the holding, is entitled to the holding.
3. No one is entitled to a holding except by (repeated) applications of 1 and 2.

Let us call principle 1 as justice in acquisition (appropriation), 2 as justice in transfer, and 3 as justice as rectification. According to Nozick, these principles work as follows.

> A distribution is just if it arises from another just distribution by legitimate means. The legitimate means of moving from one distribution to another are specified by the principle of justice in transfer. The legitimate first "moves" are specified by the principle of justice in acquisition. Whatever arises from a just situation by just

> steps is itself just. The means of change specified by the principle of justice in transfer preserve justice. (Nozick 1974, 151)

From this characteristic, this principle can be called "preservation of justice." What is important is that justice is not newly created but is preserved through the principle of 1 and 2, and if it fails to preserve justice contrary to these principles, it goes to the state of justice by 3. We need to be aware that this effect of rectification belongs to corrective justice, not distributive justice. In other words, rectification is not intended to lead to any desirable distribution pattern but is intended to correct the result of interaction that is contrary to justice and to bring it back to the state of justice to be preserved. For example, it is the purpose of rectification justice to correct a situation brought about by an unjust transfer such as stealing or fraud contrary to a voluntary exchange or gift, which Nozick assumed in justice in transfer.

Another implication of "justice is not newly created" is that an appropriate situation must exist beforehand. The argument that all situations reaching the correct transition from the correct situation are correct is not caused by the correct transition alone. Only when there is a correct situation beforehand, the correctness can be preserved. When applying this to any scene of the transition, every correct situation after transition should come from the correct situation before transition, and when going back to the transfer, it must reach to the original acquisition, where the justice in acquisition becomes a problem. In other words, it turns from the situation where natural resources are not owned privately by anyone and where no one has any private property rights to external things, into the situation where legitimate private property rights exist by adequate original acquisition. What is important here is that there is the possibility of original acquisition in the form of violating justice in acquisition. Even in the initial condition without any private property rights, obviously there is a constraint that cannot be acquired as one pleases. Nozick tried to clarify the constraint of justice in acquisition in the form of the Lockean proviso. Most of arguments of libertarianism inspired by Nozick share the paths thus far presented. Views of distributive justice of libertarians are divided on the interpretation of the Lockean proviso addressed below.

It is now necessary to consider the range of the Lockean proviso.

Nozick emphasized constraints as a condition of acquisition in the argument of Locke; "at least where there is enough, and as good left in common for others" (Locke [1690/1988], Essay 2, Ch. V, Sec. 27, 287-8[4]). Nozick interpreted the so-called Lockean proviso (sufficiency constraints) in the sense that if an acquisition worsens the situation of others, such acquisition is not permitted. The word "worsen" implies comparison. We must think of "worse" as meaning compared to what. Here, we shall call the criterion, which is compared with situations after a certain acquisition has been made, as 'baseline'. If no one is worse off from the baseline, then the acquisition is justified. Nozick draws this baseline for the state of nature that Locke supposed – namely, the state of sharing in the sense that no yet has property by acquisition.

In other words, Nozick regards justice in acquisition as being satisfied if it is established that private property on shared resources makes more access to goods than leaving it shared. Nozick thought that cases in which such justice of acquisition were not satisfied were very rare cases. This is because "the baseline for comparison is so low as compared to the productiveness of a society with private appropriation that the question of Lockean proviso being violated arises only in the case of catastrophe" (Nozick 1974, 181). In effect, the market economy by the free exercise of private property with almost no condition will be led from the argument of Nozick, and there are few (or almost no) turns to distributive justice that really work. In this case, a famous phrase "Taxation of earnings from labor is on a par with forced labor" (Nozick 1974, 169) is meaningful and even persuasive.

Although, of course, there are many criticisms from egalitarians on a way of drawing the baseline and such a low-level baseline, we will not deal with these here.[5] What we should keep in mind here is that although it seems to be of little concern, the Lockean proviso still represent a premise of the free market economy with private property. Then, Nozick thought that the Lockean proviso also restrict justice in transfer.

4. There are many negative views on whether Nozick has accepted the argument of Locke as a whole. See (Wolff 1991, 102-7) and (Cohen 1995, Ch. 3, Sec. 2).

5. For example, see (Cohen 1995, Ch. 3).

> A theory which includes this proviso in its principle of justice in acquisition must also contain a more complex principle of justice in transfer. Some reflection of the proviso about appropriation constrains later actions. If my appropriating all of a certain substance violates the Lockean proviso, then so does my appropriating some and purchasing all the rest from others who obtained it without otherwise violating the Lockean proviso. If the proviso excludes someone's appropriating all the drinkable water in the world, it also exclude his purchasing it all. [...] The total supply could not be permissibly appropriated by one person at the beginning. His later acquisition of it all does not show that the original appropriation violated the proviso. [...] Rather, it is the combination of the original appropriation plus all the later transfers and actions that violates the Lockean proviso. (Nozick 1974, 179-80)

The range of the Lockean proviso is summarized by Nozick in the following impressive words.

> Each owner's title to his holding includes the historical shadow of the Lockean proviso on appropriation. [...] Once it is known that someone's ownership runs afoul of the Lockean proviso, there are stringent limits on what he may do with (what it is difficult any longer unreservedly to call) "his property". (Nozick 1974, 180)

When anyone falls below the abovesaid baseline, a market economy that freely exercises private property, as assumed by Nozick, loses its moral foundation. Therefore, "property" will be a morally illegitimate holding in such situations. In this sense, private property in Nozick's theory can never be absolute and have full ownership (Vallentyne 2011 161-2). In this case, for pulling everyone up above the baseline, taxation of earnings from labor is not necessarily on a par with forced labor.[6] That is, to realize morally legitimate free market as Nozick assumed, people have to owe the cost to satisfy the baseline and the possibility of taxation is justified to this extent. The problem is the content of "extent". However, Nozick himself thought that "This proviso (almost?) never will come into effect" (Nozick 1974, 179) as critics regard this as a problem.

Considering the relationship between entitlement theory and the Lockean proviso, the appropriateness of the interpretation of the

6. Whether it is actually taxed depends on a practical comparison with other means, though. This point will be argued in Sec. 3 of this article.

Lockean proviso is the most morally important part for justifying free economic activities in the market within libertarian thought. Then, is Nozick's baseline as the shared state before the acquisition began a reasonable interpretation of Lockean proviso?

2.3. *Interpretation of the Lockean proviso – Nozick, suffcientarian, and egalitarian*

It is difficult to evaluate the interpretation of the Lockean proviso of Nozick, despite its mass criticism, as it is not such an unreasonable interpretation. Although Nozick almost ignores it, once it has fallen below the initial shared state, he accepts correcting the situation. In this sense, though it is different from his intention, his theory is not a historical principle in a pure sense, and it also accepts a very weak pattern. The criticisms that Nozick's interpretation does not bring equality among people or create too much of a gap are only external criticisms from critics who think that such problems are important. It is not self-evident why Nozick should accept such assumptions. At the very least, Nozick's argument can be evaluated as being internally consistent.

Of course, I do not think that Nozick's argument lacks problems. First, his assumption that the market economy by the free exercise of private property is so efficient that the market economy falls below the shared state only in the situation of catastrophe, and the proviso is rarely applied, which is not a direct answer to a question of the Lockean proviso. In other words, it is merely expressed as an empirical belief, for general affluence or wealth of society as a whole, as the average person today is richer than the medieval king and capitalism society is wealthier than socialism societies. The problem is that the Lockean proviso does not justify a free market economy with private ownership if anyone falls below the shared state.

However, Nozick gives only auxiliary material that nobody is likely below the shared state, but there is no guarantee that no one is below the shared state (Zwolinski 2015, 521). This is serious problem, but it is a criticism of Nozick's too optimistic assumption about the Lockean proviso. This does not mean that we can point out the crucial internal collapse of interpretation by Nozick. On the other hand, it is difficult to step into the interpretation of the Lockean proviso itself. Even the criticism by Vallentyne, like the following: "There is little reason to hold that those who first use or claim rights over natural resource should reap all the excess benefits that those resources provide" (Vallentyne 2009, 148[7]), does not capture the core of Nozick's argument, as the argument starts from the assumption that natural resources should be shared in some egalitarian manner. This criticism remains external to the consistency of Nozick's interpretation. Then, how can we point out that the baseline setting of Nozick is problematic for the interpretation of his argument?

I would like to point out that the nature of the person whom Nozick thinks important and the situation brought by the baseline which he draws do not mesh. As already argued, having self-ownership is not simply a matter of being born as a human. Self-ownership is a moral status and needs to be respected as a self-author as a separate person. In addition, the importance of being a self-author is that each person lives his/her life with while giving mean to his/her life. Nozick should treat people with self-ownership as such. There are two things to be guaranteed at least in order to make the existence of such a person possible. One is the ability to shape and carry out one's own life as meaningful, and the other is the distribution of resources that will enable a life like that. Things we need to keep in mind are that a meaningful life here does not mean that there are objectively determined good lives and that one should achieve that, namely, perfectionism.

Nozick mentions, "A person's shaping his life in accordance with some overall plan is *his way of giving meaning to his life*." (Nozick 1974, 50 we stress). The meaning of life here is what one gives to one's life by oneself. If we think so, the informational foundation that determines the life that people regard as meaningful to themselves will be heavily influenced by factors such as the era and society in which they actually live. If so, the baseline of the shared state indicated by Nozick should be said to be far apart, for example, from what we are supposed to live meaningful lives today. It is in each circumstance that we find meaning in our lives, not fixed in a shared state. If we think that it is important for us to live a meaningful life as having self-ownership, the baseline for us who are not living a shared state should not be living a shared state.

7. This assumption is persuasive to a degree, but what we do not necessarily have to follow is shown below.

Such understanding may be criticized as follows: you can freely decide your meaningful life instead of living a certain good life; then, for example, if you can find out the meaning of life only by being successful as a professional football player, how should we deal with that. Although the meaning of life is not an aggregate of temporary desire or well-being, if you estimate the meaning you seek for your life very high and to guarantee such a pursuit of such a life, we need too much correction of the distributive situation to achieve free economic activities of private property, and it is difficult for us to appropriately explain the distributive difference between people who want to be a football player and those who are satisfied with an ordinary life without danger.

This is similar to a case called expensive taste (Dworkin 2000, 48-59). When trying to bring about the same well-being to people, if we assume that one person can earn the well-being obtained by drinking beer while another person drinks champagne, despite the fact that they have very different value resources, should we give beer and champagne to each? I would respond to these questions as follows. Both a life becoming football player and an ordinary life without danger are meaningful to them, so it is impossible to say that someone should not to be a football player due to the need for substantial resources, but it is not necessary to carry out by the burden of others. Certainly, only the person can give the meaning of life by oneself, but that should not justify the burden of others in the resource. In this trend of argument, I am likely to advocate equality of resources, but it is not so. This is because the fact that resources are given equally themselves does not have a relationship with whether self-authors can live meaningful lives. The fact that people are given some resources does not guarantee that a person can find meaning to their lives by means of that resource or that it is an adequate treatment in the sense of appropriate respect for persons.

Given this, the degree of distribution required for a person with self-ownership needs to be objective in the sense that it is sufficient for appropriate respect for persons but not subject to individuals'life plan and preferences. There is sufficientarianism as a distribution theory that gives objective criteria in this sense. Sufficientarianism is a theory that set a threshold and combines a positive thesis that argues for the importance of living beyond that threshold and negative thesis that denies further distribution due to egalitarian reason and the like (Casal 2007, 297-304). The interpreting the Lockean proviso in such sufficientarian way is not strange for our understanding of libertarianism.[8]

Finally, I want to dismiss the argument interpreting the Lockean proviso in an egalitarian way. Peter Vallentyne, a leading left-libertarian philosopher, considers natural resources to exist in some egalitarian manner, and people have such entitlement. In particular, he defends equal opportunity for well-being, which is said to be derived from the equality of the life prospects of each person.[9] This argument seems to have considerable persuasion. If our lives are equally important, is not it natural to think that the natural resources we share also exist in some egalitarian manner? Of course, as we have discussed, what is important is whether it can be adequately treated as a self-author, and it is not necessarily the case that some kind of egalitarian distribution accords with sufficient distribution as a treatment of self-authors, there is no reason why I should adopt the egalitarian interpretation. However if we remember that justice claims to "treat equals as equal, " we should say a reason why we do not accept the egalitarian interpretation that seems persuasive at first glance. Indeed, it can be said that people should be treated as a self-author in the same way, so the same weighting should be done on their life prospects. Nonetheless, does it mean that people have to be treated equally as a person who lives life with the same weights must be an egalitarian in the distribution? The principle "treat equals as equal" requires equal treatment, which requires equals to be treated in the same way. It is certainly problematic to treat people's lives as being morally different. However, even if this principle requires our lives with the same weights to be treated according to the same rules, it does not require us to treat those in egalitarian way.[10]

In other words, although treatment according to an egalitarian rule can be one of equal treatment, demand of equal treatment does not require treatment according to an egalitarian rule. In addition, as we have seen various interpretations thus far, although all resources

8. The details of the interpretation are dealt with in the next section.

9. See Vallentyne 2009, 148-9. However, I will not deal with all arguments due to the large number.

10. See Nathan 2015, 1-6. Nagel 1979, 111 argues the distance between equal treatment and content of the treatment.

are shared only by humankind, it does not necessarily mean that we share in some egalitarian manner. Furthermore, there is no reason to assume that the argument that each person's life prospects are equal includes the claim that the sum of resources required by equal security of all human life prospects is always the same as the sum of resources shared by all humankind. Thus, the connection between equality of life prospect and sharing of resources in some egalitarian manner derives most of its conviction not from a logical strong tie but from intuitive conformity. Moreover, the argument I'm trying to advocate now does not share such an intuition and is presenting another basis as "sufficient to treat as a self-author."

From the above, I would like to conclude that I would dismiss the interpretation of the proviso both by Nozick and in some egalitarian manner. And we will explore an appropriate sufficientarian interpretation.[11]

2.4. *A variety of sufficientarian libertarianism that includes the Japanese libertarians*

In the following, I will consider some arguments in favor of sufficientarian libertarianism to articulate my theory. Actually, many libertarians and classical liberals in Japan are "sufficientarian libertarians". Susumu Morimura, a Japanese leading libertarian theorist, constructs his arguments focusing on self-ownership, but in terms of distribution, he justifies the minimum right to life through humanitarian consequential consideration. He adopts pluralism intentionally, and his greatest feature is that both self-ownership and humanitarianism are argued by moral intuition. "The judgement that anyone should not be forced to live a very miserable life without his blame and so the minimum life should be guaranteed will appeal to moral intuition as well as self-ownership." (Morimura 2001, 45).

Although there are pros and cons for his intuitionistic method, it is generally a persuasive argument in conclusion. Morimura's distributive slogan is "Do not worry about being unequal, but worry about poverty (in Japanese: 等しからざるを憂えずして、貧しきを憂

11. Of course, this is only when there are enough resources to distribute sufficiently to everyone. It does not apply to the case of catastrophe where goods are absolutely short, not a moderate scarcity. On such catastrophe case, see Mulgan (2011).

う (*Hitoshikarazaru wo ureezu shite, mazushiki wo ureu*)" (Morimura 2013, 160).

This expression is suggestive in considering our appropriate baseline. When thinking about criticism against the lowness of Nozick's baseline, we can reconsider that they ask why it is meaningful to draw such line, not lowness itself. In other words, they are seeking a positive reason for why we should put a baseline in the shared state. Nozick does not clearly answer this. Simply, it looks like he has dealt with the baseline problem by arguing that almost no situation falls below the line. The slogan above can be understood as drawing that baseline to the resolution of poverty. It also reveals that the slogan is more concerned with the problem of absolute poverty than the relative equality or economic gap. Most of Japanese libertarians, including Morimura, seek the reasons for consequentialism, including humanitarian consideration, but I do not adopt it.[12]

I would like here to submit a criterion based on the normative human view that is sufficient for dealing with self-authors. In other words, what is important in the world of libertarianism that we are discussing now is not simply that human beings live but that it is possible to live in such a way that they are properly treated as having certain moral status. In this line, it is not appropriate to use criteria that are not affected by the situation of society and the distribution pattern of goods, such as calories necessary for human beings to survive. It is also inappropriate to use criteria that are determined by the relation with others with regard to the distribution pattern of goods, for example, relative poverty and the degree of the gaps themselves. What is appropriate is the threshold that is influenced by social situations but not affected by the distribution pattern of goods. This will be a line of decency or resolution for absolute poverty, for example. Moreover, both Morimura and Fabian Wendt adopt such thresholds, while the rationale of Morimura is a humanitarian consideration – that of Wendt is in terms of securing effective self-ownership for the project pursuer (Wendt 2018, 172).

The term "project pursuer" is an expression preferred by libertarians who argue according to Nozick's argument composition. Here, I would like to explain why I will not use this concept which looks useful at first glance. The original source of this term is probably

12. For my view on Morimura's argument, see Fukuhara (2017) Ch. 3 and Ch. 5.

the argument by Loren Lomasky[13], but there are many examples of dealing with this project pursuer as an exchangeable concept of the person of Nozick. For example, Wendt says,

> Persons are purposive beings. They have the capacity to pursue all kinds of projects, including mid- or long-term projects [...] Trivially, all such projects require the use of one's body and mind, and so persons should be conceived as self-owners. But almost all such projects of course also require external resources, in one way or another, and they require being able to count on one's resources. Hence, persons as project pursuers also need the opportunity to acquire private property in external resources." (Wendt 2018, 170-1).

Then, his interpretation of the proviso (the sufficiency proviso) follows:

> [A] practice of private property should be designed in a way that makes sure that everyone has sufficient resources to live as a project pursuer. This is the basic idea behind the sufficiency proviso. Of course, the proviso does not say that everyone is to have sufficient resources to succeed in the specific projects he or she actually pursues; these projects may be very expensive or risky, and justice cannot require that everyone succeeds in his or her projects. The proviso merely requires that everyone is to have enough to live as a project pursuer, to be able to pursue projects beyond mere survival. (Wendt 2018, 172-3)

As a result, what Wendt demands are at least the basic human needs as typified by foods, clothes, and shelter.[14] The person of Nozick and the project pursuer of Wendt seem to be very close. Certainly, we will agree that mere survival is not the problem.

However, there are two points in Wendt's argument of which I am not convinced. One is that if it is supposed that the project pursuit is an essential part of humans, why does not it guarantee sufficiency sensitive to *each project contents*? Someone who wants to become a football player, even if one cannot actually become one,

13. Lomasky (1987). Yuko Hashimoto, Japanese libertarian theorist, argues according to Lomasky. However, she regards that "project pursuer" alone is not good reason to justify the right to minimum welfare. As a result, she based on three considerations including "project pursuer," humanitarian consideration, and utilitarian consideration to justify the right. See (Hashimoto 2008, Ch. 5, sec. 3).

14. See Wendt 2018, 173. Wendt, however, says that people with serious disabilities and illness are required to satisfy needs by further distribution.

should be given the "resources enough to aim for football players" that is different from someone who simply wants to live an ordinary life would be given. As Wendt says, it does not matter whether the project ultimately succeeds. However, if the project is different for each person (perhaps in reality), it should be that sufficient resources should be provided according to the project.

In this case, being that projects expensive or risky are not a good reason for reducing resource distribution: life that lives as an ordinary businessman and the life that becomes a football player should have a different resource distribution to say that there is enough opportunity to pursue each meaningful project. It seems that another stage of discussion is necessary to set an objective threshold tailored to the general "project pursuer." That is to show the reason why we can handle actually different people in a single box in terms of distribution. As I wrote above, in my argument, the reason is the ability to give meaning to one's own life. This ability does not need to mention what people actually plan for life. The important point here is whether one has such ability.[15] With such ability, you will be able to receive respect as a person. Being such a person is not affected by what kind of life plan one has or if you actually succeed.

The second point is the following: even if we can handle project pursuers in a single box, it is not clear why satisfying basic human needs can be said to be sufficient distribution for project pursuit. As Wendt says, the project pursuit is not merely for a survival, but his argument seems to get to a mere "so-so life," in other words a decent life, ultimately (Lomasky 1995, 46-8). Of course, decent life is more advantageous for project pursuit than mere survival to a considerable extent. However, is a guarantee of sufficient resources for the project pursuit to live a decent life? Or does he call lives that can be pursued by decent life as a not expensive project pursuits? If so, I cannot understand why it is necessary to argue that project pursuit is an essential part of human and that sufficient resources for project pursuit should be distributed. If we only derive sufficiency from the interpretation of proviso, we need not to mention the project pursuit (Vallentyne 2009, 148). Indeed, the guarantee of decent life is one of the persuasive interpretations of the proviso by itself. If project

15. Fukuhara (2017) Ch. 3 discusses this problem in more detail with the issue of range property.

pursuit does not mean decent life or a kind, should the term "project pursuit" be treated as a more concrete notion? In this sense, Wendt's words; "There is nothing very attractive about being formally allowed to live a life as a project pursuer when one is actually unable to live a life as a project pursuer." (Wendt 2018, 175) will rebound to himself.[16]

Wendt and I will agree that the best interpretation of the proviso is sufficientarian one. But I don't agree that the combination of project pursuer and decency is the appropriate expression of sufficientarian libertarianism, although I don't have enough words to concrete my abstract conception yet.

3. IMPLICATIONS FOR DISTRIBUTIVE POLICY

As discussed thus far, our sufficientarian-libertarianism prefers a certain pattern of distribution, allowing some distribution and sometimes even required. However, it is wrong to think that this is a correction of the consequences of a free market economy. The satisfaction of sufficiency discussed here is a condition to morally justify the free market economy with private ownership, so it is not *re*-distribution to be precise. In addition, the satisfaction of sufficiency through efforts such as relocation of goods is not satisfied, for example, by charity, but there is a right that can be legitimately required by a person who is below a sufficiency. Of course, this does not mean that we should refrain from giving donations and gifts from charity at all; it may rather be admired as virtuous. The existence of a perfect duty to respond to the demand of this right and the imperfect duty of charity are neither the same nor conflicting. However, what is important is that satisfaction of sufficiency is a duty of justice and that satisfaction must be guaranteed. This calls for measures to ensure satisfaction. On the other hand, although it is a common phrase among libertarians, ensuring the fulfillment of duty does not necessarily mean that all duties must be fulfilled by the government. If there are more effective and efficient means, there is no reason to exclude, and there is the privatization of government projects that were developed in Japan

16. While this criticism on Wendt, I do not have words to argue more in detail the distribution criteria. I can only express it requires sufficient distribution to treat as "a person with the ability to give meaning to one's own life," namely self-author, and it will be inevitable to be similar to decency. To be precise, it is not decency and decency itself is not purpose.

(whether it succeeds or not) based on such thought. Basically, the following argument assumes government policy, but this is not the purpose of denying what I have just noted.

Now, I would like to discuss the form of government distributive policies. There are various forms of policies with various purposes, then, it is difficult to argue about the significance of every forms in detail. So, firstly, I would like to argue about BI as a policy candidate to fulfill a certain threshold, not (relative) equality. Because, as explained below, BI seems to guarantee a certain standard of income and harmonize with my argument at first glance. BI is discussed not only from libertarians but from various positions and fields including egalitarians. Various things are said about the effect of this policy[17], but here I would like to argue about what this policy looks like for libertarianism that I have developed so far.

Since it sometimes carries a different meaning from "basic income" depending on theorist in the first place, I will describe the nature of BI that I will examine here. According to Guy Standing, BI is an institution that the state distributes (a) a modest amount of money (b) to the individual, (c) unconditionally and (d) regularly (Standing 2017, 3.) In addition, everyone has this as a right. It is a consistent proposal that with assuming that the distribution we have considered so far is the right as well. Let's all consider all four elements above in turn.

(a) A modest amount of money has two good meanings, modest amount, and money. To be modest, it is preferable for a libertarianism who defends the free market economy to distribute to fulfill the duty of justice but not to demand further redistribution. In addition, being that money is desirable for self-author because it does not intervene in their lives as it is not defined their uses; there is no reason to bother to select such methods, as payment in kind or food stamp will narrow their choice than money as well as giving stigma.

(b) Sharing Nozick's individualistic life image that "there are distinct individuals, each with his own life to lead" (Nozick 1974, 34), it is a truly appropriate method that distribute to individuals as a unit. Considering the difference from the case of targeting income

17. See (Bregman 2017). What is often mentioned about its effects such as crime rate or divorce rate is an interesting aspect of discussion about BI. In addition, the evaluation of BI will change depending on what kind of interest one views the results. There are various reasons why BI is required, I shall not discuss them here.

per household, for example, the appropriateness of this method becomes more prominent. In Japan, there is a certain proportion of women who become housewives, and DV is also becoming a social problem.[18] "Voice" to DV is difficult from its intimate relationship and established dominant relationship, and anxiety about economic self-reliance to "Exit" may interfere with this. Personalization of distribution may also result in byproducts that can alleviate this or others somewhat.[19]

Point (d) is no problem either: regular benefit is also a favorable condition for self-authors. Ensuring a stable economic prospect for a person planning and carrying out their life plans through a certain period of time reduces extra preparation for failure and enables life plans that one thinks more desirable. As advocates of BI say, it may extend the possibilities of more adventurous business or life.

The problem lies with (c). According to Standing, the unconditional here means that regardless of employment, use of money, amount of income (Standing 2017, 6). I agree with the problems of employment and use of money, but I cannot agree with the argument that income is irrelevant. According to Paula Casal's understanding of sufficientarianism above, distribution until satisfied the threshold is required (positive thesis), but additional distributive consideration beyond the threshold should be denied (negative thesis). If you possess goods above the threshold, it is not required to add further money to you, and you do not have the right to receive such a distribution.

Standing says, "if basic income is viewed as a "social dividend", a share of society's inherited commons and wealth should go to everyone, or to every citizen, as a right. A right is universal, or it is not a right at all" (Standing 2017, 116), but the position I defend can avoid this criticism, as those who are above the threshold already have a sufficient share of the commons. If we remember that the Lockean proviso that we derived sufficiency is a constraint on the acquisition and transfer of shared resources, that one has goods more than a threshold legitimately means that one has received a share from common resources more than enough. Standing's argument here is beside the point.

18. Nonetheless, although gender role division of labor has an influence on this, I cannot taken it up here.

19. As examples of such concrete ripple effect of BI, see (Standing 2017, 60-1).

One may question whether I have to ask employment or will to work. If one works hard with a diligent spirit, which will directly lead to economic growth, society as a whole will become enriched, which will increase living standards, threshold of sufficiency, and the prosperousness of life. However, how much essential is this to be libertarianism? In our experience, one may become wealthy if they adopt a free market economy rather than adopting a central control economy. However, adopting a free market economy is not all of the meanings of libertarian freedom, and freedom is not important only as a means of economic growth. At least, libertarians do not say (I believe so) that if freedom cannot bring about economic growth, it is useless. If diligent labor must be included in meaningful life of persons, it should be called perfectionism; a person who cannot work due to some disabilities will be unable to receive benefits as a self-author by not being able to work. This means that one is not treated as a self-author. It is obviously wrong idea that one cannot give meaning to one's life if one cannot work. In addition, as the growth of GDP in developed countries obviously slows down,[20] I cannot believe that this situation can be changed dramatically by diligence. Rather, the thing to consider is that practical use of AI probably erases largely the place to diligence. Remind the motto that "ought implies can", it is meaningless to say that people should work in the absence of work.[21]

As suggested in the discussion above, I think that the appropriate policy is something like guaranteed minimum income with a sufficientarian threshold as treating as self-authors. Of course, criticism that this will cost a considerable amount of administrative costs will be done by the advocates of BI. As a libertarianism aiming at a small government, we must admit that the problem of administrative costs is a problem that cannot be overlooked easily. In addition, when distributing, it is necessary to investigate whether the person is really below the threshold (such as means test), which itself may infringe dignity or stigmatize. Although this distribution is

20. See (Nakano (Ed.), 2010) exploring alternative visions of how to set economic policy goals when it cannot pursue economic growth. Most of the argument in this book is in the direction that it should not be an economic indicator like GDP but should be based on well-being.

21. If we call something to earn income as labor, the view of labor itself may change when AI is put into practical use more.

a fulfillment of duty of justice, it may be important that self-respect is not made in justice.[22]

At this stage, let us recall that there is a to make case that 'negative income tax' is taken up together with BI in some cases. It may seem likely to be accepted by libertarians as its strong advocator is Milton Friedman (Friedman 1962, ch. 12). I think this is an interesting proposal; however, sufficientarianism does not advocate it. As mentioned earlier, the sufficientarianism only justifies benefits up to the threshold. Then, according to the shortfall of the income up to a certain standard (tentatively 100,000 yen), we will pay benefit under negative income tax. In the absence of any income, if the negative income tax rate is 50%, there will be a benefit of 50,000 yen. Since the sum of negative income tax and earned income will continue to increase to 100,000 yen, then people will not lose the incentives to work. This would be the strength of negative income tax. However, when 100,000 yen is the threshold, positive thesis of sufficientarianism is not satisfied even if 50,000 yen is paid. In order to resolve this problem, for example, it may be considered to set the negative income tax to 100%, but it will be the same result whether you work or not until 100,000 yen. There is no point in adopting negative income tax with this. Alternatively, it may be possible to reduce the income standard to 200,000 yen in order to reach 100,000 yen at a negative income tax rate of 50%. But it collides with negative thesis that is not necessary to pay benefits for people exceeding threshold, 100,000 yen. Then, sufficientarian-libertarianism probably cannot adopt negative income tax.

4. CONCLUSION

What I have done thus far is how we can evaluate the general characteristics of BI from the viewpoint of a sufficientarian-libertarianism, which is constructed mainly by reinterpretation of Nozick.[23] Of course, I realize that efficiency, cost, and other practical problems around BI are left intact. However, I believe that although it

22. Zwolinski (2015) pp. 524-26 insists advantages of BI in practical aspects.

23. In this article, for example, I should have perhaps refered to arguments by Karl Widerquist, a great achievement of BI theory based on self-ownership. However, it goes beyond the intent of this article, and it takes too much paper to refer in this article.

is significant to discuss about data, feasibility and possibility in policy making, it is equally important to discuss the moral basis of such policies. Therefore, as I have argued above, I would like to conclude provisionally that we should advocate not BI but a system that gives each person sufficient income to live as a self-author, although there are practical problems to consider.[24]

BIBLIOGRAPHY

Askew, David. 1994-1995.「リバタリアニズム研究序説―最小国家論と無政府資本主義の論争をめぐって（一）（二）」"Libertarianism kenkyû josetsu : saishô kokkaron to museifu shihonshugi no ronsô wo megutte (1), (2)" ["Libertarianism : An Introduction to the Minimal State and Anarcho-capitalism(1) (2)"]. 法学論叢 *Kyoto Law Review*, 135(6) : 44-65 et 137(2) : 90-114.

Bregman, R. 2017. *Utopia for Realist.* London : Bloomsbury Publishing.

Brock, G. 1995. "Is Redistribution to Help the Needy Unjust?". *Analysis* 55 (1) : 50-60.

Casal, P. 2007. "Why Sufficiency is not enough." *Ethics* 117(2) : 296-326.

Cohen, G. A. 1995. *Self-Ownership, Freedom, and Equality.* Cambridge : Cambridge University Press.

Dworkin, R. 2000. *Sovereign Virtue. The Theory and Practice of Equality.* Cambridge (Mass.) : Harvard University Press.

Frankfurt, H. G. 2015. *On Inequality.* Princeton (NJ) : Princeton University Press.

Friedman, M. 1962. *Capitalism and Freedom.* Chicago : Chicago University Press.

Fukuhara, Akio. 2017.『リバタリアニズムを問い直す』*Libertarianism wo toïnaosu* [*Libertarianism Re-examined*]. Kyoto : Nakanishiya.

Hashimoto, Tsutomu. 2005.「自己所有権型リバタリアニズムの批判的検討」"Jikoshoyuuken gata libertarianism no hihanteki kentou" ["A Critical Examination on Self-ownership Oriented Libertarianism"],『法哲学年報2004』*The Annals of Legal Philosophy*, 2004 : 18-29.

– 2014.「ベーシック・インカム」"Bēshikku inkamu" ["Basic income"]. In『現代の経済思想』*Gendai no keizai shisô* [*The Contemporary Economic Thought*], T. Hashimoto (ed.), 258. Tokyo : Keisô Shobô.

Hashimoto, Yuko. 2008.『リバタリアニズムと最小福祉国家』*Libertarianism to saishô fukushi kokka* [*Libertarianism and the Minimal Welfare State*]. Tokyo : Keisou Shobou.

Inoue, Tatsuo. 1986.『共生の作法』*Kyousei no sahou* [*The Decorum of Conviviality*]. Tokyo : Sôbunsha.

Locke, J. 1988 [1690]. *Two Treatises of Government.* Cambridge : Cambridge University Press.

Lomasky, L. E. 1987. *Persons, Rights, and the Moral Community.* New York : Oxford University Press.

– 1995. "Justice to Charity." *Social Philosophy and Policy* 12 (2) : 32-53.

Morimura, Susumu. 2001『自由はどこまで可能か―リバタリアニズム入門』*Jiyû wa dokomade kanô ka : Libertarianism nyûmon* [*How Much Freedom Is Possible : Introduction to Libertarianism*]. Tokyo : Koudansha.

24. The problems about such benefits between nation and immigrant or among generations are urgent issues. But I do not discuss these here.

– 2013. 『リバタリアンはこう考える』 *Libertarian ha kou kangaeru* [*Libertarian thinks this way*]. Tokyo : Shinzansha.

MOSELEY, D. D. 2011. "A Lockean Argument for Basic Income." *Basic Income Studies* 6 (2) : 2-11.

MULGAN, T. 2011. *Ethics for a Broken World.* Montreal : McGill-Queen's University Press.

NAGEL, T. 1979. *Mortal Questions.* Cambridge : Cambridge University Press.

NAKANO, Takeshi (ed.) 2010. 『成長なき時代の「国家」を構想する』 *Seichou naki jidai no kokka wo kousousuru* [*An Alternative Vision for New Economics Policies*]. Kyoto : Nakanishiya.

NATHAN, C. 2015. "What is Basic Equality?" *Do All Persons Have Equal Moral Worth?*, U. Steinhoff (ed.), 1-16. Oxford : Oxford University Press.

NOZICK, R. 1974. *Anarchy, State and Utopia.* New-York : Basic Books Inc.

ROARK, E. 2013. *Removing the Commons.* Lanham, Maryland : Lexington Books.

SAITO, Taku. 2010. 「政治的理念としてのベーシックインカム」 "Seijiteki rinen to shite no basic income" ["Basic Income as a Political Idea"], in Shinya Tateiwa and Taku Saito 『ベーシックインカム』 [*Basic Income*]. Tokyo : Seidosha.

SCHMIDTZ, D. 2002. "The Meanings of Life." In *Robert Nozick*, D. Schmidtz (ed.), 199-216. Cambridge : Cambridge University Press.

SIMMONS, A. J. 1992. *The Lockean Theory of Rights.* Princeton (NJ) : Princeton University Press.

STANDING, G. 2017. *Basic Income : And How We Can Make It Happen.* London : Penguin Random House UK.

STEINER, H. 1994. *An Essay on Rights.* London, Blackwell.

VALLENTYNE, P. 2009. "Left-Libertarianism and Liberty." In *Debates in Political Philosophy*, Th. Christiano and J. Christman (eds.), 137-51. Chichester : Blackwell.

– 2011a. "Nozick's libertarian theory of justice." In *The Cambridge Companion to Nozick's* Anarchy, State, and Utopia, R. M. Bader and J. Meadowcroft (ed.), 145-67. Cambridge : Cambridge University Press.

– 2011b. "Libertarianism and the Justice of a Basic Income." *Basic Income Studies* vol. 6, no. 2 : 1-11.

VAN DER VOSSEN, B. and P. VALLENTYNE 2018. "Libertarianism." In *Stanford Encyclopedia of Philosophy* (http://plato.stanford.edu/entries/libertarianism/). Accessed May 28 2019.

WENDT, F. 2018. "The Sufficiency Proviso." In Routledge Handbook of Libertarianism, J. Brennan, B. van der Vossen & D. Schmidtz (eds.), 169-83. New York : Routledge.

WOLFF, J. 1991. *Robert Nozick : Property Justice and the Minimal State.* Standford : Stanford U.P.

YASUDA, Sachik. 2014. 「十分性説における閾値」 "Jūbunseisetsu ni okeru ikichi" ["The Threshold in Sufficientarianism : Doubt about Egalitarianism in Distributive Justice"]. 『政治学年報2014-Ⅱ』 *The Annuals of Japanese Political Science Association* 2014-II, 253-70.

ZWOLINSKI, M. 2008. "The Separateness of Persons and Liberty Theory." *The Journal of Value Inquiry* 42 : 147-65.

– 2011. "Classical Liberalism and the Basic Income." *Basic Income Studies* 6, no. 2 : 1-14.

– 2015. "Property Rights, Coercion, and the Welfare State; The Libertarian Case for a Basic Income for All." *The Independent Review* 19, no. 4 : 515-29.

A THEORY OF REAL FREEDOM: TOWARD A GROWTH-ORIENTED LIBERALISM

TSUTOMU HASHIMOTO*

Abstract
What is the nature of real (substantive) freedom in our society? Here, I shall present a new theory of liberalism which I call "growth-oriented liberalism." First, I examine Isaiah Berlin's concept of positive and negative freedom and raise a fundamental problem regarding freedom: Freedom is a paradoxical ideal. I shall identify two paradoxes: one concerns ordinary freedom and sophisticated values, and the other bears on "liberation" and the apathy of individuals or of groups. How can we overcome these paradoxes? To respond to this question, I shall examine Charles Taylor's argument on positive liberty (freedom) and extend its implications. The issue is all the deeper as a society is closely knitted as a community, which is a typical trait told about Japan. By going beyond Taylor's communitarian way of thinking, I shall endeavor to build a new theory of freedom by proposing three principles: the principle of virtue (self-esteem), the principle of generative change, and the principle of differentiation. I argue that the touchstone of free society depends on how we design our social governance based on these principles.
Keywords: liberty, real freedom, liberalism, principles, theory of sociology.

Résumé
Quelle est la nature de la liberté réelle (réelle) dans notre société ? Je présenterai ici une nouvelle théorie du libéralisme que j'appelle « libéralisme orienté vers la croissance ». D'abord, j'examine le concept de liberté positive et négative d'Isaiah Berlin et je pose la question fondamentale en matière de liberté, à savoir que la liberté est un idéal *paradoxal*. J'identifierai deux paradoxes : l'un porte sur la liberté ordinaire et les valeurs sophistiquées, l'autre sur la question de la libération et de l'apathie des individus ou des populations. Comment pouvons-nous surmonter ces paradoxes ? Pour répondre à cette question, j'examinerai l'argument de Charles Taylor sur la liberté positive

*. Tsutomu Hashimoto is a Professor of Economics at the University of Hokkaido (Sapporo, Hokkaido province). The Editor thanks Professor Hashimoto for his obliging help throughout the elaboration of the present issue of the *Review of Economic Philosophy*.

(liberté) et en élargirai les implications. Le paradoxe est d'autant plus lorsqu'il s'agit de communautés, comme la société japonaise. Au-delà du mode de pensée communautaire de Taylor, par exemple, je construis une nouvelle théorie de la liberté en proposant de suivre trois principes : le principe de la vertu (estime de soi), le principe du changement générateur et le principe de la différenciation. Je soutiens que la pierre de touche d'une société libre dépend de la façon dont nous concevons notre gouvernance sociale sur la base de ces principes.
Mots-clés : liberté, liberté réelle, libéralisme, principes, théorie sociologique.

JEL Codes: Z10, B25.

1. INTRODUCTION

In Japan, while traditional liberalism retreated during the period of Junichiro Koizumi's cabinet (2001-2006) under the influence of his neo-liberal philosophy regarding policies such as the privatization of the post office, the second and third Shinzo Abe cabinets (2012-present) moved policy in the opposite direction. Under Abe, neoliberal policies have receded and a big government has returned. Now, a welfare state-type of liberalism has been restored, creating a huge deficit in public finance. Shinzo Abe seems to have been successful in giving liberalism a chance, but many liberals in Japan are now apparently against his approach. For them, the Abe cabinet is seen as conservative and based on communitarian state-type ideas. What, political requests, then, do modern liberals have for the Abe cabinet? It seems that now, the identity of Japanese liberals is blurred. Additionally, it has become popular to criticize the idea of liberalism since this political philosophy does not seem to give us any alternative vision for our society.

In the context of this political situation, we must ask what the nature of liberty is and how it differs from the idea of conservatism. However, when viewed against conservatism, the theory of liberalism is sparse. Liberals today must go beyond the idea of communitarianism and construct a new philosophy of "real freedom." In this paper, I shall present my original theory of freedom in contrast to conservatism, which neglects the value of freedom. Starting with an examination of the concept of positive and negative freedom, we shall see that the words "freedom" and "liberty," which of course have many meanings, can be grasped in a new way.

I shall construct my theory of freedom based particularly on G. Simmel's insights. Then, I will present three principles of freedom with reference to the idea of growth-oriented liberalism: the principle of virtue (self-esteem), the principle of generative change, and the principle of differentiation.

The principle of virtue (self-esteem) includes discovering unknown possibilities for excellence rather than pursuing the known meaning of our lives. The principle of generative change contains a series of concepts: contingency, change, generation, growth, and evolution. The principle of differentiation involves a series of concepts, as well: criticism of uniform society, decentralization and its complementary technique, and creative diversity.

These three principles are mutually complemented in my theory. For example, the principle of virtue itself might not have a strong relationship with real freedom. However, when these principles complement one another, this contributes to providing an opportunity for substantive freedom. These principles constitute key components of what I call "growth-oriented liberalism," which pursues "positive freedom" differently from communitarianism and perfectionism. The touchstone of a free society which enjoys real freedom depends on how we design our social governance, particularly on how we activate our potentials that are unknown even to ourselves.

In what follows, I first examine Isaiah Berlin's concept of positive and negative freedom and raise a fundamental issue regarding freedom: Freedom per se is a paradoxical ideal. I shall reveal two paradoxes: one of ordinary freedom and sophisticated value, and one of liberation and apathy. How can we overcome these paradoxes? To respond to this question, I shall examine Charles Taylor's argument on positive liberty (freedom) and extend its implications. Beyond his communitarian way of thinking, I construct a new theory of freedom by proposing the three principles introduced above.

2. RECONSIDERING POSITIVE AND NEGATIVE FREEDOM

The words "freedom" and "liberty" have many meanings. For example, one might experience freedom as liberation, or might obtain liberty from subordination, compulsion, or poverty. Additionally, freedom can be absolute and can involve autonomy of choice and independence, as well as liberty from internal ego. Freedom can also exist as nonintervention, the ability to violate norms, a state without anything to lose, and as an inevitable recognition of history.

Why does the concept of freedom have so many meanings? Likely, it is because this word represents a key concept in conceiving a favorable society and a satisfying life. Socially important words are often ambiguous and people are constantly discussing their appropriate usage. Words whose interpretations are frequently disputed are called "contested concepts," and "freedom" must be one of the most important contested concepts in society since its vital meaning is constantly debated.

It might be surprising to realize that our free society has been established despite the ambiguity of the concept of freedom. Even without strictly confirming the meaning of freedom, we can maintain social order through compromising with one another. However, the question I would like to examine here is not how compromise within society is possible, but how a free society is sociologically feasible.

I shall begin by considering the famous distinction between "positive freedom" and "negative freedom," following Isaiah Berlin's division of the two concepts (Berlin 1969). Positive freedom, or "freedom to," means freedom as self-control and has the following two characteristics: individual autonomy, which controls the self, and collective autonomy, which rules the group. Conversely, negative freedom, or "freedom from," means freedom from compulsion and includes freedom from interference of others and a self-compulsive state (i.e., liberty from the lack of ability to enjoy freedom). Berlin understood that negative freedom is superior to positive freedom since the latter has historically involved the danger of turning into freedom of group control and negating individual rights. Although the concept of positive freedom is certainly appealing, it is as dangerous as other attractive concepts. According to Berlin, we should argue for a society which embraces the concept of negative rather than positive freedom.[1]

Contrary to Berlin's argument, Erich Fromm (1900-1980) believed that the concept of "negative freedom" is more dangerous

1. I. Berlin's disciple, Charles Taylor, criticized Berlin's stance advocating negative freedom in his essay, "What's Wrong with Negative Liberty?" (Taylor 1985).

(Fromm 1941). According to Fromm, people felt loneliness and anxiety and perceived liberty as an unbearable burden once they had been emancipated from various constraints in pre-modern societies. In such isolated situations, Fromm argued, people prefer authority. In fact, these scenarios have resulted in the rise of fascist political regimes throughout history. What is necessary to prevent people losing the freedom that they have only recently acquired? According to Fromm, both autonomous individuals as well as a planned economy known as "democratic socialism" must be established in society. However, Fromm's conception of freedom creates another problem in the economic field since it tends to lead to economic collectivism instead of economic liberalism.

In discussing Berlin and Fromm's interpretations, we find that freedom is a paradoxical idea. If we seek negative freedom, we will produce the desire for strong authority as an unintended consequence. However, if we pursue positive freedom, we will generate a violent collectivism as an undesired result. These paradoxes will demonstrate the difficulty involved in properly applying the concept of freedom.

3. FUNDAMENTAL ISSUES WITH FREEDOM

Is freedom an idea which paradoxically invites its opposite? A person who has acquired individual freedom sometimes seeks collective freedom to obtain more power to reform his society. Exploration of positive freedom may bring about totalitarianism as a result of individuals seeking collective power. However, once a totalitarian society is created, people realize that negative freedom is much more valuable than positive freedom. While people may feel limited when they have only negative freedom, they can understand its value when they are placed under totalitarian rule.

While realized freedom can be problematic, unrealized freedom seems beneficial. There are two paradoxes behind this contradiction: One of ordinary freedom and sophisticated value, and another of liberation and apathy. The former is a problem of negative freedom, which we will discuss in Section 3.1., and the latter is a challenge of positive freedom, which we discuss in Section 3.2.

3.1. *A Paradox of Ordinary Freedom and Sophisticated Value*

As Fromm demonstrated, when people are liberated from societal constrains, they sometimes lose their insight on how to live a meaningful life. However, such freedom *per se* is not essential to having a worthwhile existence.

It is true that people who value liberty are not necessarily culturally sophisticated. Those who defend their freedom are unable to overcome their own earthly desires and have not escaped society's judgement (*doxa*). To lead a sophisticated life, we should subject ourselves to our cultural tradition. Liberalists who strongly advocate freedom might be culturally dull. Those who claim that freedom is important are ordinary people living shrewdly and who are said to be less thoughtful from the perspective of sophisticated conservatism. Ordinary people tend to affirm secular freedom for the present. However, even when they support such freedom, they do not escape their anxiety.

If we think seriously about escaping the fear of life, we should criticize the lives of ordinary people and be prepared to escape from our secular civilization. Freedom in our secular society can never be defended as it stands. However, philosophers of liberty or liberalism tend to concentrate their deliberations on institutional conditions of freedom, where the concept of liberty is formally defined. Is this not a very paradoxical situation? Those who advocate secular freedom seem unable to escape the anxiety of crowds, and even if they know the value of liberty, they are forced to live their secular lives with many internal constraints. In this scenario, real freedom in a secular society will not be realized.

3.2. *A Paradox of Emancipation and Apathy*

Another paradox of freedom is that as liberation, it creates apathy in our mind. For example, consider a person who has recently graduated from high school and has just been emancipated from the school system's disciplinary power. For a while, he or she enjoys freedom as emancipation. However, doubts might gradually enter his or her mind. He or she might become dubious about the nature of freedom that has been acquired. After a year, he or she might lose any positive feeling regarding the value of liberty. Although this person sought freedom as emancipation eagerly, he or she might lose his or her sense of freedom altogether. What is the freedom for this individual, after all?

Freedom is a paradoxical idea. When we cannot find a good way to use it, we will become disappointed in ourselves and it is not uncommon for us to fall into self-hatred. We want to escape from liberty and thus seem to have a tradition that is anti-freedom.

Although it is said that we are living in a free society, the desire for liberty is not necessarily popular among people. It is not uncommon for individuals to fall into apathy in a free society. When people allow themselves to be free, they gradually lose their discipline and passion simultaneously. In this case, it might be better that we build a society that is replete with authority and a spirit of warmth. Binding ourselves under the power of government rule and to principles of respect will benefit us. We will find that people in our society who subject themselves to certain authority and such principles are sometimes more energetic.

Nonetheless, we are not seeking suppression. Freedom is *prima facie* regarded as desirable. Why do people pursue liberty rather than subjection? The answer is not necessarily self-evident. If freedom eventually leads to suppression, we might benefit from seeking the latter from the beginning. If human beings are incapable of enjoying freedom, then subjection is necessary in our lives.

However, saying that subjection is more important than freedom will cause a number of misunderstandings. For example, if one says that a totalitarian society is freer than a liberal one, he or she misunderstands the nature of freedom. Totalitarian society has brought various evils such as heavy assertion of political control; improper management due to excessive concentration of power; exclusion and assassination of marginal people, minorities, and rebels; purification of subordinate ethnic groups; social integration through war, bribery, and corruption; non-reflective governance by collective incorporation; authoritative oppression of people; and inefficient construction of a planned economy, etc. However, our challenge is that when we try to build a free society instead of a totalitarian state, we might become less able to enjoy the value of liberty.

The difficulty of freedom lies here. How can we construct a social order that reaffirms the value of liberty in a free society? How can we enjoy the value of freedom in an unrestricted society? Finally, how should we perceive the idea of freedom as a way of human relations, a method of managing our organizations, and as a societal rule of law? The question examining "how real freedom is possible" must be evaluated considering these questions.

4. REAL (SUBSTANTIVE) FREEDOM

As we have examined, there are two paradoxes associated with freedom: First, freedom in our secular society produces anxiety. Second, freedom as liberation cannot be properly institutionalized. How can we overcome these two paradoxes?

The answer depends on our awareness concerning social governance. Without insight, we cannot help but fall into one of the two following societies. The first is a free society in which one cannot feel free. The second is a repressed one where an individual might be able to feel free. However, neither of these societies can avoid the risk of totalitarianism. The former, which seeks liberty as an institution, easily gives up freedom because people receive no advantage from it. The latter, which seeks people's subjective feeling of freedom, might not take institutional liberty seriously from the beginning.

Is it possible to establish freedom as a real feeling and as an institution at the same time? Can we create substantive freedom both in our institutional and psychological settings? Freedom is not a regulatory condition of our actions, but a substantive condition which constitutes our lives. What kind of ideas and thoughts will bring us substantive freedom?

Let us first consider this question from the perspective of Berlin's "negative freedom." The value of negative freedom has a property of scarce goods. Generally speaking, the more one is restrained, the more one desires negative freedom. Therefore, people with various restrictions would get great value (utility) from negative freedom per unit. However, if negative freedom is established to a certain extent in our society, it will become impossible to maintain its value. In this scenario, the marginal utility of the additional unit of negative freedom will reach zero or even become negative. In such a situation, we will feel dissatisfied with ourselves because we cannot effectively utilize the abundance of freedom available.

If this is the case, we might benefit from reducing our amount of freedom through regulation and then introducing subsequent deregulation. In the phase of regulation, one will lose the negative utility that freedom brings. In deregulation, however, one will enjoy the value of liberty. Through these two operations, we might be able to perceive the greatest value of freedom. If we call institutionalized freedom "liberty," we can maximize the appreciation of freedom by cyclical manipulations of institutional authority.

However, such a policy of cyclically manipulating liberty is an unfavorable suggestion because it requires the government to increase or reduce liberty arbitrarily. We must activate our imagination to develop governance techniques that realize both institutional liberty and psychological freedom at the same time.

4.1. *Balancing Freedom and Non-Freedom*

This is a good place for us to refer to Charles Taylor's argument. Taylor, who took a different stance on liberty from I. Berlin, once argued that people in Tirana, the capital of Albania, may enjoy more freedom than people in London, the capital of the United Kingdom (Taylor 1985). Although freedom of religion is not allowed in Tiara, there are few traffic lights and traffic is smooth. However, while freedom of religion is allowed in London, traffic during the day is quite congested. Regarding daily life, citizens of London enjoy less freedom than those of Tirana. However, can we say that citizens of London are more disadvantaged than those of Tirana? The answer will depend on how freedom is evaluated. Using this example, Taylor suggests taking a specific position when evaluating various kinds of liberties.

Indeed, London's traffic jams are notorious and many professionals are late for their business meetings. Travelers sometimes move only three kilometers in 30 minutes when they get a taxi during a traffic jam. Is London worse than Tirana? Some may answer, "No, in London there are abundant business opportunities, plenty of products and cultural events, and the whole city is full of dynamic charm. London is obviously more abundant in freedom than Tirana." In addition to London, other major cities in developed countries may be said to be free and attractive places to live for similar reasons.

However, the following counterargument might be presented:

> Although people in London are free under its government, there are plenty of opportunities for businesses to be frustrated, and citizens can only engage in their desire of viewing a variety of products that cannot be bought. People cannot participate in cultural events due to the costs associated with high traffic volumes, which would leave them exhausted both financially and physically. Although it is said that the whole city is dynamic, there are large constraints. Thus, London's attractiveness is diminished. Regarding the amount of freedom available to citizens, London is the same as Tirana.

As people's freedom has certainly increased with the development of the city while the city itself has simultaneously become restrictive, we cannot regard the increase of freedom optimistically. Virginia Lee Burton's picture book *The Little House* (1942) fantastically depicts this reality. According to this story, there was a small house in a quiet place in an old country, and the house was able to enjoy the natural scenery of every season. However, with modernization, the area became surrounded by the bustle of road and housing developments, and trams and trains running over an elevated line passed in front of the house all day. When surrounded by skyscrapers, the house could no longer see the moon and stars, and it became dirty with dust and smoke. Then, the little house decided to move to the countryside, which was full of nature, stating "Oh, here is my place." Thus, the little house rediscovered its position in the natural environment.

This story makes us realize the value of nature in contrast with urbanization. Of course, if one feels comfortable in a city, one can choose to live there. However, if one feels uncomfortable, one should live in a suburb or countryside. What we can learn from this story is that a free society should be one in which people can choose their stations. When revisiting the problem of freedom in London and Tirana, we cannot say decisively which city is relatively freer. However, if there are two cities like London and Tirana in one country, or if people can become world citizens and choose either London or Tirana as their place of residence, it may be said that the freedom to choose cities constitutes a free society.[2]

2. Charles Taylor's argument on positive liberty (freedom) indicates that we must create our cities to be worthwhile places to live. Although Taylor is well-known as a communitarian thinker, the problem we face here is not an issue of community itself but how to use freedom as a valuable commodity. Liberalists will share the same concern.

However, another might respond to the question of freedom in London and Tiara with the following as indicated in Inoue (2008): "Indeed, I admit that there are a lot of traffic lights in London, but traffic lights are not the thing that constrains freedom. They merely adjust people's actions. Without traffic lights, traffic would be paralyzed even more. As far as religious freedom is concerned, citizens in London might not be so religious. However, it does not matter whether people are substantively religious or not. What matters is to permit private religious act as long as 'freedom of religion' is secured by law. Even if there are not many who use that right, this is what constitutes a free society"

According to this claim, traffic congestion is not a problem of "freedom as a right," but a matter of adjusting people's actions which the administrative authority should manage. Additionally, freedom of religion must be legally recognized, but the number of religious people does not affect the issue of freedom. Is this claim persuasive? A philosopher embracing anti-liberalism such as Charles Taylor might respond, "No, London is less comfortable than Tirana". In reality, citizens in London have not enjoyed their freedom. While giving priority to "negative freedom," society eventually becomes chaotic, symbolized by its traffic jams. This shows the great cost of negative freedom.

4.2. *Toward an Alternative Enterprise of Positive Freedom*

Is this objection persuasive? From Taylor's point of view, both "development of secularization" with declining religious faith and "progress of liberalism" with less governmental intervention deteriorate our modern society. What Taylor raises in the comparison between London and Tirana can be formulated in the following two questions:

> Question 1: When people come to live in cities seeking convenience of daily life, the unpleasantness of life increases as a result of unintended consequences. If so, should the government intervene regarding the freedom of urban residence and develop positive freedom (i.e., comfort of life) in cities?
>
> Question 2: Even though free society acknowledges "religious liberty" as a right, when the number of religious people decreases, this creates a shallow secular society. As a result, people lose some significant

> opportunities to develop valuable lives. If this is the case, our society will be deprived of positive freedom. Is this not a substantively unfree society?

The problem is not simply whether London or Tirana is the more comfortable place to live. When comparing London and Tirana, people might want to live in the former. Its intense atmosphere may add new utility and attract people. However, what if the people of London begin to exercise their religious liberty? We might be able to move our society toward such a direction in prospering citizens' lives. I would like to call such an idea of promoting substantive freedom not only in religion but also in various other areas involving the human spirit "growth-oriented liberalism."

Growth-oriented liberalism is not a position to secure freedom at its minimum. Rather, it seeks a society in which people can develop various values in a free atmosphere. Along with communitarianism, growth-oriented liberalism is interested in establishing positive freedom. However, growth-oriented liberalism is not the same as communitarianism. To clarify the difference, we must examine the problem of governance regarding what kind of positive freedom is requested and in what way. Growth-oriented liberalism is an alternative comprehensive approach to communitarianism for developing a social design for realizing positive and substantive freedom.

4.3. *Causality Determinism and Defects of Paternalism*

Thus, the question becomes what kind of social imagination is necessary to realize substantive freedom. As a foundation for considering this problem, I would like to examine "causality determinism" and "paternalism," both of which are often discussed in philosophy. Each is supposed to be an argument for denying freedom, but in fact, neither does so.

In causality determinism, freedom is considered only an illusion. Even if each person chooses based on his or her free will, an option is actually "chosen" according to one's social situation and social structure and thus there is no free choice. Suppose, for example, that I bought chewing gum at a kiosk in a building. Is this act of purchasing based on my free will? According to causality determinism, my purchase has already been determined by the advertisement of the gum company and the overall structure of capitalist society. Causality determinism does not deny the significance of "substantive freedom." Certainly, buying gum at a shop may be an involuntary act affected by the advertisement of a gum company. However, the problem here is not the causality itself, but our lifestyle orientation that requires us not to "ride too much on the logic of large capital (a large company's management strategy)."

For example, when I order high quality gum from overseas instead of buying gum at a kiosk, even if my behavior is determined by the overall structure of the capitalist society, it escapes the power of domestic large capital. Even if free will is mere fantasy, we can question what kind of purchasing style is virtually free, as a matter of one's lifestyle. Substantive freedom works as a value criterion for moral and aesthetic evaluation regarding the "quality" of our capitalist society.

Consider another example. I, as a business entrepreneur, founded a company and made profits for a while. However, the social situation changed and I was forced into bankruptcy. In this case, the main cause of bankruptcy seems to be the change of the social situation. However, is it possible for me to escape the responsibility of bankruptcy? In a free society, responsibility must be attributed to individuals. I had the option of revamping my company's management policy and avoiding bankruptcy. Thus, I must take responsibility for not making such a choice. A free society is made possible by such a "social arrangement" where responsibility is attributed to its actors. If we do not assign individual responsibility for bankruptcy, we cannot maintain a free economic order. If we can escape our responsibility when our company goes bankrupt, people will over-engage in risks and our whole economic society may fail. Freedom is not a phenomenon that is on the same level as causality determinism, but it is compatible with it. Substantive freedom depends on our social arrangements regarding risks and responsibilities. In this case, the society that allocates the responsibility of bankruptcy to the entrepreneur is a free one. In contrast, a society in which the state relieves the responsibility of bankruptcy is a collectivist one.

"Paternalism" is another concept that denies free society. According to this notion, many people cannot make autonomous decisions properly, so the government should protect them from being exposed to the freedom of choice. For example, high school teenagers who engage in prostitution have not established an autonomous self able to decide on its own. For this reason, paternalism requires that they should be restricted in their rights of self-determination (i.e., the government should regulate prostitution). However, this argument is controversial because a free society might recommend that people who do not have sufficient ability to make sound decisions for themselves learn from their own experiences through trial and error.

For paternalists, the ideal of fostering positive freedom is to develop people's self-determination abilities through, for example, the education system. However, in difficult cases such as high school teenagers'prostitution, paternalists must constrain citizens'abilities to make decisions for themselves. The problem with this logic is that it limits the scope of positive freedom to the realm in which people's self-determination ability works sufficiently. However, such freedom can also be applied to areas where citizens' self-determination power does not work very well. For example, it might be desirable for elementary school students to be given the chance to choose math classes at different levels. A free society can encourage citizens' experiences with trial and error irrespective of their self-determination ability.

It is true that the arguments of both causality determinism and paternalism criticize negative effects of freedom and harvest something substantive in our society. However, neither of these provides rich debate regarding what substantive freedom is. I would like to investigate this in the following discussion.

Generally speaking, people are not always seeking freedom. While they enjoy it as an institution, they might not appreciate liberty in a substantive sense. When people feel that they are wasting the opportunities provided by freedom, they might undervalue it. However, to establish a substantively free society, it might be necessary to limit the ability to take away freedom against citizens' will. We must have a certain outlook in our society advocating that people can enjoy substantive freedom. To that end, we must have rich political imaginations. What kinds of institutions are necessary to realize substantive freedom[3]? I would like to present three principles

3. This problem has already been thoroughly examined by the founder of sociology, Georg Simmel. However, Simmel did not propose a generalized theory of freedom, although he gave us many insights and examples of the functions of substantive freedom. Here, I would like to formulate some conditions of a substantively free society, inspired by Simmel's contribution (Simmel 1923).

of freedom from my theoretical perspective of growth-oriented liberalism in the following section.

5. THREE PRINCIPLES OF A FREE SOCIETY

In Section 3, I noted that there are two kinds of paradoxes in the concept of freedom. In Section 4, I introduced the notion of real or substantive freedom to cope with these two paradoxes. Here, I would like to investigate the nature of what we call "real freedom." I shall divide types of real or substantive freedom into the following three categories: the principle of virtue (self-esteem), the principle of generative change, and the principle of differentiation.

On one hand, the concept of real freedom represents another type of positive liberty. It is different from Berlin's concept of freedom since it does not refer to any particular purpose of individual life or social group, any notion of self-control, or any idea of planning. On the other hand, real freedom represents another type of negative freedom. It differs from Berlin's concept of negative freedom since it promotes the government's role of making people feel more esteemed, changing social situations, and differentiating social conditions.

Additionally, the concept of real freedom will give us insight regarding how to overcome the two paradoxes of liberty discussed above (i.e., that of ordinary freedom and sophisticated value, and that of liberation and apathy). Furthermore, the concept of real freedom will give us solutions to the following questions stated previously (e.g., How can we construct a social order that reaffirms the value of liberty in a free society? How can we establish the value of freedom where it ceases to be felt? How should we perceive the idea of freedom as a way of human relations, a method of managing our organizations, and as a societal rule of law?

5.1. *The Principle of Virtue (Self-Esteem)*

Freedom can pave the way for fostering human excellence. This is the principle of the excellence or virtue of freedom. Freedom is important because it first gives each person a minimum amount of dignity as an individual. When people receive this dignity, they can start developing feelings of self-esteem through mutual recognition.

This feeling will ultimately lead people to excellence. Here, I would like to note that there is a chain of values from dignity to self-esteem which ends in excellence.

The scope of this chain can be expressed by the word "decency." Decency has two meanings in our lives: ordinariness and elegance. Use of this word shows that there is no clear division in the value chain from minimum dignity (negative freedom) to the highest degree of prominence (positive freedom). We interpret the meaning of excellence in the word "dignity," and in the practice of excellence, there is an opportunity for us to admit true dignity. Of course, we can draw artificial distinctions in this concept. However, growth-oriented liberalism would rather focus on a society that seeks minimum dignity, which enables simultaneously seeking the highest degree of excellence. Negative freedom, which is given by institutions in our society, would lead us to realize substantive freedom through various circuits. The logic that searches for such a society forms the principle of virtue (self-esteem) in relation to freedom.

What is necessary for this purpose (which seems to be irrelevant at first glance) is the behavioral principle that each person follows non-personal and super-personal forms of guidance (such as money, rule of law, bureaucratic communication style, etc.). For example, people can accept non-personal influences such as money in the market as super-personal forms of guidance. People can also learn how to handle anonymous relationships such as those seen in social dancing by eliminating private and emotional communications. In this way, converting the way of communication from a human and emotional one to a non-personal and super-personal method will enrich the range of people's actions.

The reason these forms of communication become factors of freedom is that people can secure personal independence by accepting non-personal and super-personal principles of human discourse. If we value exclusively personal transmission, it will lead us to narrowing the scope of communication, sacrificing our inner self and excluding marginal persons. According to Georg Simmel, approving non-personal and therefore symbolic authority is more important than approving "prestige," which derives from personal relations since the former secures the internal freedom of individuals (Simmel 1923). Additionally, to approve of the dominance of abstract rules is to agree with the prohibition clause regarding what should not be done, and this guarantees freedom about what one must do. Of course, to establish the rule of law based on the realization of freedom, we need a geographically sufficient area for its dominance. If the dominant sphere is wide, the authority (ruler) can control only a smaller portion of each individual's behavior. In such a situation, people can freely develop their own personality.

In this way, we acquire substantive personal freedom by accepting the authority of non-personal and super-personal entities. To free ourselves, we must first be prepared to obey an abstract entity. However, this does not mean that real freedom will be fostered only by making us slaves to abstract entities. Here, I would like to propose my observation regarding how to foster our real freedom beyond accepting abstract entities: Real freedom can be symbolically represented by satisfying the dignity of the most oppressed people in a way that realizes their excellence. In an adversarial situation, one can fortify his or her passion to become a noble soul. Oppressed sufferers care for their souls and thereby have great influence on other people through their noble spirit. In this case, it is effective to support the activities of oppressed people to foster various kinds of human virtues in our society. Supporting a marginal person in adversity, for example, provides new possibilities to vulnerable people who tend to be excluded (such as the Ainu), stimulates other people's activities, and nurtures their real freedom in activating their own potentialities.

Marginal persons experience discomfort in their daily lives, and it is not uncommon for them to be excluded from other people. A free society should be inclusive of such marginal persons and should support their outstanding spirits, which are sometimes sublimated through their suffering. By supporting them, our society can make freedom more valuable. A substantively free society reveals that a life which at first glance is not regarded as virtuous has dignity, and it also realizes excellence at the same time. The realization of various values that do not fit into the existing concept of civil virtue is substantively important in making our society free.

The value of freedom lies in excellence that is not constrained by existing virtues. While such excellence is inspired by others, each person can discover its nature through an inherent understanding of liberty. The value of freedom is realized by discovering unknown possibilities of excellence in the process of searching for the meaning of life. Freedom has such an irreplaceable significance. People who seek excellence or virtue often lose sight of the significance of liberty because they tend to try escaping from narrow types of freedom, i.e., the autonomy to choose in a social system. However, for those who seek excellence, freedom must have substantive significance. The question that remains examines what kind of governance technique constitutes the principle of virtue in a free society.

Thus far, I have argued that the real value of freedom lies in the realization of human virtue in a different manner. However, the objection that freedom is possible without seeking excellence may arise. In reality, every individual can have distinction to the extent that it is suitable for him or her. However, from an ethical perspective, real freedom is defined as human growth where people can foster their own assets. Although this can be done to a broad extent, there is no objection regarding this ideal. The question we must ask is how to position this ethical ideal in our free society. For example, this will allow us to design our society to receive various benefits and inspiration from individuals who seek their own excellence, while we honor them. Particularly, when we have a good attitude and recognize the potential excellence of marginal people, we will foster various virtues and therefore real freedom in our society in which communitarians are not deeply interested.

5.2. *The Principle of Generative Change*

The second principle for establishing real freedom is generative change. Real freedom is brought when society is constantly mobilized. To give freedom its substantive value, for example, it is necessary to secure a situation in which authorities are regularly changing. When various dominant values and influences are always shifting, real freedom will flourish spontaneously. Freedom becomes real when we escape from the dominant power and established values, since we can then expect new values and power relations in such a changing situation (e.g., negative freedom). For that purpose, our society must incorporate the element of change in principle. "Generative change" means change which is generated spontaneously without our arbitrary will but that is nonetheless capable of being stimulated institutionally.

The principle of generative change involves the human understanding necessary to make our society flourish. It requires not only changing people's communication, but also saving them from being disconnected. If people do not care about each other, society will not thrive. However, liberty is the value that inspires constant change in human relations. Freedom does not involve qualities that each person has inherently, and it is not an acquired property. Instead, freedom is a process that is generated in people's communication in which they are constantly achieving self-liberation, both physically and spiritually (i.e., positive freedom).

Of course, a society rich in change tends to fall into instability, such that a certain system design is necessary. For example, we must establish a political system for implementing regime change to make rotation of rulers a peaceful process. To make a bad ruler retire as soon as possible and in a peaceful manner, it is desirable to have a system that limits the terms of administrative power. Additionally, we must establish a system that gradually rotates influential persons in politics (e.g., a two-party system that institutionalizes the substitution of the ruling party, or a single-seat constituency system that dramatically changes the outcome of a vote).

Such institutional design can be regarded as a competitive order. In fact, an order which incorporates various competitions changes people's relations within a certain institutional framework. People no longer live in a cooperative structure, nor do they live with master-slave relationships. Instead, people will live with a fluid relationship of control in a competitive environment. To build a competitive order, we can propose various ideas such as activating free public debate, rotating leaders, etc.

The principle of generative change is attractive because we sometimes want to review our lives from a novel perspective, and it can be said that novelty is the source of vitality in our life. The first step is to recognize contingent reality, or to identify that a situation is potentially different from what was expected. The principle of generative change in real freedom begins with encouraging the recognition of this unintentional aspect. Next, the principle of generative change encourages advancement that enhances growth and development and ultimately leads us to a desire for omnipotence and evolution. Real freedom with generative change will guide us to novelty as a source of a rewarding life and will promote transformative use of free opportunities.

While concepts such as contingency, change, generation, growth, and evolution have different meanings, our desires and aspirations for generative change are not limited to any one of these concepts. Since our desire is amorphous, the principle of generative change will require a broad philosophy which leads us to the idea of growth-oriented liberalism. The principle of generative change demonstrates that real freedom must be subjected to social transformation. This idea is different from other normative stances such as communitarianism or perfectionism.

The competitive order mentioned above is one device for encouraging such generative change. Such an order can be organized in various aspects of our society. This would, for example, require governance techniques such as encouraging alternative policy recommendations (submission of legislation) or promoting cultural maturity through commerce in a competitive market. However, the principle of generative change does not necessarily defend the market principle based on private property rights. For example, this position may recommend restricting the idea of self-ownership and permit transactions of body parts. It also advocates destroying intellectual property rights associated with the development of AIDS treatment drugs. Additionally, this principle will require institutional design to impose constraints on the demand for economic freedom and develop various values supporting the growth of our society.

However, the principle of generative change recommends that we transplant artificial market mechanisms and administrative laws in such areas where the market mechanism does not function well.

A free society is one that has created a system that stimulates change and expects the substantive value of freedom to be fostered in our social order. The mechanism of generative change is one of the means by which we can discover substantive freedom. However, we do not know enough in advance regarding the nature of real freedom. We must take the change itself as worthwhile. Otherwise, we cannot grasp the potentials of substantive freedom.

At the outset, I examined various forms of unknown purposes (value) to be nurtured and realized rather than assuming a certain substantive purpose (value) or adopting the optimum means for that purpose. I would like to call such a method of governance "spontanietism." "Spontanietism" is the idea of proposing a social design for fostering potential virtues by activating the spontaneous power of the people. A gardener cares for vegetation by nurturing rich soil. In the same way, we as the gardeners of society will foster fruitful changes by cultivating a rich environment in our social order. Real freedom as substantive value will flourish when we reorganize our governance based on such a perspective.

5.3. *The Principle of Differentiation*

The third principle for establishing substantive freedom is differentiation. Differentiation represents division, insertion of noise, cracks, pluralization, and criticism of overwhelming elements. Through differentiation, real freedom is fostered in our society. The following is a discussion of the differentiation principle of freedom introduced above.

The concept of differentiation involves the following sequence. First, differentiation calls for practices which seek to escape from the dominant ideas which have stagnated in our society. Next, it entails establishing a system which decentralizes the dominant power. Third, differentiation proposes various pieces of wisdom regarding governance to cope with the risk of decentralization. If decentralized governance goes well, this principle proposes that we divide our inner spaces to foster our potentialities. Ultimately, differentiation expects the occurrence of spontaneous creative activities. In this way, the concept of differentiation has a semantic sequence ranging from criticizing a non-creative and uniform society to advocating creativity and non-uniformity.

The principle of differentiation is similar to that of generative change mentioned above regarding seeking a shift or a transformation toward a new society. Differentiation is avant-garde in its spirit. It is not a means for achieving freedom, but instead constitutes freedom in itself. In the process of differentiation, a person will gain his real freedom. While the principle of generative change provides a condition for realizing substantive freedom, the principle of differentiation gives us real freedom directly.

The method of differentiation has already been examined in the sociology of Simmel, who suggests division of the system's dominant power (Simmel 1923). It has also been examined in the anarchist movement, which seeks differentiation as a means of creation (Graeber 2004). Modern anarchists would not be satisfied with the principle of generative change, which produces real freedom spontaneously. Instead, they would try to bring substantive freedom through their practice. For example, anarchists gain substantive freedom through expression of resistance to the dominant power. Resistance constitutes real freedom by itself since it indicates that its adherents are not involved in the dominant power structure, therefore expressing the conduct of real freedom.

The principles of generative change and differentiation can be distinguished from other concepts. For example, the principle of generative change is favored since it accords with the principle of hedonistic pleasure, but it does not constitute substantive freedom. In contrast, the principle of differentiation is not necessarily desired by people, but it constitutes substantive freedom. Substantive freedom does not mean realizing human desires as they are. When one develops desire in a certain direction, freedom will appear to be substantive. For the sake of substantive freedom, some type of wisdom is necessary to guide the principle of hedonistic pleasure.

First, the principle of differentiation calls for departure from the stagnant dominance of uniformity. As an ethical guideline of this principle, we are recommended to evaluate outstanding, unusual, or extraordinary things instead of ordinary, uniform, or obsolete ones. In politics, this principle recommends that we listen to the voices of minorities to avoid the tyranny of the majority. Additionally, this principle promotes us constantly handling our own intimate affairs through exchanges with minorities. Through such practices, we can expect better governance regarding freedom.

Second, the principle of differentiation proposes a certain institutional design for decentralized governance. For example, this could include a proposal for privatization of the post office or private consignment of the public library. Furthermore, the principle of differentiation must propose complementary systems and practices to reduce the risks associated with decentralized governance. What is ethically required in a decentralized society, for example, is trust among strangers, ethics for welcoming guests with hospitality, or an attempt to belong to multiple groups. Such ethical practices are not recommended in a centralized and bureaucratic social order. However, in a constantly changing society, they provide prudential wisdom for enhancing our freedom.

According to Simmel, freedom is made possible through affiliation with multiple groups (Simmel 1923). When a person becomes subordinate to more than one authority, this ensures his or her independence of personality rather than subordination to one authority. Specifically, if people live in locations where the practices of various groups conflict, they will acquire freedom from a single authority and a sense of balance in following multiple systems. Furthermore, a person who belongs to multiple organizations can easily break apart from one of them if it brings him disadvantage. Unfavorable communities will be selected out under the condition of multiple affiliations. In this way, belonging to various organizations constitutes a substantive value in a free society.

The principle of differentiation involves the wisdom of nurturing a decentralized society. This principle will ultimately lead to differentiating even the internal psychological orientation of each person by imitating the technique of decentralized governance to enhance our potential creative activities. To become creative, one must not stick to an established sense of identity, but rather examine his or her inner self and enhance new potentialities. Furthermore, to improve creativity, it is necessary to maximize the practice of trial and error, examine ways to make good use of novel factors of genes, explore human abilities through the educational system, and restrict monitoring measures.

In this way, the principle of differentiation contains a series of concepts: criticism of a uniform society, decentralization and its complementary technique, and creative diversity. In contrast, the principle of generative change involves the following concepts: contingency, change, generation, growth, and evolution.

6. CONCLUDING REMARKS (ON THE THREE PRINCIPLES ABOVE)

Based on Simmel's insights, I presented three principles of freedom which constitute the idea of growth-oriented liberalism: the principle of virtue (self-esteem), the principle of generative change, and the principle of differentiation. The principle of virtue values freedom involving positive attributes that do not fit into the existing categories of merits. The value of freedom is recognized through discovering unknown possibilities for excellence in the process of searching for the meaning of life. The second principle, that of generative change, values freedom in the condition of the constant mobilization of society. To give freedom its substantive value, it is necessary to secure a situation where rulers are continually changing. The third principle, differentiation, values freedom in division, insertion of noise, cracks, pluralization, and criticism of overwhelming elements. Through such varied dimensions of differentiation, real freedom can appear in our society.

These principles have mutually complementary relationships. Specifically, reasons for pursuing one of these principles in the search for real freedom are established by the other principles. For example, the principle of virtue itself might not have a strong relationship with real liberty. However, when this principle is supported by the others, it creates substantive freedom. These principles sustain one another and constitute key components of growth-oriented liberalism, which pursues positive freedom in a different way from communitarianism and perfectionism. Real freedom should activate our potentialities. The touchstone of a free society which enjoys real liberty depends on how social governance is designed to activate the potentialities that are unknown even to ourselves.

Worldwide and even in Japan, the real-existing liberalism will emphasize values such as tolerance and opportunities to express a diversity of opinions. However, the perspective of real freedom or growth-oriented liberalism emphasizes not only these values of negative liberty, but it also promotes the values of obtaining high self-esteem, enhancing the spontaneous process of social change, and differentiating one's own opinion from that of others.

REFERENCES

BERLIN, I. 1969. *Four Essays on Liberty.* New York : Oxford University Press.
FROMM, E. 1941. *Escape from Freedom.* New York : Holt, Rinehart and Winston.
GRAEBER, D. 2004. *Fragments of an Anarchist Anthropology.* Chicago : Prickly Paradigm Press.
INOUE, Tatsuo. 2008. 自由論 *Jiyûron* ["On Liberty"]. Tokyo : Iwanami Shoten.
SIMMEL, G. 1923. *Soziologie : Untersuchungen über die Formen der Vergesellschaftung.* München und Leipzig : Duncker & Humblot.
TAYLOR, Ch. 1985. "What's Wrong with Negative Liberty?". In *Philosophy and the Human Sciences : Philosophical Papers*, vol. 2, 211-19. Cambridge : Cambridge University Press.

CONTINUITÉ ET RUPTURE DANS LES THÉORIES SOCIO-ÉCONOMIQUES DE YASUMA TAKATA

SHIGERU KITAJIMA ET HIROKI YOKOTA*

Abstract

This article has the following three objectives. The first is to display the thought and behavior of Japanese thinker Yasuma Takata (1883-1972), almost unknown in the West, who formulated a sociological theory and a socio-economic theory. The second is to examine how his thought and his behavior related to Japan wrong-doing during World War II and the issue of "responsibility/irresponsibility". The third goal is to show that Takata's thought actually remains deeply connected with modern Japanese currents of thought, as indicate thinker Masao Maruyama and fiction-writers Kenzaburo Ôe and Yasunari Kawabata.

Keywords: Community, Japan ("ambiguous Japan"), Socio-economics, WW II, war responsibility (and the idea of non-responsibility).

Résumé

Nous avons trois objectifs dans cet article. Le premier est de montrer la pensée et le comportement de Yasuma Takata (1883-1972), auteur quasiment inconnu en Occident, mais qui donna pourtant au Japon ses premières théories sociologiques et socio-économiques générales. Le deuxième est d'examiner comment ces pensée et comportement sont liés à la responsabilité de la guerre dans la seconde guerre mondiale. Le troisième consiste à montrer que cette pensée est profondément connectée au courant de la pensée japonaise moderne à travers la théorie de Maruyama et des opinions des Ôe et Kawabata.

Mots-clefs : Communauté, Japon (« Japon ambigu »), responsabilité de guerre (et idée de l'absence de), Seconde guerre mondiale, socio-économie.

Classification JEL : B15, B31, N45

*. Shigeru Kitajima est professeur de sociologie et vice-président de l'université d'Asahikawa (ville d'Asahikawa, Hokkaïdo).

Hiroki Yokota est maître de conférences en sciences économiques à l'université de Shizuoka (ville et département de Shizuoka). La pensée socio-économique présentée est celle du penseur nationaliste Takata (prénom Yasuma). Les auteurs remercient Gilles Campagnolo pour sa révision de leur texte en langue française.

1. INTRODUCTION

Selon l'essayiste Masao Maruyama (1961, 1964), les sciences sociales japonaises, y compris l'économie et la sociologie, après qu'elles furent importées d'Europe, ont ignoré, ou plutôt manqué la relation avec la pensée qui inspirait le cœur de la construction des sciences sociales en Europe. L'objectif du présent texte est de montrer comment la structure et les caractéristiques de la sociologie et de la socio-économie du penseur Yasuma Takata sont reprises par des universitaires japonais aujourd'hui, notamment parfois à propos de questions socio-économiques. Il s'agit d'examiner comment la construction de la théorie et de la structure de la sociologie de Takata fut influencée par le fait que l'on semblait accorder de l'importance seulement à la « théorie » (ses concepts et sa constitution) dans les sciences sociales japonaises, comme si une expression spécialisée et individualisée dans leur champ devait constituer une nouvelle étape après leur importation depuis l'Europe à la fin du XIXe siècle et au début de XXe siècle.

Pour notre part, sur ce point, nous ne regardons pas la sociologie de Takata comme une théorie « dénuée de réflexion » et nous cherchons plutôt à savoir quel sens Takata donnait à la théorie abstraite importée au Japon. Dans ce contexte, la présente étude devrait selon nous contribuer à déterminer non seulement la position et le rôle de Takata lui-même, mais aussi la reprise de sa théorie, encore ambiguë dans l'histoire du développement de la socio-économie japonaise, notamment en raison d'affinités idéologiques dont la Seconde guerre mondiale montra tous les effets délétères.

D'abord, une morale ambiguë régit la sociologie de Takata quant à la question de la responsabilité. Plusieurs sociologues japonais soulignent de nos jours que la théorie sociologique de Takata mérite un grand crédit. Isamu Kaneko et Kenichi Tominaga souhaitent notamment reprendre sa théorie[1]. Leurs idées influencent non

1. Kaneko et Tominaga voient en Takata le fondateur historique d'une théorie sociologique générale. La question est plus incertaine quant à la socio-économie au Japon. Sa méthode n'est pas « générale » au sens d'immuable, car elle change de logique et de signification selon la « réalité » traité (mode d'existence familial, l'État ou la relation des deux), ce qui constitue la « société communautaire » comme concept essentiel dans sa sociologie. Takata caractérise sa méthode comme fondée sur une « intuition essentielle ». C'est son « existentialisme méthodologique », pour ainsi dire, qui donne l'importance primordiale à l'objet examiné. Les méthodes de Takata et de Weber diffèrent tout à fait. Pour former son fameux « idéal-type »,

seulement des courants de recherche en sociologie, mais aussi des acteurs de l'administration concernant des politiques économiques publiques. S'ils n'osent pas toujours examiner ouvertement la « doctrine Takata », insérée dans sa théorie, ni les propositions politiques qu'il avait formulées avant-guerre et pendant celle-ci, la raison est que ces critiques concernant l'économie, la société et la politique, exprimées du milieu des années 1920 jusqu'en 1945, se liaient à la politique belliciste du gouvernement japonais. En outre, ces auteurs laissent planer l'ambiguïté sur l'idée de soi-disant « conversion démocratique » que Takata aurait opérée, une attitude qui structure en réalité l'idée d'une irresponsabilité devant les horreurs perpétrées pendant la guerre, qu'il avait alors soutenue.

On peut certes observer une conversion dans le comportement de Takata, qui prit tout soudain un caractère démocratique dans un article de 1946 où il défendait la validité de sa théorie dans le cadre post-1945 ; cet essai reviendra sur ce texte. Mais nous souhaitons discuter, autant que possible, la mentalité selon laquelle Takata avait écrit es œuvres, sous l'angle de ce que Maruyama a pu nommer le « régime d'irresponsabilité » (Maruyama 1964, 111) chez les fauteurs de guerre japonais – ou encore ce que Kenzaburô Ôe a appelé un « Japon ambigu » (Ôe 1995). Nous interrogeons pour ce faire les idées et l'« attitude » souvent exprimées dans le Japon d'aujourd'hui, au XXIe siècle, où l'on n'est peut-être pas encore sorti du régime d'irresponsabilité dont Maruyama soulignait le caractère délétère.

2. LA FORMATION DE LA PENSÉE DE TAKATA

2.1. *Milieu d'origine, influences familiale et locale sur Takata*

Il existait chez Takata à la fois un profond attachement et une haine rentrée pour la région où il était né. Il étendit ensuite cette ambivalence bien au-delà, et elle devait teinter ses sentiments quant aux différences de culture et de race qu'il allait découvrir. Ce sentiment partagé (mi-amour mi-haine) se forgea au long de sa vie entière.

Weber abstrait un objet significatif en sélectionnant un point de vue fondé sur une valeur au sein de l'infini des phénomènes sociaux. Une tension se crée entre le « point de vue de la valeur » comme heuristique du chercheur et l'analyse de l'activité sociale chez Weber : ce n'est jamais le cas chez Takata.

Takata était né en 1883, le troisième et dernier fils d'une famille (qui comptait aussi trois filles) d'un village du canton d'Ogi-gun, bourg de Mikazuki-mura dans la préfecture de Saga, c'est-à-dire l'île de Kyûshû, au sud du Japon. Son père, Kiyoto Takata, était prêtre de la secte bouddhiste Tendai et cultivateur propriétaire. Sa mère appartenait aussi à une famille de bonzes. Kiyoto confia la gérance de son bien agricole à un fermier, puis il céda sa vaste rizière au village. La récolte devint une ressource majeure pour ce village.

Comme l'aîné de la famille, du nom de Kiyotoshi, (aîné de vingt-deux ans de Yasuma) avait certaines connaissances en médecine, en mathématiques japonaises et pouvait passer pour un lettré (il écrivait des poèmes dans le style *waka*), il devint médecin. Yasuma, très attaché à son village et à cette vie fondée sur la famille et les liens de parenté au sein du village, reçut l'influence de l'importance particulière de la vie commune et il allait donner à la notion de communauté un rôle fondamental dans ses théories ultérieures.

La position hiérarchique occupée par la famille de Takata au village comptait passablement à cet égard. Son père s'y connaissait un peu en médecine, en mathématiques japonaises et il écrivait des *waka*. Ces savoirs, pas strictement indispensables à un prêtre, formaient ses loisirs. Assurément, le père de Takata était l'« intellectuel » du bourg de Mikazuki et du village de Tônoé où il vivait. Père et fils aîné accordant une importance énorme à l'éducation, l'atmosphère familiale conduisit à inscrire à son tour Yasuma au collège, à Saga, où l'on suivait l'ancien système d'éducation[2]. Bien qu'élevé dans un village « à la campagne », Takata n'était pas un simple « fils de paysan » : à la fin du XIXe siècle, il n'était possible de s'inscrire au collège, pour les enfants des villages ruraux, que si leurs parents possédaient déjà notablement un certain bien.

En 1902, Takata allait avoir vingt ans. Il entra en faculté de médecine à Kumamoto, une ville majeure de la région méridionale de Kyûshû. Son frère lui avait fortement recommandé cette voie. Toutefois, Takata s'inscrivit à la faculté des sciences humaines et sociales peu de temps après, car il s'intéressait aux questions sociales, en particulier l'inégalité entre pauvres et riches. La question l'intriguait au moins depuis son entrée au collège, sans qu'il soit très clair pourquoi, et son intérêt se

2. C'est-à-dire le système préalable à la réforme de l'éducation primaire et secondaire dans le Japon de la fin de la période dite d'Edo et durant l'ère *Meiji*.

porta sur les inégalités de fortune. Entre 1907 et 1911, le taux des mises en fermage de rizières atteignait 50 % dans le canton d'Ogi-gun, tandis qu'entre 1922 et 1925, ce taux atteignait 65,7 % dans le bourg de Mikazuki, celui de Takata. Le seigneur local, du clan des Nabeshima, gouverneur de la région à l'époque d'Edo (soit, avant l'ère *Meiji* ouverte en 1868), possédait, avec ses vassaux, la vaste majorité des terres cultivées. La propriété tendait à se concentrer encore plus, le fermage progressait en conséquence. Cet essor des relations propriétaires-fermiers entraînait la paupérisation des paysans : la précocité de l'intérêt, encore tout intellectuel de Takata, pour la question des inégalités s'explique en partie par l'observation de cette situation, une première intuition de l'approche socio-économique.

Pour Takata, le village de Tônoé était donc, d'une part, l'objet de son attachement à sa famille, aux siens, et, d'autre part, d'un intérêt déjà presque savant pour le problème de la pauvreté et l'impact négatif causé par le développement du fermage dans les villages. Dans la formation du jeune Takata, le premier point allait rester à l'arrière-plan d'un fort intérêt pour la notion de communauté à la base de la société japonaise, et le second devait le faire se soucier de la pauvreté causant l'effondrement des communautés villageoises.

2.2. *La rencontre de Takata avec Yoneda*

Shôtarô Yoneda jouit d'un grand prestige dans l'histoire de la théorie sociologique au Japon. La rencontre entre Yoneda et Takata eut lieu en 1907 ; elle joua un rôle majeur pour l'évolution de Takata. En effet, jusque-là, celui-ci avait compris la société sur des bases théoriques, exactement à l'opposé de la vision que formait Yoneda, qui allait influencer Takata jusqu'à lui faire renverser sa perspective. Takata prit une nouvelle orientation sous l'influence de Yoneda. Yoneda enseignait à Kyôto, au lycée renommé Dôshisha, puis à la Faculté des Lettres de l'Université de Kyoto, en spécialité « philosophie »[3]. Yoneda avait non seulement une bonne connaissance des questions d'actualité touchant

3. Yoneda était né à Nara en 1873. Inscrit au lycée chrétien de Nara Eiwa, il devait se faire baptiser ultérieurement. Il reçut l'enseignement du missionnaire américain Isaac Dooman (1857-1931), professeur et prêtre à Nara. Après sa sortie du lycée, Yoneda traduisit des livres de Dooman, dont il fut le secrétaire. À l'âge de dix-neuf ans, Yoneda accompagna Dooman aux États-Unis. Yoneda suivit un séminaire à New York, fit des études de sociologie à l'Université Columbia, sous la direction de F. H. Giddings (1855-1931) puis il se rendit en France, où Gabriel Tarde le dirigea (1843-1904) au Collège de France.

la société, l'économie et la politique, mais aussi de la sociologie et des sciences économiques occidentales. Il maîtrisait passablement les langues anglaise, française, allemande et russe, et il avait des rudiments de latin et de grec ancien. Takata rencontra Yoneda lorsque celui-ci commençait d'enseigner à l'Université de Kyoto.

L'impression créée mutuellement chez les deux jeunes hommes fut vive : ils reprirent leurs idées l'un de l'autre puis ils rompirent pour former leurs théories respectives. Takata était entré à l'Université de Kyoto en apportant un esprit pratique, il n'entendait pas moins que résoudre le problème du paupérisme, avec l'espoir que la sociologie jouât un rôle à cet égard. Or, Yoneda fit voir à Takata dans la sociologie une théorie *pure* plutôt qu'une pratique. Là où Takata tendait *a priori* vers une conception pratique du monde, il aperçut alors les limites de sa conception.

Yoneda, quant à lui, avait notamment soigneusement repéré le positif et le négatif du concept de société civile venu d'Occident, sur l'arrière-fond de théories sociologiques variées. D'une part, l'aspect positif comportait le respect des droits humains, la liberté individuelle et l'esprit de réforme : graduellement, la pauvreté diminue sous l'effet de la lutte incessante contre des hiérarchies héritées. Cette idée de société civile s'est constituée dans l'histoire occidentale, quoique déjà en germe au sein même des sociétés hiérarchisées. D'autre part, la part d'ombre concerne précisément l'inégalité, entérinée par les hiérarchies, et l'existence de la discrimination, dont une expression est le racisme.

Bien plus tard, Maruyama (1961) devait à son tour critiquer le fait que les sciences sociales avaient été importées au Japon en ayant l'œil fixé sur la seule constitution *logique* des concepts et leurs relations, sans les examiner assez pour saisir les pensées critiques qui accompagnaient le développement des théories « *pures* ». La théorie de Yoneda aurait sans doute été épargnée dans la critique de Maruyama, mais les a-t-il pour autant bien comprises dans leur ensemble, et quant à la thèse de l'individualisation qu'on jugeait devoir les caractériser inévitablement ? Yoneda proposait une sociologie synthétique, qui liait la compréhension des réalités par la sociologie à sa saisie à travers d'autres sciences sociales, où l'économie jouait un rôle selon le commentateur Naka (1998).

Takata reprit des éléments de la théorie de Yoneda, en premier lieu, sa « théorie pure » (« pure » au sens où elle approfondit les principes, loin de toute « visée pratique de la théorie »). Deuxièmement, Takata regardait la sociologie pure comme une science *individualisée* (Kitajima 2002). Troisièmement, Yoneda avait osé donner activement son opinion sur les problèmes sociaux de son temps, à partir d'une perspective sociologique, dans un style qui n'était pas journalistique, mais au titre de résultats démontrés dans son travail de chercheur, du point de vue des sciences sociales. Yoneda insistait pour améliorer progressivement la société ; il se focalisait sur la classe ouvrière, suivant une tendance alors prédominante (Yoneda 1921). Takata allait, lui aussi, s'exprimer activement sur la question sociale, suivant en cela Yoneda et développant des positions politiques critiques depuis les points de vue de la socio-économie. Les opinions des deux hommes devaient cependant diverger de plus en plus au fur et à mesure des guerres que le Japon allait mener contre la Chine (1895), la Corée (entièrement colonisée dès 1910) et la Russie (1905).

Ainsi Takata ne reprenait-il pas certains autres éléments présents chez Yoneda. Premièrement, il écartait sa « sociologie synthétique ». Yoneda ressaisissait le processus de transformation du paradigme d'une « science sociale unifiée » en sciences spécialisées en suivant l'histoire de l'Occident des XVIIIe et XIXe siècles. C'est pourquoi il tenait à préserver une sociologie qu'il disait « synthétique ». Yoneda avait certainement enseigné à Takata les orientations suivies par la recherche lui en Occident. Takata retint que la sociologie *spécialisée et individualisée* avait le vent en poupe. N'était-elle pas l'aboutissement de cette mutation sociologique ? Takata portait peu d'intérêt aux causes réelles comme idéelles de cette mutation dans la société occidentale, mais il entendait restructurer la théorie sociologique en insérant des théories venues d'Occident. Il ne remettait frontalement en cause aucune des tendances observables dans la société, l'économie et la politique de l'Occident. Ces idées résultaient des changements qu'il y voyait : ils constituaient autant de *faits* à ses yeux. Non seulement Takata ne reprenait pas la direction que Yoneda imprimait à la théorie sociologique, sur la base de considérations nées de l'observation de la culture humaniste chrétienne, sur la société civile notamment, (en bref, ce que Yoneda avait retenu de ses voyages d'études en Europe et aux États-Unis), mais Takata n'essaya même pas du tout de leur donner de suite. Cette différence dans la formation de leurs idées forgea assurément leur différence de fond dans l'appréciation des « valeurs » importantes : ils le sentaient sans doute dans leur for intérieur et cela avait des répercussions sur leurs théories. Chez Takata, toute valeur doit s'ajuster avant tout à la vie de la communauté rurale (représentée par son village de Tônoé) ainsi qu'au foyer, à la « maisonnée », regardée comme la composante fondamentale de la communauté.

Une seconde différence de méthode concerne la formation des concepts différenciée entre les deux auteurs[4]. Takata les forme en les tirant avant tout de faits empiriques, auxquels il ajoute des connaissances courantes acquises après coup au gré de ses besoins et de ses intérêts : par exemple, l'approche « relationnelle » qui nourrit sa réflexion aboutit à l'idée qu'il existe une « forte solidarité entre pauvres ». Elle s'observe chez les pèlerins qui, pauvres eux-mêmes, font la charité aux mendiants (que les riches ne regardent même pas) (Usui 1981). Takata considérait que cette formation des concepts constituait l'apport essentiel de l'*intuition* du savant, le regard qu'il porte en propre. De la sorte, le sens d'un concept peut varier passablement selon le rapport entre un point de vue et la réalité du fait correspondant observé : au final, le choix d'observer tel ou tel cas influe sur la formation du concept.

3. THÉORIE SOCIOLOGIQUE ET SOCIO-ÉCONOMIE CHEZ TAKATA

3.1 *Le rapport aux sciences sociales importées d'Europe*

Rappelons ici les caractéristiques de l'importation des sciences sociales européennes au Japon pour comprendre comment Takata construisait ses théories.

4. Si l'on compare la méthode par laquelle Takata constitue ses concepts à celle de Yoneda, ce dernier élabore par exemple son concept de classe ouvrière en observant et en ressaisissant statistiquement le rapport salarial réel selon Marx, le droit naturel et la question des personnes improductives. Yoneda constitue ses concepts en combinant le classement des concepts selon une documentation et la méthode inductive. Au contraire, Takata adopte la méthode déductive et définit, par exemple, le concept de classe comme l'« écart de force dû à la richesse basé sur le désir de puissance et le pouvoir ». Il choisit et abstrait depuis l'existant, renforce son point de vue en effectuant des choix habiles ou reclasse si besoin ses concepts et les théories qu'il développe à partir de documents extérieurs pour une redéfinition *ad hoc*. Sa méthode de l'intuition de l'essence des phénomènes est l'occasion de sortir du concept constitué, sa conceptualisation conséquente suit fondamentalement les mêmes voies.

Maruyama a montré que l'importation au Japon de sciences sociales développées en Europe a rencontré l'obstacle suivant : alors qu'il existait en Occident une communauté de pensée à la « racine » de ces sciences, une unité synthétique qui s'était forgée depuis l'Antiquité grecque en passant par le Moyen-Âge, la Renaissance et les Temps modernes, ces sciences se spécialisèrent à partir du XIXe siècle pour répondre à de profondes mutations économiques et sociales. Le Japon importa les sciences spécialisées, mais en les coupant des réalités économiques et sociales et des idées sociales qui avaient été leur terreau et qui avaient suscité à la fois leur essor et cette mutation de paradigme. Autrement dit, les sciences sociales spécialisées étaient complètement « déracinées » au Japon, sans même une langue commune pour communiquer mutuellement : entre elles, toutes individualisées et spécialisées, rien n'existait plus une fois au Japon de leur sol commun d'Occident. Aussi chaque science transplantée dans ce nouveau lieu d'accueil y suivait-elle une sorte d'existence semblable à celle de ces poulpes que les marins pêchent pour les enfermer dans une boîte, c'est-à-dire que chacune se constituait sa propre sphère, sa « société académique » propre (Maruyama 1961). Maruyama soulignait encore que ces sciences sociales européennes liées les unes les autres par une origine commune de pensée trouvaient dans cette racine commun de quoi les relier même une fois spécialisées[5].

Alors que les théories importées s'accumulaient, elles étaient comme neutralisées une fois resituées dans un espace théorique sans réflexivité critique ni perspective théorique que l'on pourrait rapporter à des racines. Cela caractérise aussi la sociologie de Takata. Maruyama mentionne encore un autre trait de l'importation au Japon des sciences sociales ou d'idées qui les sous-tendent : cette « accumulation » de théories adoptées sans critique et sans débat sur les principes de ces théories a caractérisé ces sciences importées sans confrontation véritable aux pensées japonaises traditionnelles, que sont le bouddhisme et le confucianisme (eux-mêmes importés,

5. L'expression utilisée par Maruyama (1961) « *sasaragata* » renvoie à un type traditionnel de balayette constituée des fibres serrées par une corde sur le manche de bambou : cette « racine » évoque le fonds commun de disciplines occidentales, ce qui manque précisément au Japon à ces disciplines importées.

de Chine, en leur temps), le shintoïsme, les « études nationales » traditionnelles, notamment[6].

De ce fait, les idées venues de l'étranger ne se sont donc pas « structurées » au Japon. Elles échouent à forger une pensée vraiment nouvelle. Elles s'accumulent seulement, sans ordre ni perspective historique, dans un champ vite encombré. Maruyama considère (négativement, donc) que c'est même l'essence de cette fameuse « tolérance » si vantée par quoi l'on qualifie parfois la pensée japonaise : si elle est censée « accepter à l'infini » toutes les philosophies, religions et sciences venues de l'étranger, c'est qu'elle s'abstient d'en donner de critique théorique sérieuse, comme de les relier les unes aux autres en saisissant des principes qui pourraient régir la société dans son ensemble.

Le cas de Takata illustre bien le processus dénoncé par Maruyama. En 1908, sous la direction de Yoneda, à l'Université de Kyoto, Takata avait rédigé deux articles sur les rapports sociaux, des textes en apparence introductifs aux idées de deux Occidentaux : « J. G. de Tarde : théorie des lois sociales » et « F. H. Giddings : une étude sociologique ». En 1910, le mémoire de licence de Takata devait porter sur la sociologie d'Émile Durkheim sous le titre « Théorie de la division du travail : une étude sur É. Durkheim ». Ces études s'inscrivaient dans un courant alors naissant, à l'époque où l'on tentait de produire au Japon une « sociologie psychologique » qui conjuguerait les idées des trois sociologues susnommés, avec en outre celles de Georg Simmel. Il s'agissait de placer la sociologie au rang de science sociale reconnue dans l'université la plus prestigieuse du pays, l'Université impériale de Tokyo. Dans ce contexte, le concept de rapports sociaux devint l'objet par excellence de la sociologie japonaise, fondé sur les besoins psychologiques inter-individuels.

3.2. *Concepts fondamentaux de la sociologie et de la socio-économie de Takata*

Takata était très attaché à saisir les réalités sociales, dont il tirait l'objet d'une contemplation infinie. Cela explique l'intérêt qu'il devait ensuite porter à l'économie « politique » – et d'ailleurs à une économie

6. Les études nationales (*kokugaku*) sont le nom de la tradition revivifiée par Motoori Norinaga au XVIIIe siècle, à la recherche des origines des premières chroniques japonaises, le *Nihon shoki* et le *Kojiki*.

très *politisée*. Takata procédait par généralisation depuis un point de vue spécifique qu'il élisait sur un objet donné et qu'il reportait ensuite sur de nombreux cas d'instanciation ; il constituait ainsi des règles, qui n'équivalaient guère à des lois naturelles, mais qu'il faisait cadrer avec des probabilités fournies par les observations qu'il menait. Cette méthode est essentiellement « intuitive ». Elle pouvait faire office d'attitude raisonnable tant qu'elle dépassait l'expérience d'un temps et d'un lieu donnés, le point qui était important aux yeux de Takata dans la théorie[7].

Si l'on repart de la comparaison entre les méthodes pour constituer les concepts chez Takata et chez Yoneda, ce dernier les formait par observation et avec des statistiques qui liaient les concepts dans la théorie. Ainsi, concernant la classe ouvrière et la notion de rapport salarial[8], Yoneda croisait-il les notions du droit naturel et l'observation des agents dits « improductifs ». Il s'agissait de constituer les concepts de la sociologie par combinaison et croisement des concepts avec les documents tirés du terrain et pris dans une méthode inductive. Tout au contraire, Takata allait développer une méthode *déductive*. Il définissait le concept de « classe » comme l'« écart d'influence entre la richesse et la puissance, fondé sur les besoins ». Takata choisit et abstrait ce qui existe réellement, puis il appuie ce facteur extrait ou il le reclasse les concepts dans les théories qu'il a forgées sur d'autres documents afin d'obtenir une redéfinition. Sa méthode d'« intuition essentielle » poursuit une conceptualisation *ad hoc* suivant au fond cette démarche. C'est ainsi qu'il définit le concept de société comme une « coexistence désirée ». Il part en cela d'une généralisation de l'objet qu'est la « relation sociale ». Dans le processus de constitution qui mène à sa définition, il s'appuie sur un modèle dyadique « simmélien » :

1°) Takata suppose d'abord qu'il existe, pour toute paire d'individus pris au hasard, quelques besoins fondamentaux socialisés sous la triple forme d'un besoin matériel (économique), d'un besoin de protection et d'un besoin sexuel ;

7. Le rôle de l'« intuition » dans la saisie socio-économique du monde, même dans la théorie scientifique, doit se comprendre dans un contexte qui n'est pas spécifique au Japon : à la même époque en Allemagne, sous l'influence du cercle réactionnaire qui entourait le poète charismatique Stefan George, l'économiste Edgar Salin proposait l'*anschauuliche Theorie*, ou « théorie intuitive » (Nolo et Schefold 2007).

8. Une notion présente dans le marxisme également, voir plus bas la section consacrée à ce courant.

2°) Quand les deux individus considérés se rencontrent (dans leur *interaction* sociale, donc), il naît entre eux une tendance à souhaiter le contact mutuel. Le besoin de se grouper surgit sous l'effet du besoin de se rapprocher et d'échanger, il prend des formes variées ;

3°) Du fait de cette différenciation du besoin initial de se grouper les besoins de coexister, de vivre ensemble surgissent, c'est-à-dire la « coexistence désirée » susmentionnée, qui forme la société, vue dans la forme sous laquelle elle s'est structurée.

Ce modèle de « rencontre » de deux individus et d'interaction sociale reste fondé sur le cadre théorique que Simmel avait développé en son temps[9]. En outre, Takata développait une théorie de la diversification des besoins, sur le modèle des propositions formulées par Simmel. Takata forgea sa vision de la diversification des besoins à partir de l'interaction sociale, du besoin de se grouper, de la tendance au travail collaboratif, qui contrebalancent tous la tendance, qui existe aussi et qui pousse à l'affrontement et au conflit ouvert. Cette tendance au combat s'autonomise d'ailleurs, puis elle se différencie elle aussi en un besoin d'exercer du pouvoir sur la société ; cela tourne finalement au besoin d'entrer en compétition (concurrence) et de dominer autrui (Takata 1919). Cette logique sociologique, que Takata appuie sur la pensée de Simmel, constitue également essentiellement la conception profonde de ce penseur japonais. Mais elle ne suffisait pas comme telle. Avec sa théorie sociologique, Takata se proposait de fournir pour la première fois un complément à la théorie qui lie les besoins diffus et l'état de la relation sociale.

Selon Takata, la relation structurée par l'interaction sociale entre deux individus (il considère toujours des paires d'individus) est homogène de par sa nature (c'est une relation d'attachement), ce qui signifie que la relation même est l'objectif que l'on souhaite atteindre. Cette relation homogène se différencie en une relation avec l'extérieur du groupe social (lequel y est inévitablement poussé par la croissance de sa population), et une relation interne de progrès graduel dans la collaboration existant au sein du groupe. Le besoin de vivre en groupe et cette relation homogène sont les instruments pour édifier la société toute entière. La croissance de la population et le besoin du pouvoir

9. Pour mieux comprendre ce modèle « dyadique », le lecteur pourra consulter l'avis émis sur la sociologie de Simmel par Max Weber, on trouvera dans la *Revue de philosophie économique* (Campagnolo 2006).

se combinent pour stimuler la division du travail et hiérarchiser les classes sociales au sein de la société en son entier. En outre, cette société se différencie de l'État car la conquête et l'assimilation des sociétés extérieures vont de soi : le besoin de conquêtes provient du besoin des individus de s'affronter autant qu'ils coopèrent – et les sociétés de même.

Takata présente cette méthodologie de sa sociologie sous la forme d'une « loi du *quantum* de relations » (Takata 1922). C'est assurément un apport car c'est un concept sociologique original qui est produit là par Takata. Toutefois, on peut s'interroger si sa vision est bien convaincante par rapport à des concepts concurrents promis, eux, à plus amples développement, comme celui d'urbanisation – cette lacune expliquerait d'ailleurs les limites de la loi formulée par Takata. Ce manque s'expliquerait à son tour par les conditions de la formation des vues de Takata dans son époque[10].

Quoi qu'il en soit, le sens de la structure et du changement de la conception que Takata prend de la communauté, sur le modèle allemand, (*Gemeinschaft*) par rapport à la société (vue sur le type de la *Gesellschaft*) explique en grande partie la sociologie de Takata. C'est donc maintenant l'examen de cette structure et des mutations des rapports entre communauté et société qui doivent être considérés au titre des thèmes principaux dans le développement de la théorie sociologique et socio-économique de Takata.

3.3. *Communauté et société (*Gemeinschaft und Gesellschaft*) dans la sociologie de Takata*

L'interaction sociale entre deux individus est homogène et mutuelle selon Takata car c'est une relation d'attachement. Elle se différencie en relation d'hétérogénéité en raison de la croissance de la population,

10. L'expression 結合定量の法則 (*ketsugô teiryô no hôsoku*) désigne une « règle » (*hôsoku*) exprimant le « *quantum* » de relations existantes distribuées dans la société prise dans son ensemble à un moment donné. Ce *quantum* est déterminé par la relation entre les membres de cette société ; celle-ci tend à s'affaiblir avec le temps, au fur et à mesure de l'expansion du champ d'interaction des membres. La « loi du *quantum* des relations » accorde une importance extrême au facteur démographique, mais sans mentionner pour autant le concept d'urbanisation, ce qui est pour le moins gênant. Takata élit la méthode de tirer les concepts de son intuition formée à partir de l'état empirique des choses. Il souligne cependant que, plus une société s'est différenciée en ses composantes, quand on la considère dans son ensemble, plus la relation entre ce tout et les parties *doit* s'affaiblir. Cette logique transcende des circonstances de temps et d'espace donnés.

d'une part, et des progrès dans la coopération au sein du groupe, d'autre part. La relation d'origine est regardée comme fondée sur le sacrifice : on s'y sacrifie à l'autre et l'on peut y être sacrifié pour lui dans la mesure où le but est de maintenir la relation à l'intérieur du groupe. Cette relation vient satisfaire un besoin profond et précis, celui de la communauté à persister dans son être de groupe reclus sur soi. Cette société est formée sur un sentiment *illimité* d'attachement de chaque membre, cette *communauté* en tant que telle ne forme pas une « société » mais un *groupe*. En elle, le Tout intègre absolument chaque individu. Le Tout a la priorité absolue (Kitajima 2002).

En revanche, la « société » se constitue, quant à elle, selon une relation hétérogène qui s'explique de manière naturelle par la cupidité, ou l'attraction que le profit exerce. Le fait est que la société est donc dispersée, anonyme : c'est ainsi que s'établit un rapport à l'initiative privée dans la vie économique de la société, qui reste un moyen (de réaliser des objectifs individuels). Autrui dans la société n'est pour chacun que le moyen de réaliser son propre objectif. Une telle société peut d'ailleurs ainsi conduire à accroître la liberté individuelle, à former de nouvelles identités et à développer une nouvelle culture.

Comment Takata saisit-il cette dernière image de société ? Il la voit comme une « société du profit ». Il en voit le modèle définitif dans la recherche du profit comme elle se pratique dans l'entreprise, précisément nommée une « société anonyme ». Il voit là une relation sociale entre des agents économiques qui sont autant de commerçants, relation où tous se considèrent les uns les autres strictement comme des moyens de parvenir à leurs fins ; cette relation est mutuelle entre tous. Dans la « société », la déréglementation est donc la règle : la contrainte et le contrôle par la « conscience collective » sociale sont déconstruits, et l'organisation sociale communautaire avec. Logiquement, le manque des normes sociales et culturelles au long du processus de formation de la « société du profit » entraîne l'image d'une société « anomique » dont Takata reprend l'expression de Durkheim, société au sein de laquelle les individus « libres » et indépendants vivent dans le désordre et où ils se comportent comme des commerçants pour qui le profit pécuniaire constitue le seul critère concret de réussite, et où sa quête infinie donne donc la norme absolue de leur comportement. Cette « société du désordre » perd tout esprit de cohésion.

Takata détestait profondément le type de cette « société du profit », où les individus ne font aucun effort pour promouvoir le tout, ce qui résulte inévitablement de la croissance démographique et de sa « loi du quantum de relations ». La cohésion sociale ne peut que décroître « depuis la société communautaire jusqu'à la société du profit », insiste Takata, qui convoque à cet égard les concepts de *Gemeinschaft* et de *Gesellschaft* de Ferdinand Tönnies. Il voit dans ces concepts et la théorie systématiquement dichotomique de Tönnies le reflet de la crise de la société civile en Europe. Il la redoute pour le Japon. L'idée que la société civile puisse être une bonne chose et son concept même, tel que l'Europe l'avait illustré, ne prirent jamais racine dans la pensée de Takata. Cela est surprenant alors qu'il en avait étudié le concept sous la direction de Yoneda. La raison tient sans doute à ce que la « vision » que Takata prend de ces choses reste focalisée sur son « pays », sa région natale, le village de Tônoé. Il craint la crise qui mènera à l'effondrement de la communauté.

Considérée comme une science sociale spécialisée parmi tant d'autres en Europe, la sociologie, une fois introduite au Japon dans la seconde moitié du XIXe siècle, a produit assez naturellement, nous semble-t-il, ce type de réaction. Simmel avait pris comme objet de l'analyse sociologique la « forme » que les objets sociaux revêtent. Cette conception eut un fort impact sur les sociologues japonais à l'aube du développement autochtone de leur science. Si Takata a pu développer sa théorie en s'appuyant sur les idées européennes, ce fut sans les saisir toutefois dans leur ensemble : sans l'effort de théorisation de Simmel, sans les thèmes de division du travail et d'anomie chez Durkheim, sans celui de mutation de la *Gemeinschaft* en *Gesellschaft* chez Tönnies. Cela échappait à Takata, comme le fond du processus de formation de la société civile en Europe lui échappait, avec les mutations qu'elle avait entraînées dans les conceptions fondamentales du mouvement de la société.

Il est passablement ironique de constater que Takata a introduit une interprétation *originale* en ce sens des concepts théoriques *importés*. Précisons : d'abord, Takata regarde l'expansion des libertés individuelle et d'une identité personnelle libérée au sein de la « société du profit » (c'est-à-dire, la société civile) comme le signe d'un relâchement des mœurs et, au final, de la perte de toute norme morale. Ensuite, Takata accorde surtout du poids à la logique associant mécaniquement progrès de ce type de société et déclin (voire démantèlement) de la société communautaire, celle où chacun acceptait de sacrifier ses propres désirs individuels pour le tout communautaire. Takata suit simplement la « loi du quantum des relations » de cohésion sociale qu'il a formulée. Mais, enfin, Takata échoue à saisir les aspects positifs de la « société du profit », les normes et les cultures nouvelles.

4. LA MUTATION DE LA THÉORIE EN POLITIQUE CHEZ TAKATA

4.1 *Un vœu : ralentir la marche vers la « société du profit » pour préserver la vie en communauté*

En rédigeant ses *Principes de sociologie*, Takata pensait établir sa propre « théorie » de manière analytique en formulant la loi de la transition inévitable d'une société communautaire vers la « société anonyme du profit ». Takata songeait ainsi à préserver le rôle de la communauté comme telle. En conséquence, l'outillage de sa compréhension théorique a évolué vers une conception qui prenait de plus en plus appui sur la valeur de la « réalité existante » (la communauté villageoise originelle). Et l'on parle en effet parfois à ce propos d'une méthode appuyée sur la « réalité existante ». Elle donnerait du sens à ce qui « est là », ce qui existe, tout en permettant d'expliquer comment renforcer la cohésion homogène censée prévaloir au sein de l'État nippon et de la famille japonaise. Le but est de construire ou de contribuer à consolider du moins ces deux communautés. Mais la manière dont Takata saisit dans sa sociologie la nature de ce qui « existe » déjà de la sorte n'est toutefois à son tour qu'un reflet de ce que lui prend pour le réel même.

La relation de cohésion au sein de la « société du profit » est toute hétérogène même si elle dérive de la relation homogène originelle de cohésion au sein de la communauté. Autrement dit, la « société communautaire » se faisait voir quand les facteurs de cohésion homogènes étaient mis en avant, qu'ils avaient la priorité, tandis que les facteurs de cohésion hétérogènes restaient secondaires (Takata 1926). Pour cette raison, Takata remarque qu'il doit être possible de retarder la dérive vers l'hétérogénéité par l'opération (d'essence politique) portant sur le facteur d'homogénéisation/« hétérogénéisation ».

À partir de là, Takata édifie une théorie visant à retarder la socialisation appelée par (et pour) le profit. Selon la théorie qu'il vise à élaborer dès le milieu des années 1920, État et famille composant la « société communautaire » ne pourront échapper ni l'un ni l'autre au déclin ; ils doivent donc tous deux faire face au changement qui affecte sur le long-terme les structures sociales de la société communautaire, la menant à la « société du profit ». Pour Takata, déclins de l'État et de la famille sont des soucis majeurs. Il établit une proposition secondaire, qui vient cependant contredire son affirmation générale, à savoir que, si les principes de cohésion de l'État et de la famille sont identiques, ils se stimulent aussi réciproquement. Cette proposition est assurément logiquement intenable, car elle vient au contraire battre en brèche l'idée que la théorie de Takata puisse être considérée comme une théorie vraiment générale.

Dans le Japon des années 1920, l'on pouvait observer les progrès de l'industrie lourde, le développement d'un capitalisme vivace et l'établissement d'une politique de parti virulente. L'époque entre 1919 et 1926 se caractérisait par l'émergence de la société civile et le développement de ce qui se nomme la « démocratie Taïsho »[11]. Le point de vue de Takata est hostile aux libertés et à la diversification de l'identité culturelle, des nouveautés de cette ère. Takata suppose que le développement de la démocratie et la démocratie même font progresser ces aspects qu'il réprouve ; on se dirige donc, selon lui, vers ce qui est le plus périlleux pour l'idéal communautaire. La théorie sociologique de Takata se développe contre la démocratie de Taïsho : à la même époque, elles vont en sens opposé. La pensée de Takata peut donc être qualifiée de « réactionnaire », sauf à indiquer qu'il n'a jamais mentionné explicitement la démocratie dans ses écrits avant l'après-guerre.

C'est donc par nature que la « théorie sociologique » de Takata tend à prendre une teinte « politique » en proposant des politiques de substitution appuyées sur des critiques de la modernité. On le voit surtout après la publication de ses *Études sur la notion de relation sociale* en 1926. Le processus était enclenché qui devait lier le destin de Takata aux politiques de guerre du gouvernement nationaliste et de l'armée, en particulier après les événements de l'« incident de

11. Il s'agit de l'ère impériale et calendaire (1912-1926) qui a succédé à l'ère *Meiji* (1868-1912) et qui vient avant celle de *Shôwa* (1926-1989).

Manchourie », la guerre ouverte contre la Chine et la marche à la guerre mondiale. Takata en était très conscient, et pas opposé à la marche des événements. C'est qu'il en attendait une solution à la crise de la société communautaire.

4.2 *La portée au Japon de l'introduction du marxisme dans les années 1920*

Un point concernant l'impact de l'introduction du marxisme au Japon s'impose, car il y joua un rôle majeur dans les sciences sociales. Takata avait lui-même été influencé par le socialisme durant ses années de lycéen, toutefois avec une compréhension superficielle. Les études sérieuses commencèrent avec son article « La théorie de l'accumulation du capital » paru en 1914 (il était étudiant). Takata fut certainement un précurseur si l'on prend en compte le fait que le marxisme fut vraiment introduit au Japon seulement à partir des années 1920. Il n'a cependant pas su comprendre l'impact que ce courant allait avoir sur les sciences sociales japonaises. Les critiques qu'il lui adresse dans son article de 1925, intitulé « Hiérarchie et conception d'une troisième voie historique », qui présente sa vision de la sociologie en perspective historique, montrent assez qu'il considérait le marxisme pour son analyse de l'histoire économique, sans plus. Les conférences critiques qu'il donna sur le marxisme après 1931 ne dépassent guère cette première impression et sa propre incompréhension théorique s'y entend car il se rabat sur des critiques idéologiques, tandis que la véritable question est l'impact et la signification de ce mouvement marxiste sur l'ensemble des sciences sociales japonaises.

Maruyama souligne les points suivants : d'abord, le fait que le marxisme offrit une compréhension globale et une méthode pour enseigner aux érudits japonais à examiner méthodiquement la vie sociale en relation avec la politique et le droit. Ensuite, le marxisme prête une attention toute particulière à l'arrière-plan de l'histoire : il analyse les causes fondamentales transformant l'histoire et il indique les causes sociales de manière synthétique. Il structure l'histoire et voit l'histoire *structurellement*. Or, les sciences sociales introduites au Japon étaient individualisées et spécialisées à l'extrême : le marxisme fixa la perspective dont ces sciences sociales et économiques avaient besoin.

Troisièmement, le marxisme met en débat la science même, qui n'est jamais dépourvue de prémisses ni de choix philosophiques. Les scientifiques doivent opérer intellectuellement sur la base de choix axiologiques, explicites ou pas. Or, sur la question des valeurs, les débats firent rage dans le milieu universitaire japonais nourri de théories allemandes. L'intérêt pour Max Weber au Japon l'illustre. En outre, les années 1920 virent l'essor de ce que l'on nommait précisément la « philosophie économique », avec les théories de Kiichirô Sôda et Kôzô Sugimura, qui prenaient la science économique comme objet de leurs réflexions [12]. Ces derniers n'étaient certainement pas marxistes. Mais leur inspiration néo-kantienne nourrie aux sources de langue allemande, comme celles de Takata, faisait à sa manière une place à la vision marxiste. En économie comme en sciences sociales, la promesse marxiste était d'éclairer la tension qui lie inséparablement les sciences et l'exercice de la pensée rationnelle critique. Il émerge une « conscience de parti » [13] dont l'effet se fait sentir dans la théorie, soulignant que l'on peut changer effectivement la réalité des conditions sociales (Maruyama 1961).

En concentrant exclusivement l'attention sur l'analyse des concepts et sur les cadres théorique de la sociologie, Takata répétait en quelque sorte l'argumentaire « bourgeois » dans sa critique même du marxisme... Les critiques que Takata portait contre Marx provenaient ainsi d'une inspiration nuancée d'arguments marxistes, sans toujours en saisir le sens. Il les critiquait plus qu'à son tour alors même que le marxisme commençait d'imprégner les sciences sociales en donnant à son combat le sens d'efforts pour juguler ce qu'il voyait comme essor de la modernité et abandon graduel de la vie communautaire. Il souffrait en somme de ces processus que Weber nommait pour sa part le « désenchantement du monde » et la « sociétalisation » [14].

12. Voir dans ce numéro, la traduction du texte de Yûichi Shionoya consacré à ces deux auteurs.

13. La notion de « conscience de parti » (党派性 *tohasei*) est prise ici dans son sens marxiste, à savoir que l'apparente indifférence politique des classes dirigeantes est un leurre qui sert leur domination sur les classes inférieures. Il s'agit pour le savant *marxiste* de rendre consciente l'illusion volontairement suscitée et de dénoncer les intérêts de classe, afin d'intégrer l'accusation sociologique à la politique partisane.

14. Le terme japonais de « changement méthodologique » désigne le processus de mutation structurelle faisant passer de la société communautaire originelle à la société moderne « du profit ». En termes de sociologie wébérienne, qui serait ici parfaitement adaptée, le terme « *Vergesellschaftlichung* » s'imposerait. Il accompagne la plus connue *Entzauberung*, devenue plus fameuse que l'autre terme technique en français.

4.3. La « socio-économie » proposée par Takata

À partir du milieu des années 1920, Takata passe véritablement de ses recherches sociologiques à l'étude des sciences économiques. On le regarde depuis lors comme le précurseur qui a « importé » la théorie de l'équilibre général au Japon, même s'il est délicat de retracer ses études de la pensée de Léon Walras, par exemple. Après 1925, Takata inclinait de plus en plus vers les recherches en sciences économiques *stricto sensu*. Il tenta de combiner la théorie de l'équilibre général avec une « sociologie de la domination » pour élaborer ce qu'il nomma l'« économie de la puissance »[15]. En 1941, Takata publia ce livre. En 1995, une version anglaise parut sous le titre *Power Theory of Economics*, éditée par Michio Morishima, qui avait été l'élève de Takata à l'Université de Kyoto[16]. Il s'agit d'une somme de « socio-économie » et Morishima la regarde comme une économie politique de plein droit. Où se situait alors le but des recherches que Takata menait à partir de la théorie de l'équilibre générale ?

Takata a publié une *Nouvelle lecture des sciences économiques* (en cinq tomes) de 1929 à 1932. Le deuxième tome, intitulé « La théorie des prix », consistait en une introduction au « courant européen » des sciences économiques développées par le Français Léon Walras, l'Allemand Karl Cassel et le Britannique Stanley Jevons. Là, Takata entendait lier la théorie de l'équilibre général à sa théorie de la domination en sociologie afin d'expliquer des cas précis : par exemple, les inégalités salariales entre métiers – ou celles entre hommes et femmes, et surtout celles entre les nations et les « races » qui les peuplent. Sa vision se porte à l'échelle du monde. Et la théorie de l'utilité marginale développée dans l'équilibre général et appliquée à la notion de productivité n'y suffisant pas selon Takata (1947), il concluait qu'il fallait la dépasser. Si elle ne suffisait pas, c'est qu'elle ne déterminait pas précisément le salaire par sa productivité marginale.

15. Des parallèles peuvent se profiler avec des travaux de langue allemande de la même époque, comme *Das Gesetz der Macht* de Friedrich von Wieser. Ces rapports ne sont ni consciemment mis en avant par Takata, ni prouvés par les archives, mais il est notoire qu'un « esprit du temps » (*Zeitgeist*) lie en somme les mondes de la « république de Weimar » (autant que la situation en Autriche) et la « démocratie Taïsho ».

16. Michio Morishima (1923-2004) est internationalement bien plus connu (comme mathématicien marxiste) que son maître dont il reçut l'influence quant aux théories sociales (et pas politiques).

Il fallait en outre prendre en compte l'existence du chômage de manière ou d'autre. Pour autant, Takata ne copie ni n'anticipe John Maynard Keynes. Mais il identifie des problèmes et il envisage un facteur de « domination » à même d'expliquer les inégalités salariales. Il tente de connecter la théorie de l'équilibre général avec une conception du rapport de domination, en liant les motifs intéressés du côté des dirigeants avec l'offre de travail par les travailleurs. Il ne développa toutefois pas beaucoup plus avant son analyse.

Takata vit dans la théorie de l'équilibre général une théorie qui traitait des seules « situations-limite » (le terme « à la marge » étant pris dans un sens assez naïf pour le coup), celles où la relation de pouvoir ne s'exercerait pas. Autrement dit, au final, Takata pensait catégoriser la théorie de l'équilibre général comme une théorie spécifique (un « sous-régime ») au sein de sa « théorie générale » propre, plus vaste, à savoir sa socio-économie. Takata dit que cette socio-économie devrait véritablement devenir l'économie standard, le « *mainstream* » en somme (Hayasaka 1981). Cette grande ambition ne devait évidemment pas se réaliser. Takata échoua dans son entreprise et personne ne reprit ses vues ni son approche, quasiment complètement ignorée, sinon de son élève Morishima.

Morishima mit sa réputation internationale au service d'une réappréciation des vues de Takata, car il pensait que l'échec subi était dû avant tout à l'incapacité de son maître à présenter sous forme de modèle mathématisé les propositions qui devaient en effet servir à mieux expliquer la détermination des salaires sous l'effet des facteurs de pouvoir. Il fallait une explication mathématique que Takata, qui ne maîtrisait pas cet outil, était bien incapable de donner. Takata n'avait absolument pas participé au processus de mathématisation des sciences économiques dans les années 1930-1950. Mais, après les années 1970, une fois que les sciences économiques se libérèrent un peu de leur « fièvre de quantification » (une expression qui existe au Japon), que la « socio-économie » de Takata restât cependant encore ignorée était à déplorer pour Hayasaka (1981), qui explique ainsi que les économistes japonais ont très généralement l'habitude, qu'il juge déplorable, de prêter attention aux seules théories développées à l'étranger – et, dans le champ économique, avant tout aux États-Unis.

Il est vrai que la littérature scientifique japonaise originale est quasiment absente du domaine économique. C'est un constat. La contribution originale du Japon se manifeste donc ailleurs que dans les vues économiques *stricto* sensu et elle vient notamment de l'alliance de l'économie avec la sociologie. Ce recours est récurrent dans les approches non-standard des économistes japonais qui s'aventurent à une production originale. Une raison majeure de leurs échecs reste qu'eux, comme Takata, n'ont le plus souvent pas la capacité de mathématiser leur approche. Or Morishima avait cette capacité. Et il ne la surestime pas : en 1995, quand il édite en anglais *Power theory of economics*, il pense même que l'ère que l'économie mathématisée a dominée complètement tire à sa fin. Il lui semble alors qu'il est donc temps de mettre en avant de nouveau les idées d'une « économie de la puissance » (bref, la socio-économie) de Takata.

On peut synthétiser en trois points l'intérêt de Morishima à publier ce travail. Premièrement, les sciences économiques étaient selon lui en train de se libérer de la vision unilatérale d'une quantification exclusive. Deuxièmement, le courant critique au sein de l'économie moderne reprochant à juste titre au *mainstream* de s'être séparé de la réalité de la vie économique, la socio-économie pouvait donc jouer un rôle renouvelé à cet égard. Troisièmement, selon Morishima (1995), la socio-économie de Takata pouvait fournir une explication théorique supérieure concernant les décennies de forte croissance de l'économie japonaise (de la fin des années cinquante au premier choc pétrolier). Ces trois points faisaient espérer à Morishima, qui mit sa renommée internationale dans la balance, que la socio-économie de Takata serait remarquée et appréciée dans le monde.

Une intuition de Morishima, pour prendre un exemple en revenant aux inégalités salariales, était que l'analyse des facteurs de la domination dans la relation industrielle devait prendre en compte des facettes typiquement culturelles : ainsi, au Japon, la négociation salariale dépend notamment du « salaire à l'ancienneté », de la fameuse politique d'emploi à très long terme (« à vie » selon l'expression) au sein des grandes entreprises, de la relation des syndicats à la direction de l'entreprise[17]. Il reste difficile de juger si l'analyse produite sur cette question fournit vraiment une clef de compréhension supérieure

17. Il est possible d'expliquer la forte croissance de ces années par le « cercle vertueux » de la hausse du salaire *via* la négociation collective *Shuntô* (春闘), qui stimule la consommation et donc la demande, qui tire à son tour la production. Il est aussi possible d'expliquer le lien entre l'investissement public, dirigé par l'État, et l'investissement privé porté par les entreprises sur le mode des cartels (*zaïbatsu*) (Kitajima 1998).

aux autres théories (Kitajima 2002). En effet, de nombreuses autres directions de recherche, outre celle de Takata, introduisent ces notions de relation de pouvoir entre patronat et syndicats ou d'analyse sociologique du travail industriel et de la gestion des relations au sein du monde du travail en général. Il n'est pas forcément besoin de s'appuyer sur la socio-économie de Takata, comme le voulait Morishima. Sur ce point, la socio-économie de Takata reste en fait incomplète, et un signe ne trompe pas à cet égard : Takata lui-même appliquait de préférence sa théorie de la domination au domaine de l'ethnologie, ce qui le conduisit à « raciser » sa conception de la socio-économie.

5. UNE VISION FAUSSE DE L'ETHNOLOGIE FONDÉE SUR DES PRÉSUPPOSÉS IDÉOLOGIQUES

5.1 *Le développement d'une ethnologie « raciste » faussement cohérente*

Nous prenons sciemment dans la suite pour méthode de ne focaliser l'attention ni sur les seuls concepts ni sur la seule théorie qu'exprime Takata et d'après lesquels tout chercheur en histoire de la pensée et en philosophie économique devrait se guider. C'est qu'il est raisonnable de penser qu'un penseur ne développe pas ses idées indépendamment des théories et des courants de pensée auxquels il se trouve confronté dans sa position historique, et que, de fait, et quoi qu'il en dise, il les lie dans son esprit. Dans le cas de Takata, on ne trouve aucune mention explicite de la constitution nationale japonaise, ni du système impérial, mais on lit dans son œuvre tardive la discussion abondante de la notion de *race* qui vise clairement à discerner parmi les races celles qui forment des sociétés de type communautaires et méritent la préservation.

Takata fut (et se voulut) un penseur de la « race » (et de la « race jaune ») au sens où il la définissait et où il s'appuyait sur cette définition. La race est la base même du groupe. Le groupe veut s'assurer de vivre en formant communauté, pour réunir une vaste quantité de semblables. Ce besoin est *subjectif*, il apparaît comme l'impératif de tout individu dans le groupe. Le sentiment s'appuie à son tour sur des déterminations objectives, celles de la communauté comme telle, à commencer par le lien du sang (l'homogénéité soulignée plus haut se prouve par ces « liens du sang ») et une culture commune, qui s'exprime dans la communauté de langage, de religion, d'us et de coutumes, de mœurs, de vues morales partagées, notamment (Takata 1942). Le besoin qu'une race éprouve de mesurer son influence collective se mue en une « identité de soi raciale ». Le besoin de « progresser » se comprend comme expansion du « soi racial » et l'impulsion illimitée vers le maintien et l'extension de son être. Une race ne peut pas s'empêcher de « déborder » sur les autres.

Cette logique fournit la base d'un nationalisme extensif sur lequel Takata a insisté. Dans l'impérialisme, compris dans ses sens économique, politique et social à la fois, la race veut, selon Takata, l'extension de ses objectifs inévitables d'influencer le monde : l'État en est le moyen, et non la fin, chez Takata. Cet État réalise l'expansion du territoire en annexant les races conquises à la race conquérante. La guerre ou la fusion pacifique des races peuvent valoir comme autant de moyens typiques de cette expansion selon les situations – souvent, la version pacifique de cette expansion consiste dans l'extension du commerce. Takata insiste sur le fait que le nationalisme japonais (pris en un sens large) se fonde sur une fusion pacifique de ce genre, sans prendre les armes. La guerre consiste en effet plutôt au contraire à exclure la volonté d'autrui ; elle n'est un recours que lorsque l'on viole le souhait de la race à se diffuser de manière prioritaire.

Comme toute race construit un État qui manifeste son « soi racial », elle tient certainement à exclure les races autres qui violent son espace (« vital », pour ainsi dire). C'est la cause des guerres, qui seraient superflues si les conditions de développement de chaque race, y compris les conditions économiques, étaient respectées avant tout. La guerre est en somme un malheur parfois inévitable. La logique de Takata, qui peut rappeler la logique déployée en Allemagne vers la même époque. L'idée d'un espace propre à ce nationalisme « élargi », fondé d'abord sur une vision pacifique de la fusion des races dans le creuset japonais, contredit violemment la formulation de la théorie de Takata lui-même quand il partait du point de vue d'une expansion illimitée censément souhaitée par le « soi racial ». Si le conflit menace d'emblée, alors la proposition pacifique n'est qu'illusoire. Il n'y a qu'un « pseudo-pacifisme » dans les nationalismes.

Takata soulignait encore que les guerres menées par le Japon jouaient un rôle historique : mettre fin à la domination des pays occidentaux sur les pays orientaux. Il s'agissait donc, contre les Européens, d'une autodéfense des « races orientales ». Takata se plaçait dans la perspective d'une « guerre sacrée ». C'est dans cette logique qu'il traita du fameux « incident de Manchourie » (1931) et de la guerre sino-japonaise ouverte (à partir de 1937) : selon lui, le premier incident est fondamentalement lié au souci qu'ont l'État japonais et la race japonaise de survivre, et la seconde s'explique à son tour comme le résultat inévitable des politiques d'une Chine hostile à l'égard du Japon, le ressentiment national chinois ne connaissant plus de bornes après la création de l'État de Manchourie (*Manchukuo*) établi après l'incident de 1931 (Takata 1943)[18]. Takata arrivait ainsi, par exemple, à conclure que la Chine devait lutter (commercialement et militairement) contre les Occidentaux en s'alliant au Japon, dont la mission était de libérer tous les peuples de couleur du joug des Occidentaux. Pour Takata, le Japon peut et doit unir les races d'Extrême-Orient contre les « Blancs », qu'il faut combattre et vaincre par toutes les voies économiques et militaires (si nécessaires). À cet égard, Japon, Manchourie et Chine sont liés par le sang et un même type commun de culture communautaire (Takata 1939)[19].

Quel est dès lors le type racial japonais qui doit prendre le rôle dirigeant dans la « ligue anti-occidentale » ? Selon Takata, la race japonaise se caractérise par son entière consanguinité pure, ce qui est très positif (et non une tare), au sens où le signe d'une race capable d'élargir son domaine par son effort conscient est cette homogénéité, avec la très forte solidarité qu'elle fonde. La question des unions dites « inter-raciales » est cependant plus complexe qu'il paraîtrait car Takata ne les condamne pas si « le sang japonais l'emporte » (quoi que cela signifie : alors ces unions ne sont pas forcément néfastes). L'idée

18. On sait que l'incident avait été fabriqué de toutes pièces par les services secrets japonais pour justifier l'intervention ouverte et établir la mainmise japonaise sur l'État-fantoche du *Manchukuo*, prolongeant la colonisation de la péninsule coréenne et une extension vers les territoires chinois. Dans ses textes, Takata veut intégrer cet aspect sans renoncer à y voir une expansion légitime du « soi racial » nippon.

19. Takata distingue la Manchourie (qui comprend, dans cette acception, les populations mongoloïdes) et la Chine (les Chinois sont des Han). Il les englobe dans les « races d'Asie orientale » dans la mesure où celles-ci sont liées par le sang et par la culture. La Corée déjà colonisée par le Japon à partir de 1910 n'est pas discutée et Takata considérait cette colonisation comme une « fusion pacifique », alors qu'existait toujours une résistance active contre le Japon qui l'éliminait férocement. Takata manquait complètement de réalisme au plan international : son ethnologie relève d'une invention fantastique de la mythologie nationaliste.

d'homogénéité dans la « pureté » du sang sert de base à l'idéologie qui superpose nationalisme d'État, vision idéalisée de la famille traditionnelle et discours raciste. La famille japonaise s'établirait sur le même modèle que l'État impérial et chaque famille du Japon est donc à son tour comme un des multiples rejetons de la lignée principale, la famille dynastique impériale. L'empereur est donc non seulement monarque, mais aussi maître absolu, comme l'est tout chef de la branche aînée de toue famille dans la tradition extrême-orientale (où les branches cadettes doivent dévouement entier et sans limite à a branche aînée) – et donc toute famille japonaise le doit à l'Empereur divinisé.

5.2 *Théorie ethnologique et critique de la théorie sociologique chez Takata*

Une remarque sera ici éclairante dans ce paysage, sans doute peu familier pour un lecteur occidental. Revenons pour cela à l'analyse de Maruyama, dont les options politiques et idéologiques étaient évidemment aux antipodes de celles de Takata. Pourtant Maruyama n'a jamais critiqué de manière directe la logique *comme telle* que suivait Takata dans la cohérence de son raisonnement logique dont il réprouvait les attendus.

Dans son livre de 1964, Maruyama décrit en effet ce raisonnement comme suit : l'empereur du Japon constitue la personnification absolue des valeurs nippones (dans la forme traditionnelle du pouvoir au Japon) et cette valeur se décline à l'infini, d'abord dans la noblesse japonaise, puis chez les bureaucrates au service de l'État, enfin chez tous les sujets pris un par un, dans l'ordre de leur distance vis-à-vis de la position centrale occupée par l'empereur. D'un point de vue global, lorsque la valeur absolue que représente l'empereur s'élargit en politiques internationales qui s'exercent sur le monde entier, c'est la nation japonaise (dans le corps de l'empereur) qui deviendrait à terme maîtresse des pays du monde entier, hiérarchiquement positionnés autour d'elle compte tenu de leur distance de l'empereur. Cette vision, au final étrangement proche de celle de la Chine ancienne pour en être héritée, signifierait une paix mondiale enfin trouvée.

C'est pourquoi les lois internationales n'ont, dans cette perspective, *pas même lieu d'exister*. Le Japon pouvait quitter la Société des Nations sans que la crédibilité d'une telle « vision du monde » soit entamée aux yeux de ses élites : c'est au contraire le reste du monde qui échouait à comprendre cette vision supérieure, toute nippone. La « forme spirituelle du militarisme japonais dominateur » et l'oppression exercée par les Japonais, en tant que « race », sur les autres peuples doivent se comprendre dans ce cadre. Il faut constamment répandre au loin le système impérial, qui a valeur absolue. Étendu aux autres pays, il liera les « races jaunes » de sang commun pour jouir de la « faveur » de participer à la sphère de la race dominante ; les peuples bénéficiaires au final devraient être reconnaissants pour ce qui constituera en somme une *pax japonica*, à sa manière.

Maruyama (1964) démonta la logique de cet argument en remarquant que l'oppression des autres races fut toujours acceptée sans aucune critique par Takata (et par tant d'autres), parce que, chez Takata, ces vues se superposent à sa version de l'ethnologie. Un autre commentateur, Kiichirô Yagi (1999), a énoncé une vue critique des théories de Takata en repartant de la notion de société communautaire et de « société du profit », ainsi que de son ethnologie. Dans un premier temps, Yagi remarque que l'autodétermination et la reconnaissance mutuelle « au sein de la même race » n'ont pas pu fournir une base solide à l'ethnologie de Takata, tout simplement en raison du manque d'« égalité » et de « reconnaissance mutuelle » dans son concept du « désir de vivre-ensemble ». Dans un second temps, Yagi critique la compréhension que les membres de cette société prennent des normes universelles et de la moralité car la sociologie de Takata ouvre la porte à l'essor d'une volonté de puissance, et en vérité à rien d'autre.

Il manque précisément à la théorie de la transition depuis la société communautaire jusque vers la « société du profit », dans la sociologie de Takata, une théorie *économique* significative du *profit*, justement ! Sa théorie de la société civile laisse complètement échapper l'analyse de la liberté individuelle, du rôle et du sens des processus de formation de la « société du profit », quand bien même il existe forcément un tel processus dès l'origine puisque c'est la raison pour critiquer cette « société du profit », dont il est dit qu'elle doit forcément émerger. Il doit même y avoir une loi socio-économique de l'*accélération* de sa mise en place. Enfin, quant à la reconnaissance mutuelle des races, il est impossible qu'elle vienne d'un processus d'extension du système impérial, qui procède par conquêtes, rendant impossible que chaque « race » ne s'autodétermine (Kitajima 2002).

Un autre commentateur, Takeshi Inagami, a lui aussi porté des critiques similaires à celles de Yagi envers Takata. Elles rejoignent celles que nous formulons quant à nous. Inagami adresse ses remarques non seulement à l'ethnologie de Takata, mais aussi à sa méthodologie et à ses vues historiques. Parmi diverses critiques, il vient préciser la discussion sur la relation entre le chercheur et son objet d'analyse. Inagami prête attention au « point de vue » que Takata prend sur ses objets de réflexion pour souligner que les principes de cohésion valant dans la famille et dans l'État sont différents et que l'on ne peut pas étendre le point de vue de l'une à l'autre sans autre justification. Impossible alors d'appuyer des propositions politiques, *a fortiori* très discutables, dans ce cas : tout cela doit susciter la plus grande réserve. Inagami souligne que cette déviation indue opère déjà dans le *Précis de sociologie générale* de Takata de 1922. La transformation de la notion produit en effet une position incompatible avec l'autre loi, tout à fait générale et originaire dans la sociologie de Takata, de la relation de groupe, ce qui crée une incohérence de fond.

Le livre de 1922 fut en effet l'occasion du tournant de Takata, d'un positionnement théorique vers la « politique ». Inagami montre que ce changement de méthode de la part de Takata vient bouleverser son point de vue sur la valeur dans les recherches qu'il mène sur le cadre social « réellement existant ». En poursuivant, Inagami (1972) note que ce changement de méthode poussa Takata à se tourner vers des propositions de plus en plus « politiques ». La critique touche tout à fait juste selon nous. Pour le dire dans nos propres mots, il s'agit de la « connexion non-intermédiée de la socio-économie et de la politique ». Ajoutons que c'est aussi le moyen que Takata trouva pour s'enfoncer toujours sciemment plus loin dans une apologie d'une autre dimension de la réalité, à savoir la *guerre*.

6. L'HÉRITAGE D'UN « RÉGIME D'IRRESPONSABILITÉ », DE TAKATA AU JAPON D'AUJOURD'HUI

6.1 *La responsabilité devant la guerre et l'attitude de Takata*

C'est tout à fait clair : Takata a proposé activement des politiques bellicistes et des plans pour la guerre depuis un point de vue nationaliste qu'il assumait. Il devint directeur de l'Institut d'ethnologie, établi en

1943 dans le cadre des politiques pour soutenir les théories raciales bellicistes[20]. Il est cependant plus pertinent de porter plutôt attention à l'opinion exprimée par Takata (1946) *après-guerre*, pour clarifier cette « mentalité de l'irresponsabilité ».

Takata explique alors tout de bon la guerre en lui attribuant la cause suivante : dès avant l'incident de Manchourie de 1931, la voix des intellectuels japonais aurait été étouffée et l'opinion publique était comme morte. Non seulement les partis politiques ne pouvaient pas publier les opinions, mais le monde de la pensée était muselé. Une partie des penseurs suivit le courant et changea de vues pour adopter la direction indiquée par l'armée – il y eut effectivement un « tournant » (転換 *tenkan*) majeur dans la philosophie de l'École de Kyôto, par exemple (京都学派 *Kyôto Gakuha*). En outre, il cite au titre d'une des causes de la défaite japonaise, le fait que l'on n'avait connaissance que des vues nationalistes, d'ailleurs censément déployées par tous les pays du monde, sans prendre en compte aucune enquête objective ni sur les niveaux de développement ni sur la taille relative des nations, ni sur l'état de leurs technologies ni sur celui de leur industrie. Bref, Takata souligne l'abaissement systématique des intellectuels et de la science qui visait à répandre l'esprit nationaliste fondé sur des bases de nature fantasmée, et des mythes propres à la civilisation japonaise.

Trouve-t-on dans ces lignes de Takata les éléments d'une grande variation avec ses opinions formulées avant-guerre ? La « remarque » qu'il émet en 1946 surgit comme si cela n'avait rien à voir avec les opinions que, lui, Takata avaient lui-même déjà présentées. Il serait donc assez logique de critiquer sa posture comme assez honteuse : le penseur n'aurait même pas le courage moral de prendre ses responsabilités. Comment analyser la « structure mentale » qui conduit Takata à développer cette ligne de raisonnement ?

Le cœur du régime des valeurs que Takata prône se situe dans ce qu'il nomme « communauté ». Il en est fier comme patriote, mais plus : c'est la clef de sa fidélité à l'empereur et à l'État nippons. Le premier mot qui vient est la protection de l'État national. Rappelons que, dans la culture japonaise (et dans la langue même), il va entièrement de soi

20. Nombre de critiques ont porté sur l'installation de Takata au poste de directeur de cet Institut. Les critiques ne voient cependant souvent en lui qu'un savant plutôt « louche » qui se serait plié aux politiques nationalistes. Cette vision borne leur critique de manière regrettable, ainsi chez Kizaemon Aruga (1897-1979), un spécialiste du mode de vie villageois et de l'économie rurale au Japon (Kitagawa 2000).

qu'un « inférieur » offre sa personne en protection à son « supérieur » au prix même de sa vie pour le servir le plus fidèlement possible[21].

6.2 *Décryptage du discours d'absence de responsabilité*

Citons derechef un passage des théories de Takata sur la race japonaise en expansion (économique et politique) :

> La Chine doit lutter contre les pays occidentaux en s'unissant au Japon, et le Japon a la mission de libérer les races de couleur [jaune] du joug des pays occidentaux. […] Il est possible d'unir les races asiatiques à leur racine parce que le Japon, la Manchourie et la Chine sont proches par les liens du sang et parce qu'elles ont une culture communautaire proche (Takata 1939, 114-7).

Juxtaposons alors à cette citation de Takata, cette autre, de Maruyama qui la décrypte :

> La domination du Japon sur les autres races doit consister à faire reconnaître aux autres la valeur absolue du système impérial, car c'est une faveur à leur faire (Maruyama 1964, 96).

Les opinions de Takata sur la nature de la race japonaise sont présentées, non dans un cadre de patriotisme inspiré par l'amour des siens, mais comme une idéologie, erronée et embellie à dessein, qui prétend s'appuyer sur « la science » dans le cadre d'une ethnologie faussée. Existe-t-il quelque motif pour Takata de prendre part à la responsabilité quant aux méfaits accomplis, en particulier sur les peuples asiatiques ? La structure de responsabilité qu'il propose se lit aisément comme une prétention à l'*irresponsabilité*. En outre, Takata rendant responsable de la guerre les « autres », en particulier l'« Occidental », il s'ensuit forcément qu'il publie ses opinions concernant les causes de la guerre et la défaite comme s'il pouvait en juger de manière neutre, voire quasiment en victime, parmi d'autres, de la répression contre les intellectuels par le régime militariste.

Or il est assez évident que Takata n'était pas un citoyen ordinaire. Professeur de l'Université de Kyoto, directeur de l'Institut d'ethnologie, lu et cité, sa voix portait. Il a certes déclaré assumer la responsabilité de ses opinions politiques, de ses vues en économie, sur la société et

21. Ce n'est donc pas le « supérieur » qui étend sa protection sur l'« inférieur », mais le sacrifice du second qui doit servir à perpétuer la hiérarchie : ce rapport du féal, du vassal a ici une illustration toute particulière.

sur la guerre. Mais il n'a jamais précisé *quelles vues* ni ce dont il prenait exactement la responsabilité. Ses actes s'expliqueraient (sans s'excuser pour autant) s'il se disait au moins responsable des vues impérialistes qu'il a portée haut. Mais il ne l'a jamais fait. Et *quid* de la responsabilité à l'égard des peuples asiatiques dominés d'abord économiquement, puis militairement (souvent sauvagement) ? Il semble que la question ne vint même jamais à l'esprit de Takata.

Maruyama dit de cette attitude mentale que Takata illustre au plus haut degré qu'elle s'inscrit dans « la structure mentale du militarisme dominateur », celle des élites militaires qui assistaient aux réunions avec l'empereur. Les décisions devaient habituellement être déjà préparées par la bureaucratie militaire, de sorte que les élites n'ont apparemment même pas besoin d'émettre d'opinion ; elles se défaussent plus tard de l'approbation qu'elles apportaient alors. Les vues rédigées par les bureaucrates sont pourtant à regarder comme exprimant les idées de ces mêmes élites. Mais le processus conduit à l'apparition d'une « structure mentale de déni de responsabilité », attitude par laquelle personne ne prend jamais de responsabilité des décisions qui émergent des réunions. Takata mit ainsi les responsabilités sur le compte de « ceux qui ne l'écoutaient pas bien, ou pas assez ». Il n'en sort pas grandi, mais « sauf » en un sens qu'il convient pourtant de dénoncer : c'est pourquoi Maruyama insistait si fort sur l'attitude structurelle mentale détestable qui était présente non seulement chez Takata mais encore chez les élites militaires et économiques nippones, qui ne se considéraient ni responsables, ni coupables. Cette « structure mentale du déni de responsabilité (ou *irresponsabilité*) » les portait à se dédouaner des faits inqualifiables innombrables commis sur les plans économique, militaire, idéologique.

7. CONCLUSION

Lors de sa conférence de réception du prix Nobel de littérature 1994, Kenzaburô Ôe a prononcé un discours célèbre, intitulé « Moi, d'un Japon ambigu ». Au tournant du XXe au XXIe siècle, la conception du déni de responsabilité constituait un courant majeur dans les représentations japonaises sur la période menant à la Seconde guerre mondiale et sur celle-ci. Dans ce contexte, Ôe plaça le point de départ de son travail dans une critique approfondie du fascisme japonais, qui avait imposé les horreurs que l'on saut dans la guerre menée contre les peuples d'Asie. Ôe exprima des excuses et ses regrets à leur égard. Il insista sur le fait que la rédaction de la nouvelle constitution japonaise et l'instauration de la démocratie après-guerre étaient une « preuve » de la sincérité des excuses et des regrets du peuple nippon. On peut trouver là des similarités avec le ton de la dénonciation par Maruyama de la « mentalité du déni de responsabilité ». Le Japon laisse toujours dans l'« ambiguïté » ce qui s'est passé durant la guerre faite aux peuples d'Asie : des crimes, des violations des droits de l'homme et du droit de la guerre, des massacres. La critique du régime fasciste japonais doit inclure le fait que ce régime a également opprimé l'homme et la femme du peuple japonais, niés dans leur vie (à disposition du pouvoir) et dans tous leurs droits. Pour autant, même la constitution et la démocratie demeurent également « ambiguëes » au Japon. C'est là que doit se situer la réflexion sur ce qui constitue un grand problème pour le Japon.

Il est évident que, dans son discours, Ôe faisait écho, par son titre déjà, au discours tenu par Yasunari Kawabata vingt-cinq ans avant lui (en 1968), le premier Prix Nobel de littérature japonais. Ce discours s'intitulait « Moi, d'un beau Japon ». D'une part, Ôe prêtait attention à la réflexion sur le « beau Japon » formulée par Kawabata, sans tenir compte de l'histoire du tout, et, d'autre part, il tournait un œil critique vers ces « idées » de Kawabata, qui avait quant à lui sciemment fermé les yeux sur cette histoire comme sur toute excuse ou regret à formuler à l'égard des peuples du monde et d'Asie, en particulier, comme en s'abritant derrière ce paravent de son « beau Japon ».

Les idées et les comportements de Takata, liés à une attitude qui parvient toujours à finir par s'accommoder de l'irresponsabilité, à dénier sa responsabilité, voilà tout ce qui converge dans la logique selon laquelle un Japon oppresseur des autres « races » devait soi-disant les faire bénéficier, à leur tour, de sa domination. Dans cette logique, la responsabilité est toujours reportée sur ceux qui avaient fait la guerre au Japon ou qui l'avaient poussé, à son corps défendant, à faire la guerre. On chercherait en vain une véritable reconnaissance de la responsabilité japonaise pour les horreurs de la guerre chez ces gens-là. Takata les représente : il incarnait bien ce « Japonais ambigu » dont parlait le grand écrivain. Au gré des vœux de sa « communauté », Takata, et ceux dont il représente l'infamie, peuvent toujours s'envelopper dans leur « beau Japon ». La vérité doit cependant apparaître.

La position de Takata dans l'histoire de la pensée sociologique et économique au Japon consiste donc en une double évidence. Introducteur de la théorie de l'équilibre au Japon, Takata a clairement échoué à fournir ce qu'il souhaitait être *sa* théorie générale. On le considère aujourd'hui comme activement mêlé aux politiques nationalistes racistes. On a beau jeu de le rejeter à bon compte, sans remarquer à la fois son apport en sociologie, avec ses impasses, et surtout que c'est toutefois son type de pensée dont le « beau Japon » a hérité en évoluant depuis l'après-guerre sans parvenir à trouver la structure morale pour faire face à ses propres responsabilités.

La « structure mentale de l'absence ou du déni de responsabilité » dénoncée par Maruyama, comme ce « Japon ambigu » évoqué par Ôe sont aujourd'hui des conceptions qui prévalent au Japon. On y accepte à l'infini non seulement des recherches qui jouent sciemment constamment sur les ambiguïtés de « l'histoire » (que ces recherches dévoyées discréditent à son tour), mais encore une activité pratique effective de nombreux éducateurs, politiciens et responsables religieux qui se situent en fait dans la lignée de Takata en même temps qu'ils prétendent faire valoir (et apprécier aux étrangers) leur « beau Japon ». Il est possible de considérer que cette pente glissante de la vie socio-politique au Japon et la fragilisation des libertés civiles (avec celle des syndicats et des partis progressistes) vont de pair. Au-delà des considérations socio-économiques, la philosophie sous-jacente est claire : il s'agit pour lors d'une crise profonde de la pensée dans le Japon contemporain.

RÉFÉRENCES

CAMPAGNOLO, G. 2006. "Max Weber : Georg Simmel, sociologue et théoricien de l'économie monétaire." *Revue de philosophie économique* 7/2 (numéroté 14) : 53-67.

— et B. SCHEFOLD. 2007. "Théories de la connaissance en économie : théories rationnelles appliquées à l'économie et théorie intuitive selon Edgar Salin." *Asterion* 5 : 265-97 (e n ligne : http://asterion.revues.org).

HAYASAKA, Tadashi. 1981. 日本経済学史における高田保馬博士 *Nihon Keizai Gakushi ni okeru Takata Yasuma Hakase.* ["Yasuma Takata dans l'histoire des sciences économiques au Japon"]. In 高田保馬博士の生涯と学説 *Takata Yasuma Hakase no Shôgai to Gakusetsu.* [*Vie et Doctrine de Yasuma Takata*], Takata Yasuma Hakase, Tsuisôroku Kankôkai (dir.), 112-55. Tokyo : Sôbunsha.

Inagami, Takeshi. 1972. 高田社会学の理論的下部構造, *Takata shakaigaku no rironteki kabukôzô*, ["Sub-structure théorique de la sociologie de Takata"]. *Shakaigaku Hyôron* 23/2 : 65-82. Société de la sociologie au Japon.

Kawabata, Yasunari. 1969. 美しい日本の私 *Utsukushii Nihon no Watashi*, [*Moi qui vient d'un beau Japon*]. Tokyo : Kôdansha.

Kaneko, Isamu (dir.). 2003. 高田保馬リカバリー *Takata Yasuma Recovery* [*Redécouvrir Yasuma Takata*]. Tokyo : Minerva Shôbo.

Kitagawa, Takayoshi (dir.). 2000. 有賀喜左衛門研究 *Aruka Kizaemon Kenkyû* [*Études sur Kizaemon Aruka*]. Tokyo : Tôshindô.

Kitajima, Shigeru. 1998. 開発と地域変動 *Kaihatsu to Chiikihendou* [*Développement et changement régional*]. Tokyo : Tôshindô.

– 2002. 高田保馬 *Takata Yasuma.* Tokyo : Tôshindô.

Maruyama, Masao. 1961. 日本の思想 *Nihon no Shisou* [*Pensées sur le Japon*]. Tokyo : Iwanami shoten.

– 1964. 現代政治の思想と行動 *Gendai Seiji no Shisô to Kôdô* [*Pensée et comportement dans la politique comtemporaine*]. Tokyo : Miraisha.

Morishima, Michio. 1995. "Foreword : Yasuma Takata (1883-1971)." In Takata, Yasuma (1995), *Power Theory of Economics*, ed. by M. Morishima, xi-xxv. London : Palgrave Macmillan.

Naka, Hisao. 1998. 米田庄太郎の社会学 *Yoneda Shôtarô no Syakaigaku* [*La sociologie de Shôtarô Yoneda*]. Tokyo : Inaho shobô.

Ôe, Kenzaburo. 1995. あいまいな日本の私 *Aimaina Nihon no Watashi.* Tokyo : Iwanami Shoten ; *Moi, d'un Japon ambigu* trad. fr R. De Ceccatty et R. Nakamura. Paris : Gallimard, 2001.

Takata, Yasuma. 1919. 社会学原理 *Shakaigaku Genri* [*Principes de sociologie*]. Tokyo : Iwanami Shoten.

– 1922. 社会学概論 *Shakaigaku Gairon*, [*Théorie de la sociologie*]. Tokyo : Iwanami Shoten.

– 1925. 階級及び第三史観 *Kaikyû oyobi Daisanshikan* [*Hiérarchie et point de vue de la troisième histoire*]. Tokyo : Kaizôsha.

– 1926. 社会関係の研究 *Shakaikankei no Kenkyû* [*Études sur la relation sociale*]. Tokyo : Iwanami Shoten.

– 1929-32. 経済学新講（全5巻） *Keizaigaku Shinkô zengokan* [*Nouvelle lecture des sciences économiques* (5 tomes)]. Tokyo : Iwanami Shoten.

– 1939. 東亜民族論 *Tôa Minzoku ron* [*Ethnologie de l'Asie orientale*]. Tokyo : Iwanami Shoten.

– 1942. 民族論 *Minzokuron* [*Théorie de l'ethnologie*]. Tokyo : Iwanami Shoten.

– 1943. 民族と経済 *Minzoku to Keizai* [*Race et économie*]. Tokyo : Yûhikaku.

– 1946. 終戦三論 *Shûsen Sanron* [*Trois théories de la fin de la guerre*]. Tokyo : Yûkôsha.

– 1947. 経済の勢力理論. *Keizai no Seiryokuriron* [*La théorie de la force en économie*]. Tokyo : Jitsugyô no Nihonsha.

Usui, Jishô. 1981. 高田保馬博士の生涯と社会学 *Takata Yasuma Hakase no Shôgai to Syakaigaku* [« Vie et sociologie de Yasuma Takata »]. In *Takata Yasuma Hakase Tsuisôroku Kankôkai* (dir.) (1981), 1-88. Tokyo : Sobunsha.

Yagi, Kiichirô. 1999. 近代日本の社会経済学. *Kindai Nihon no Syakaikeizaigaku.* [*Socio-économie au Japon contemporain*]. Tokyo : Chikuma shobô.

Yoneda, Shôtarô. 1921. 現代社会問題の社会学的考察 *Gendai syakai mondai no syakaigakuteki kousatsu* [*Études sociologiques sur les problèmes de la société contemporaine*]. Tokyo : Kôbundô shobô.

A NOTE ON JUST TAXATION

SUSUMU MORIMURA *

Résumé
L'imposition est l'un des principaux sujets de la théorie de la propriété des droits, mais il a pourtant été assez négligé jusque récemment. La communauté académique des philosophes avance de nos jours des arguments pour discuter avec ardeur des types d'imposition qui sont légitimes, s'il en est, et l'on doit beaucoup en ce domaine à l'ouvrage de Liam Murphy et Thomas Nagel *The Myth of Ownership*. Dans leur ouvrage polémique, les auteurs soutiennent qu'il n'existe pas de droit légitime permettant d'imposer par préemption ni la propriété ni les droits naturels à la propriété et que le processus d'imposition n'empiète certes jamais sur les droits de propriété, qui sont le fruit d'une institution par décret gouvernemental. Murphy et Nagel prennent pour cible principale Richard Epstein qui prône une vue libertarienne ou « libérale classique » contraire à ce propos. Epstein compare l'imposition à une expropriation publique et argumente en faveur de l'impôt sur le revenu.
Nous discutons ici la thèse d'Epstein sur la propriété privée, avec laquelle nous nous trouvons en accord quoique moyennant des nuances notables. Nous examinons la théorie étatiste de la propriété de Murphy et Nagel et nous soutenons que leur égalitarisme est surtout le fait d'un présupposé. Nous concluons que l'impôt sur la propriété foncière est la forme d'imposition la plus apte à être légitimée à partir de la perspective libertarienne sur les droits naturels, plus en tous cas que l'impôt sur le revenu et que la taxe sur la valeur ajoutée, formes d'impôt qui sont les plus habituelles. Surtout, nous soutenons qu'il y a là une forme d'imposition que la Constitution du Japon autorise.
Mots clefs : Constitution du Japon, expropriation, imposition, propriété privée, libertarisme, taxe foncière.

Abstract
Taxation is one of the fundamental topics in property right theory, but it is rather neglected one until quite recently. Today there are fervent arguments advanced in philosophical academia on what kind of, in any, taxation is

* Susumu Morimura is a Professor at the University of Hitotsubashi (Kunitachi, Tokyo). He is known for supporting libertarian views on the Japanese academic scene

justifiable, largely owing to Liam Murphy and Thomas Nagel's *The Myth of Ownership*. In this controversial book, they claims that there are no such things as a morally legitimate right to pretax property or natural property rights and that taxation never infringes upon property rights because they are only institutionally created by governmental decree. Murphy and Nagel's main target is Richard Epstein's opposite libertarian or classical liberal view on tax. Epstein likens taxation to public expropriation or eminent domain and argues for proportionate income tax.
Here, after concurring with Epstein's view on private property with some important qualifications, I critically examine Murphy and Nagel's statist property theory and claim that their overall egalitarianism is not argued for but merely presupposed. I conclude that estate tax is more justifiable kind of tax from the natural rights libertarian perspective than both income tax and consumption tax, which are the most common form of taxation today. I also claim this conclusion is consistent with the natural reading of the Japanese Constitution.
Keywords: Constitution of Japan, taxation, expropriation, private property, libertarianism, estate tax.

JEL Codes: E62, G28, H24

1 FOREWORD

In this note, I endeavor to determine the rationale of taxation in the context of property theory by examining two opposite contemporary views in this field. One of them was developed by libertarian or classical liberal legal theorist Richard Epstein in his book *Takings* (Epstein 1985, esp. ch. 18) and his later writings. It argues that since taxation can be regarded as just another kind of "taking" (that is, levying specific private property. also known as "expropriation" or "eminent domain"), it also requires just compensation, which, according to Epstein, ought to be proportionate to the amount a taxpayer is taxed. The other view was developed by philosophers Liam Murphy and Thomas Nagel in their influential work *The Myth of Ownership* (Murphy and Nagel 2002). They claim there is no such thing as a morally legitimate right to pretax property and that taxation never infringes upon property rights because they are only institutionally created by governmental decree.

I focus on these two views because they make explicit the basic, usually unspoken beliefs many people have concerning taxation. My view is somewhere between them, but closer to Epstein's.

2. THE CASE OF THE CONSTITUTION OF JAPAN AND EPSTEIN'S UNITARY UNDERSTANDING OF TAXATION AND TAKING

Epstein conceives expropriation or eminent domain and taxation in a similar way and tries to apply the same constitutional principles of "public use" and "just compensation" from Amendment V to the U.S. Constitution to them. (According to that Amendment, private property shall not "be taken for public use, without just compensation". Both phrases are also used in Article 29 (3) of the Constitution of Japan, which provides for private property rights. Hence I believe Epstein's theory is applicable not only to the American Constitution but also to the Japanese Constitution.) But Epstein is fully aware his view is not a dominant one. He writes:

> The proposition that all taxes are subject to scrutiny under the eminent domain clause receives not a whisper of current support. The taxation power is placed in one compartment; taking power in another. The first power is wholly untouched by the limitation imposed upon the other. (Epstein 1985, 283f.)

The situation is almost the same in Japan. As far as I know, there are very few authors in Japan who seriously compare taxation to taking. Indeed, both precedents and constitutional scholarship in Japan seem to accept any policies and function as legitimate aims of taxation. Thus, in the "Salaries Workers'Taxation Case" (1985), a Japanese leading case in tax law, the Supreme Court famously held as follows:

> Tax today has, in addition to its original function to fulfil the financial needs of the State, various functions such as income redistribution, optimum allocation of resources, economic adjustment and so on, and to this end, it is obviously necessary not only to make a comprehensive decision in light of policy requirement for the whole field of national administration including fiscal, economic, social and other policies so as to determine the tax burden on the people, but also take a highly specialized and technical decision so as to provide for taxation and other requirements. Hence, it is held that when it comes to enactment of the Tax Code, there is no other way than to leave to the technical decision of the legislature in line with policy based on accurate material and data for the real state of national finance, socio-economy, national income, the people's living and the like, and that the court basically has no choice but to respect such

> legislative discretional decision. (Supreme Court Judgment 1980 (*Gyo-Tsu*) No. 15 rendered by the Grand Bench on March 27, 1985, *Minshu* Vol. 39, No. 2, at 247) [1].

The Supreme Court of Japan has been so completely deferential to the legislature concerning the rationale of taxation, and the majority of legal scholars in Japan are of the similar persuaion. I suspect that legislative discretion in tax policies is more or less taken for granted not only in Japan but almost all over the world.

However, Epstein claims that the conventional distinction between taxation and expropriation is merely a legal technicality.

> The arguments for using the just compensation principle to constrain state regulation apply with equal force to the area of taxation. After all, a tax is only a threat to take specific property unless its owner pays a certain portion of income or wealth to the government. (Epstein 1995, 137)

It is usually claimed that expropriation is different from taxation in that the former is exercised for the sake of certain public enterprises, while the latter is for general financial purposes. However, that difference is only a matter of degree, since tax is levied nowadays not only for financial purposes but also for some policy reasons (as frankly admitted by the Japanese Supreme Court decision above) and some taxes have particular people as their targets, while the professed, if not real, purpose of most expropriations is the public good and not a certain group interest. Thus, it seems that not only expropriation, but also taxation requires some justification to those who are burdened, and not to citizens in general. Moreover, just as "just compensation" to the original owner is required for expropriation in general, so some kind of "just compensation" to the taxpayers is needed in the case of taxation.

There is, however, a practical difference between expropriation and taxation here. It is impossible to compensate taxpayers'loss by paying them money. If it were possible, then there would be no reason for taxation from the start. But Epstein believes that all taxpayers must at least benefit overall as a consequence of taxation. For example,

1. [Editor's Note] 民集 *Minshu* : The volumes of this publication gather the judgments rendered by the Supreme Court of Japan. They are ordered through the system listing cases by year of submission, followed by (*Gyo-Tsu*) and a serial number. The judgment in this case was rendered on March 27, 1985 by the Grand Bench, or Japan's highest ranking court.

they would obtain a net benefit in kind by increased public security in exchange for paying taxes. However, justifiable tax must, according to Epstein, be a flat tax (by which he means tax proportionate to each taxpayer's benefit), and neither a progressive tax nor a tax levied on particular people, since the latter kind of taxes would inflict net loss on some taxpayers and give the government arbitrary power. He writes:

> When the degree of progression is allowed to vary freely, an important constitutional bulwark against uncompensated taking is removed. The progressive tax increases the frequency and intensity of legislative rent seeking by increasing the expected gains of factions. (Epstein 1985, 299)

Indeed, in real politics both progressive and policy-oriented taxes are liable to violate the requirement of universality of legal rules, which is arguably a major component of the rule of law.

Nevertheless, Epstein does not deny altogether the justifiability of redistribution of wealth by taxation since it could increase the overall societal utility, on the problematic but popular assumption of interpersonal diminishing marginal utilities – that is, "a unit of wealth is worth more to a poor person than a richer one" (Epstein 1995, 141). Yet Epstein insists that the burden of redistributive taxation must be not shared progressively, but rather, proportionately.

I personally tend to agree with many of Epstein's claims, subject to some qualification.

First, Epstein accepts taxation mainly as the means of supplying public goods on the ground that every citizen would obtain some benefit – perhaps benefit proportionate to each person's payment – from public goods and services which would not be supplied by voluntary private enterprises. But I doubt that current public welfare payments always satisfy this condition since rich people do not seem to benefit from this system. Indeed, Epstein writes:

> Countless programs of redistribution have [...] perverse effects, but income or wealth redistribution from rich to poor lays a far greater claim on the social conscience and cannot be dismissed in a cavalier fashion. (*ibid.*)

Epstein's acceptance of redistribution is thus only pragmatic, not principled. Moreover, it is not at all clear how much redistribution he is ready to admit.

I differ from Epstein in considering that it is more plausible to accept as natural human rights – not only negative liberty rights and private property, but also positive claim rights to a minimum standard of living – for humanitarian reasons. True, the people who are taxed in order to provide welfare payments do not gain a benefit from it. But it is a burden necessary in order to meet the pressing interest of guaranteeing a minimum standard of living for all. And if the burden is distributed proportionately as Epstein proposes, there is little danger of the rent-seeking or arbitrary abuse of political power that he is understandably afraid of.

I agree with Epstein that private ownership is a vital natural right, but also believe there are other kinds of natural rights. The positive right to subsistence is one of them. In this point the Japanese Constitution is favorably different from the American one, as Article 25 of the former explicitly provides that "[a]ll people shall have the right to minimum standards of wholesome and cultured living", while the latter is silent on such rights. I admit it cannot be easily determined what the minimum standards of living should be in a concrete social condition and how to secure it to everyone.

Concerning the ways of financing the government, I am inclined to support the system of negative income tax, which is also compatible with Epstein's proportionality principle, but what tax system is the best or least objectionable certainly depends on contingent social conditions.

Secondly, I regard the proportionality requirement of Epstein itself as being unreasonably strict. It seems that taxpayers cannot justifiably complain if the post-tax condition is much better than the pre-tax one for the worse-off and only marginally preferable for everyone, even though the benefit to each and every taxpayer is not proportionate to his or her payment. In this way, there can be some range for the government's justifiable policies. One may therefore think more about the case in Japan. We shall investigate some more on adverse positions that have been upheld as well.

3. PROPERTY THEORY ACCORDING TO MURPHY AND NAGEL

The diametrical opposite stand to Epstein's view on property and taxation is the one upheld and advocated by Murphy and Nagel. They write:

> There is no market without government and no government without taxes; and what type of market there is depends on laws and policy decisions that government must make. In the absence of a legal system supported by taxes, there couldn't be money, banks, corporation, stock exchanges, patents, or a modern market economy – none of the institutions that make possible the existence of almost all contemporary forms of income and wealth.
> It is therefore logically impossible that people should have any kind of entitlement to all their pretax income. All they can be entitled to is what they would be left with after taxes under a legitimate system, supported by legitimate taxation – and this shows that we cannot evaluate the legitimacy of taxes by reference to pretax income. [...] The logical order of priority between taxes and property rights is the reverse of that assumed by libertarianism. (Murphy and Nagel 2002, 32)

Murphy and Nagel call the Epstein-like view of private property "everyday libertarianism" and criticize it as "an unexamined and generally non-explicit assumption that does not bear examination" (*ibid.*, 36). In their view, it is just in the same way that slave owners in the antebellum South believed in the justice of slavery and people today believe in everyday libertarianism (*ibid.*, 7). What determines the shape of property rights are not entitlements of individual persons, but rather, "the legitimate aims of society" (*ibid.*, 75). From this premise, Murphy and Nagel reach the conclusion that such common concepts as "vertical equity" and "horizontal equity" and "the general idea that taxes should be levied in accordance with ability to pay" (*ibid.*, 28) should be abandoned altogether, since those concepts presuppose the everyday libertarian idea that one is morally entitled to one's pre-tax income.

While it is not altogether perfectly clear in their book, it seems to me, what kind of social justice Murphy and Nagel endorse as an alternative to "everyday libertarianism", they are certainly critical of both utilitarianism and the idea of efficiency and sympathetic to the Rawlsian difference principle and equality of opportunity. They believe that morally arbitrary inequality of result should be eliminated from a just society (*ibid.*, 56).

Murphy and Nagel state in a crystal-clear manner the view on property rights that is usually, albeit implicitly, adopted by many contemporary distributive egalitarians and which is the one also outlined by John Rawls in *A Theory of Justice* (Rawls 1999, see especially section 43 discussing the "Background Institution for Distributive Justice"). They seem to hold the view that property is a state-made system from top to bottom and that the contents of property rights are to be determined by the state for the legitimate aims of society. Not only welfare benefits, but also markets, property rights, and taxation are all institutions for implementing distributive justice. In their social justice fundamentalist view, there is not a single hint of the familiar idea that one is morally entitled to what one produces by one's work. Indeed, this idea is censured as being a harmful false myth. They assume that all goods, including wealth produced individually or collectively by human beings as well as natural resources, are morally owned by the state. I shall call that assumption "implicit statism".

While Murphy and Nagel's view is approved by egalitarians, it has been severely criticized in many ways. Some critiques are rather superficial or trivial, but some are more fundamental (e.g. Huemer 2013, 40-3; Biron 2018, esp. 86-7; Brennan and van der Vossen 2018, 203-5). I shall focus on the latter.

What Murphy and Nagel call "everyday libertarianism" is exemplified in the Lockean property theory adopted in the main by Robert Nozick in *Anarchy, State, and Utopia* (Nozick 1974) and Epstein. In fact, both Nozick and Epstein are many times explicitly criticized in Murphy and Nagel's book. Thus, it is helpful to examine whether Lockean property theory is sound or not. It is remarkable that Murphy and Nagel do not try to refute "everyday libertarianism" squarely in their book. They claim (1) that "everyday libertarianism" would make all the property rights almost inviolable and consequently deny many activities which modern governments are engaged in, and (2) that the idea of "desert", which everyday libertarianism often appeals to, is unsound. Their attempted rebuttal of everyday libertarianism is, however, not successful.

I shall contest their view. First, I shall begin by pointing out that Murphy and Nagel's implicit "statism" (or likeness for an expanded role of the state) and their explicit egalitarian distributive policy are both opposed by many authors, whether liberal or conservative. Such opponents are not persuaded by notions of the strong political authority of state or egalitarianism in distributive justice. These views are to be argued for, with stronger arguments, in my view, and they are not simply to be presupposed.

Since I do not intend to use the idea of desert, I shall not deal with their opposition to it (their second claim). Instead, I wish to refute their first claim that "everyday libertarianism" leads to unacceptable consequences. In general, those consequences seem unacceptable only for such egalitarian statists as Murphy and Nagel, and not for those of us who are skeptical of big government. We should not take existing systems for granted.

More specifically, if "everyday libertarianism" completely denies the justifiability of taxation, it may certainly be unconvincing. But we need not take such an extreme position in order to be an everyday libertarian: we can accept taxation for supplying genuine public goods and minimum welfare while believing in robust property rights and resisting more extensive governments. Murphy and Nagel suppose that everyday libertarians must regard every kind of taxation as theft, but that is a false dichotomy. Everyday libertarians can admit without contradiction that everyone has a right to subsistence as well as rights of self-ownership and personal freedom and that government has a legitimate power to collect taxes in order to realize those basic human rights and supply public goods.

Most libertarians tend to believe that everyone has natural property rights in his or her person and what he or she produces (self-ownership thesis) and that the free market is a system of natural liberty. It is those beliefs that Murphy and Nagel attempt to demolish. On what grounds do they attempt to do so? They first claim that property rights cannot exist without protection by the state, and secondly, that the market system is an artifact which includes such state-made institutions as contract law, intellectual property, limited liability, anti-trust law, legal tender, and stock exchange. But, according to us, neither claim denies the concept of natural property rights.

Regarding the first claim, we can argue that if property rights are said to be nonexistent without governmental protection, then all natural rights must also be so, since freedoms of association, movement, religion, thought and expression may need governmental protection for their full exercise, too. But that does not mean that the government exists prior to natural rights. Rather, natural rights are conceptually precedent to, and independent of, the state, and the foremost aim of the state is to protect and implement natural rights. If Murphy and Nagel are consistent in their opposition to everyday libertarianism, they must also criticize that basic doctrine of natural rights in general.

As to the second claim above, we can argue that although states today adopt such institutions as limited liability and legal tender, it does not follow that every public institution is in harmony with the free market. For example, certain public institutions in the real world, such as government monopolies and restrictions on trade, are incompatible with the free market. And some libertarian economists even advocate such anti-statist proposals as the denationalization of money and abolition or radical curtailment of intellectual property, thereby opposing many current public institutions.

True, some public institutions, such as enforcement of property and contract, strengthen the free market, but that does not mean that without such public institutions, property rights and free market cannot exist. Property rights and markets are possible without public institutions, just as we can have the concept of health without any medical system. Just as the medical system was established in order to improve public health, so property and contract law have developed (partly) to make natural property rights more concrete and solid. Moreover, there are a great number of examples of customary property law, such as law merchant (domestic and international) and customary rules among farmers, fishermen, and ranchers, which are born and grow independently of, or sometimes even in conflict with, state law.

So-called "everyday libertarians" believe in such natural property rights. Rights to one's wage and work – that is, property rights one obtains through free exchange or by voluntary gift, in what one produces, in what one finds and catches in commons – are modern-day natural property rights, as distinct from privileges and benefits given by government for some policy or more dubious reason. Therefore, everyday libertarianism is not uncritical conservative thinking in favor of the economic status quo as Murphy and Nagel misleadingly represent, but radical thought which questions the legitimacy of many existing political and legal systems, including taxation.

4. IMPLICATIONS FOR TAXES

What normative implications do the arguments above have for taxation? Even most libertarians admit it is justifiable for governments to levy taxes in order to finance their legitimate functions, even though they are much more modest than those of today's states. Many pragmatically minded libertarians such as Epstein advocate proportional income tax or consumption tax as the least evils because they seem to fit best the benefit theory of taxation, according to which the government is justified in levying taxes on taxpayers only for the services it provides. In contrast, corporation tax is regarded as inappropriate, because income tax on individual basis would be sufficient since a corporation's benefits ultimately belong to its shareholders.

On further reflection, however, estate taxation (that is, taxation on the estate of a decedent, as distinct from inheritance taxation on the recipient of an inheritance, which is adopted in Japan) is still less objectionable from the natural property rights perspective, since income tax taxes living persons who are bearers of natural rights, while estate tax taxes deceased persons who no longer have natural rights. Though estate tax is much less popular than income tax in modern states including Japan (see, e. g., Scheve and Stasavage 2016, ch. 4), it is probably only because even today many people regard human beings chiefly as members belonging to their respective families or dynasties, not as free independent individuals.

Thus, I agree with Jennifer Bird-Pollan's recent assertion that wealth transfer taxation is endorsed by four major different ideologies so different as socialism, egalitarian liberalism, libertarianism, and Millian utilitarianism. Referring to libertarians'strong view of property rights, she writes:

> The estate tax provides a unique opportunity for just taxation under the libertarian model. Because the entity subject to taxation (the estate) is not a person with natural rights, the normal libertarian arguments regarding unassailable property rights and the requirements of consent do not apply. (Bird-Pollan 2017, 227)

Bird-Pollan also argues that estate tax is as consistent with the libertarian benefit theory of taxation as income tax since the former charges the taxpayer for the service in a lifetime instead of some time period (*ibid.*, 228). In other words, estate tax can be regarded as *postmortem* income tax.

I agree with Bird-Pollan on this point as well. Nevertheless, I do differ with her when she writes that the gift tax ought to complement the estate tax because "without the gift tax, the estate tax would be all too easy to avoid" (*ibid.*, 221f) by *inter vivos* gifts. It is true that almost all tax theorists believe gift tax is pragmatically on a par with estate tax or inheritance tax. On natural rights theories in pure forms, however, living persons are essentially different from dead, non-existing ones. The gift tax is a restriction on property rights to the same degree as income tax and consumption tax. Although estate taxation would be avoided by *inter vivos* gifts to some degree, yet that alone does not justify gift tax. It may only justify the estate tax being complemented by proportional income tax or consumption tax in order to fill the deficit, because gifts are only one kind of income (for the donee) and consumption (for the donor). There are no needs for gift tax in addition to income tax or consumption tax.

REFERENCES

Bird-Pollan, J. 2017. "The Philosophical Foundations of Wealth Transfer Taxation." In *Philosophical Foundations of Tax Law*, M. Bhandari (ed.), 217-32. Oxford : Oxford University Press.

Biron, L. 2018. "Taxing or Taking? Property Rhetoric and the Justice of Taxation." In *Taxation : Philosophical Perspectives*, M. O'Neill and S. Orr (eds.), 81-97. Oxford : Oxford University Press.

Brennan, J. and B. van der Vossen. 2018. "The Myths of the Self-Ownership Thesis." In *The Routledge Handbook of Libertarianism*, J. Brennan, B. van der Vossen and D. Schmidtz (eds.), 199-211. New York and London : Routledge.

Epstein, R. A. 1985. *Takings : Private Property and the Power of Eminent Domain.* Cambridge (MA) : Harvard University Press.

– 1995. *Simple Rules for a Complex World.* Cambridge (MA) : Harvard University Press.
– 2003. *Skepticism and Freedom.* Chicago : The University of Chicago Press.
HUEMER, M. 2013. *The Problem of Political Authority : An Examination of the Right to Coerce and the Duty to Obey.* New York : Palgrave.
MURPHY, L. and T. NAGEL. 2002. *The Myth of Ownership : Taxes and Justice.* New York : Oxford University Press.
NOZICK, R. 1974. *Anarchy, State, and Utopia.* New York : Basic Books.
RAWLS, J. 1999. *A Theory of Justice, Revised Edition.* Cambridge (MA) : Harvard University Press.
SCHEVE, K. and D. STASAVAGE. 2016. *Taxing the Rich : A History of Fiscal Fairness in the United States and Europe.* Princeton : Princeton University Press.

A PROPOS DES ERRANCES DANS LA RÉCEPTION JAPONAISE DE L'ŒUVRE D'ADAM SMITH

MASATAKA MURAMATSU*

Résumé
La réception d'Adam Smith au Japon est l'occasion d'expériences variées de comparaison internationale et interdisciplinaire. Smith paraît ce que l'on pourrait déjà nommer un « philosophe-économiste » tout en étant regardé comme « l'économiste par excellence » et, au Japon aussi, le « professeur de tous les économistes ». Il continue d'y être considéré comme un représentant du libéralisme économique, ce qui prête à des erreurs et des errances que cet essai entend dénoncer. L'objet principal de ce texte est de présenter comment la doctrine smithienne a été conceptualisée au Japon sur les plans historique, social et intellectuel : ce n'est pas seulement la réception de sa théorie économique, mais aussi la relation à sa philosophie qui est questionnée.
Mots-clefs : Adam Smith, histoire de la pensée économique au Japon, philosophie sensualiste au Japon.

Abstract
The reception of Adam Smith, the Scottish founder of modern political economy, in Japan offers many opportunities for international and interdisciplinary comparisons. In such a perspective, Smith may well appear as a so-called early "economic philosopher" as much as the "father of economics" or "*the* economist *par excellence*". As far as Japan is concerned, he remains "the Professor of Japanese economists" as the latter regard him as the embodiment of the liberal way of looking at economics. The main purpose of this essay is to introduce to a Western audience how, despite an honorable tradition of scholarship, Smith's ideas at a historical, social and

* Université du Hokkaido, Faculté des Sciences sociales et des Humanités, Département de philosophie, Sapporo, Japon. Maître de conférences, M. Muramatsu a coordonné la partie japonaise du réseau LIBEAC de 2013 à 2016 depuis l'université du Hokkaido (une des sept anciennes universités impériales du Japon) : ce texte fut élaboré dans ce cadre. La version française en a été révisée par Gilles Campagnolo.

intellectual level, were distorted, not only due to his economic doctrine, but in relationship with the latter's philosophical tenets.
Keywords: Adam Smith, history of economic thought in Japan, sensualistic philosophy in Japan.

Classification JEL : B12, B31, N01, N35

1. PRÉLIMINAIRE

Le spiritualisme français est passablement étudié au Japon. Ces études ont également pu conduire à s'intéresser à la philosophie écossaise du XVIIIe siècle, qui est l'une des racines de ce courant philosophique et, de ce fait naturellement, aux travaux d'Adam Smith, plus exactement à sa *Théorie des sentiments moraux*. Le présent essai est consacré à analyser les éléments qui, dans cette réception, peuvent mal tourner. Pourquoi s'intéresser à la réception de Smith au Japon ? Parce qu'elle est essentielle pour comprendre l'attitude des Japonais face à la perspective occidentale sur les questions et les sciences économiques. Et aussi parce que la réception de Smith peut s'apprécier comme un facteur-clef du processus de modernisation du Japon.

Cet essai débutera par l'évocation historique sommaire de la réception de Smith au Japon à partir de la fin du XIXe siècle, source d'informations indispensable pour saisir la thématique philosophique que nous développerons – autant qu'elle est sans doute nécessaire pour nombre de lecteurs occidentaux peu au courant de la réception des auteurs, même les plus classiques, sur un sol si loin d'eux que le Japon. Ensuite, nous traiterons ce que l'on peut nommer une véritable *« renaissance » contemporaine* de la *philosophie* de Smith auprès du grand public nippon. La contribution de cette renaissance à une meilleure compréhension de la doctrine smithienne sera décrite en soulignant le risque d'un malentendu, que l'on dirait presque « traditionnel » tant il est récurrent, et qui demande examen, car il pourrait, malgré une démarche plus réflexive sur ce sujet dans le champ de la recherche japonaise récemment, subsister au cœur même de cette renaissance.

2. LE STATUT SPECIAL ACQUIS PAR L'ŒUVRE D'ADAM SMITH AU JAPON

Adam Smith est particulièrement populaire au Japon. Dans toute bibliothèque universitaire japonaise, ou dans une grande librairie, on trouve facilement plus d'une centaine de titres traitant de la pensée ou de l'économie politique de Smith. Sur les bancs des facultés d'économie politique japonaises, les travaux de ce philosophe sont ceux que l'on étudie en premier encore de nos jours.

Pourquoi Smith jouit-il d'une telle popularité ? Qu'est-ce que qui peut expliquer un engouement qui n'est pas seulement académique ? Dans cet essai, pour apporter des éléments de réponse, nous porterons d'abord l'attention sur le statut spécial de ce penseur au Japon. Là, Smith est vénéré. On dira, sans emphase excessive, qu'il est « idolâtré ». Illustrons par une anecdote cet état de fait. Dans les années 1930, le professeur Charles Ryle Fey, spécialiste de Smith, rapporte qu'il rencontra par hasard deux gentilshommes japonais à Edinburgh. Ils lui demandèrent où se trouvait la tombe du philosophe. Fey les y emmena et les vit tomber en adoration devant sa tombe.

Cette anecdote est, selon nous, révélatrice de l'attitude japonaise à l'égard de Smith. Or cette « idolâtrie » reste d'actualité. Ainsi, l'on peut souvent entendre le raisonnement suivant : « Smith est juste, ce qu'il dit est juste, ce qui est juste est vrai, et cela vaut pour tout ce qui découle de sa pensée ». Dans les années 1990, on pouvait aussi entendre des avis du type « Smith explique que le libéralisme absolu est juste en raison de son autorégulation, c'est-à-dire la main invisible divine ». Smith dirait ainsi toujours « juste » et donc, le libéralisme est juste. Le lecteur pensera peut-être qu'il est exagéré d'utiliser le terme d'« idolâtrie ». Ne devrait-on pas parler de science ? Les pages qui suivent montreront au lecteur que c'est souvent le contraire.

Pour comprendre la genèse de cette « idolâtrie », il faut revenir à l'histoire de la réception de Smith au Japon. On peut distinguer quatre périodes dans ce processus. Il existe donc une très importante et très ancienne tradition d'études smithiennes au Japon. Elle a été brillamment illustrée, par exemple par Hiroshi Mizuta, dont il suffit de citer le travail de collation intégrale de la bibliothèque d'Adam Smith (Mizuta 1967 ; 2000) qui venait compléter et parachever avec toute la précision minutieuse requise et une érudition prodigieuse le travail accompli en Occident par Bonar sur cette même bibliothèque. Les travaux de Mizuta à l'international (Mizuta 2009) sont assez reconnus pour ne pas avoir ici besoin d'y revenir : nous le mentionnons (et nous le citerons en conclusion) pour corriger l'image assez sévère que nous allons donner de la recherche japonaise dans les pages qui suivent. Mais reprenons dans l'ordre.

La réception inaugurale a lieu à l'époque dite « *Meiji* », notamment dans les années 1880. À cette époque, deux courants s'opposent violemment au Japon en économie politique. D'un côté, la position officielle, défendue par le gouvernement Meiji : après avoir observé la guerre franco-prussienne de 1871, il décida d'adopter et d'imiter le système politique et économique allemand. Cette décision conduisit à établir les sciences politiques et économiques en sciences « officielles ». Elles devaient justifier l'ensemble des choix politiques et économiques au nom du développement, même lorsque les décisions « pour le pays » étaient arbitraires. L'histoire allait se répéter puisque, les thèses économiques de l'Allemand Friedrich List, qui furent adoptées par les autorités notamment à partir des années 1890, servirent d'alibi à une politique conservatrice et belliciste.

De l'autre côté se dressait un groupe composé d'intellectuels et de journalistes aux idées libérales et antiprotectionnistes, voire antigouvernementales. Il s'agissait d'anciens officiels du *Bakufu* (ou gouvernement de la période dite d'Edô), de leurs héritiers et de leur disciples. Citons ainsi Ukichi Taguchi, qui fut surnommé l'« Adam Smith japonais ». En 1880, c'est grâce aux travaux de ce journaliste, politicien et grand prêcheur du libre-échange dans le commerce, que le nom de Smith se propagea dans les milieux intellectuels libéraux ainsi que dans le grand public. Taguchi donna notamment la première traduction en japonais des *Recherches sur la nature et les causes de la richesse des nations*. Le groupe libéral refusa d'intégrer le nouveau gouvernement, il se divisait en positions revendicatives relatives aux idées libérales françaises ou britanniques, en opposition à la politique gouvernementale – les courants de pensée venant de France ou d'Angleterre étaient parfois assimilés à des formes de résistance contre la toute-puissance de l'État.

Le groupe se disait « libéral » au sens où il s'opposait à la réglementation commerciale excessive du gouvernement et où il défendait avec ardeur le principe du libre-échange. À cette époque, l'économie libérale était vue comme une science hostile au gouvernement ; elle était « patriotique » car elle était la seule en mesure de mener le Japon vers la prospérité économique. Au sein de ce courant, Smith était regardé comme le héros historique qui avait combattu avec courage pour les libertés civiles et commerciales. Il devint le héros du libéralisme, image qui s'est naturellement muée progressivement en « icône » du libéralisme.

Une deuxième étape fut franchie dans les années 1920, une époque cruciale pour le développement de l'économie politique au Japon. La faculté d'économie politique acquit l'indépendance vis-à-vis de la faculté de politique et de droit dans les universités de Tokyo et de Kyoto. Ce changement entraîna la reconnaissance de l'économie politique comme science à part entière. Cette révolution académique eut des conséquences encore visibles de nos jours pour le pays. On se persuadera aisément que cette décision était loin d'être anodine : en fait, il était espéré alors que la science pût aider à solutionner efficacement les maux économiques de la pauvreté et du chômage. Hasard du calendrier, cette prise d'indépendance coïncidait en 1923 avec le 200e anniversaire de la naissance de Smith. Quoi qu'il en soit, les deux événements ont largement contribué à approfondir les recherches menées sur Smith au Japon. Smith demeurait un symbole du libéralisme et de la théorie économique, mais l'on se penchait enfin sur d'autres travaux du penseur que la *Richesse des nations*, en particulier sa jurisprudence et sa philosophie morale.

Les années de la deuxième Guerre Mondiale vont asseoir définitivement cette idolâtrie. Pendant la guerre l'étude du marxisme fut prohibée par le gouvernent, alors qu'elle avait connu une grande vogue au début des années 1930. Nombre des économistes forcés d'abandonner l'étude de Marx se retranchèrent derrière celle des écrits de Smith : estimant que la doctrine de ce dernier constituait une des sources majeures du marxisme, ils poursuivaient leur étude de Marx sous le couvert de Smith. Ici, l'idolâtrie de Smith gagnait une symbolique neuve, la liberté d'expression mise à rude épreuve durant cette période tragique. Déjà un symbole du libéralisme, Smith devint le symbole des libertés fondamentales. Cette facette vint s'ajouter, non se substituer, à la première. Il faut dire que la doctrine économique de Smith fut aussi vue comme une forme de résistance contre l'impérialisme japonais, contre son militarisme et contre une direction exclusivement protectionniste de la politique économique.

Après sa défaite dans la deuxième Guerre Mondiale, le Japon passa sous contrôle américain. Il incorpora le modèle économique américain. Son application alla de pair avec la démilitarisation forcée du pays. Elle permit le grand retour à la pensée de Smith, comme idéologie du libéralisme. À partir de ce moment, tous les esprits allaient converger pour soutenir la thèse du « laissez-faire » selon Smith. Le monde académique allait se concentrer sur le système de Smith pour la première fois conçu en son entier, notamment dans le rapport entre la *Théorie des sentiments moraux* de 1759 et la *Richesse des nations* de 1776. Le Japon découvrait en somme, à son tour et tard venu, le « problème d'Oncken »[1]. Dans le monde non-académique toutefois, à mesure que le nom de Smith était mis en vedette, on le traitait toujours exclusivement en idéologue d'un libéralisme absolu.

Ici devait commencer une simplification excessive des thèses de Smith, qui allait conduire par la suite à de nombreux malentendus sur lesquels nous vivons encore. En général, bien des Japonais imaginent, sans même avoir lu un seul ouvrage de ce penseur, qu'il prêche un libéralisme dépourvu de toute idée de régulation. Cette simplification devait s'aggraver dans les années 1980, période charnière du néo-libéralisme au Japon, en lien au grand boom économique connu par le pays. Nombre d'idéologues néo-libéraux citent alors le nom de Smith comme un *mantra* et dans le seul but de justifier leurs arguments, quels qu'ils puissent être, en faisant simplement et totalement fi du système de Smith. Il convient de souligner la gravité des erreurs causées par une telle simplification et de délimiter le malentendu central, c'est l'objet principal du propos dans cet essai.

En résumé de ces rappels historiques trop brefs, il existe une tradition ancienne, et elle fut riche, qui établit la perspective de la réception de Smith au Japon. Nous en retenons sciemment pour notre propos que Smith y est avant tout vu, non seulement comme le penseur qui eut raison « le premier et pour toujours » dans son combat en faveur du libéralisme, mais encore comme un symbole des libertés fondamentales, et tout à la fois un prédécesseur du marxisme en même temps qu'un idéologue du néo-libéralisme. En fait, on est

1. D'abord formulé par Gustav Oncken (1898) dans le premier numéro du *Zeitschrift für Sozialwissenschaft*, « das Adam Smith Problem » demandait : le fondement de la doctrine morale smithienne, à savoir la sympathie, tel qu'il apparaît dans la *Théorie*, contredit-il le « *self-love* » de la Richesse des nations (« amour-propre » ou « amour de soi », souvent compris – et improprement traduit – comme « égoïsme ») ?

souvent arrivé au Japon à avancer tout et son contraire au nom de Smith. Il est notoire que nombre d'économistes essaient de légitimer leurs arguments de son autorité mais il reste frappant de voir combien c'est fort le cas au Japon.

Ce sont des idolâtres, ces économistes qui cherchent à légitimer leurs positions en s'appuyant sur l'autorité de Smith. Plus encore qu'un savoir, ils semblent invoquer une idole. Ce qu'il faut remarquer, c'est que l'image de Smith, en tant que reflet de l'époque où l'on utilise son nom, change par conséquent foncièrement avec les temps. Dans notre temps, où le vent se retourne contre le néolibéralisme, elle évolue encore. Ce vent d'« anti-néolibéralisme », qui souffle aussi au Japon, s'accompagne de manière prévisible de la renaissance d'un intérêt pour Smith. Il donne lieu à une énième réinterprétation de ses idées, surtout auprès du grand public.

3. LA « RENAISSANCE-SMITH » : DES RESSOURCES POUR UNE ÉTHIQUE DE L'ÉCONOMIE POLITIQUE

L'ancien idéologue du libéralisme fait peau neuve après la crise majeure suivant 2008. Ou plutôt, on peut parler d'une « renaissance Smith (*Smith revival*) » qui voit sa réinterprétation au Japon, avec la publication d'ouvrages aux titres évocateurs, dont nous citons, à titre purement générique, les expressions de réclame qui y apparaissent, comme « le véritable Adam Smith », « Adam Smith et le monde contemporain », « Smith, notre contemporain », etc., autant de formulations publicitaires destinées à hameçonner l'acheteur, mais qui n'en marquent pas moins son regain réel dans l'actualité.

Les auteurs d'ouvrages de ce genre tentent, en général, de corriger l'image trop simplifiée de Smith mentionnée plus haut et ils réfutent l'image du Smith idéologue d'un libéralisme économique « absolu » en insistant sur l'importance de sa philosophie morale. Pour atténuer l'étiquette libérale qui a été collée au philosophe écossais, ils axent leur réflexion sur la relation étroite entre ses différentes œuvres, notamment entre la *Théorie des sentiments moraux* et la *Richesse des nations*.

Ainsi l'ouvrage *Adam Smith. Le monde de la « Théorie des sentiments moraux » et les « Recherches sur la nature et les causes de la richesse des nations »*, du professeur Dôme de l'université d'Osaka a manifesté dès 2008 une renaissance de ce type. Il s'en est vendu beaucoup d'exemplaires en peu d'années et ce « best-seller » reçut le Prix académique Suntory, accordé aux ouvrages dont l'excellence académique n'empêche pas qu'ils soient adressés au grand public. De nombreux économistes recommandent cet ouvrage jusqu'en cours, le présentant même comme un modèle de guide pour entrer dans la philosophie de Smith. L'analyse des caractéristiques de la renaissance de l'intérêt pour Smith renvoient, dans les pages qui suivent, principalement à ce livre.

La « renaissance » de la pensée de Smith a sa source dans sa *Théorie des sentiments moraux*. L'ouvrage de Dôme contribue à en donner une compréhension plus exacte. Dans le monde non-académique, la philosophie de Smith fut toujours trop simplifiée, souvent en rapport avec la réalité économique : avant l'éclatement de la bulle économique de l'économie japonaise, dans les années 1980, beaucoup citaient le nom de Smith à tort et à travers comme modèle d'un laissez-faire intégral, en négligeant les œuvres qui venaient contredire cette affirmation, notamment sa *Théorie* de 1759. Ils voyaient en Smith l'auteur qui a pensé que les hommes ne commettent jamais de mauvaise action quand ils font ce qu'ils veulent. Et cet « optimisme » était censé manifester sa grande confiance dans l'humanité, ce pourquoi on pouvait l'apprécier.

Certes, personne ne disconviendra que Smith pouvait sans doute avoir confiance en l'humanité. Mais on ne devrait pas oublier qu'il analyse les circonstances qui poussent les hommes à commettre de mauvaises actions. Cette analyse est, selon nous, un des legs majeurs du penseur écossais. Malheureusement, l'économiste cité omet ce point cardinal. Dôme essayait, de son côté, de corriger cette image simpliste de Smith, en présentant le système élaboré par celui-ci dans son entièreté. Dôme présentait ainsi sa visée :

> [Mon] livre présente une nouvelle image de Smith, qui respectera son point de vue sur l'homme et sur la société, tel qu'exprimé dans sa *Théorie des sentiments moraux* [...] Je traiterai des arguments de Smith développés dans sa *Théorie* ainsi que dans sa *Richesse des nations* comme d'un système globalement cohérent de l'ordre et de la prospérité de la société. (Dôme 2008, II, notre traduction)

Le but avoué de Dôme consiste à se défaire de l'image de l'agent « utilitariste égoïste » que l'on prétend trouver dans la *Richesse des nations*, tout en démontrant le rôle central joué par la « sympathie » dans la doctrine de Smith. Dôme cite, au début de son argumentation, cette phrase très connue de Smith :

> Aussi égoïste que l'homme puisse être supposé, il y a évidemment certains principes dans sa nature qui le conduisent à s'intéresser à la fortune des autres et qui lui rendent nécessaire leur bonheur, quoiqu'il n'en retire rien d'autre que le plaisir de les voir heureux. (Smith 2014, 23).

Il commente cette phrase comme suit :

> On apprend que Smith ne pense pas que l'homme soit simplement égoïste. L'homme considère, bien sûr, son propre intérêt. Mais il y a aussi un autre principe dans la nature humaine. C'est qu'il s'intéresse aux autres. (Dôme 2008, 28, notre traduction).

Dôme met au cœur du système de Smith l'intérêt pour autrui, né de la sympathie. Les sentiments humains sont expliqués en se référant aux arguments de Smith à partir de la sympathie. L'auteur consacre plusieurs pages à la genèse de la « propriété », qui peut servir de mesure aux actions humaines et au sens du devoir. En cela, il tente de resituer à leur juste place l'égoïsme (ou l'amour-propre, *self-love*) promu par Smith, mais que l'on a utilisé, au nom de Smith, depuis très longtemps hors de leur contexte d'origine. La « renaissance Smith » passe donc par la clarification de la « hiérarchisation » des sentiments moraux fondés sur la sympathie, ainsi que par le refus d'un libéralisme simplificateur à l'excès qui exploite les notions des sentiments smithiens, comme l'amour-propre ou l'ambition, sans absolument tenir aucun compte d'une telle hiérarchisation.

Pour illustrer notre propos, prenons deux exemples, les notions d'amour propre et d'ambition, sentiments qui ont été surexploités et/ou utilisés arbitrairement par bien des idéologues japonais du libéralisme, que l'on peut aussi bien qualifier de « néo-libéraux ». Il est cardinal de revenir au texte original pour saisir dans leur authenticité la véritable nature de ces sentiments, car Smith écrit en vérité que « c'est la tâche spécifique des facultés que nous considérons ici de juger, de censurer ou d'applaudir tous les autres principes de notre nature. (Smith 2014, 233). Les « facultés » que Smith mentionne se fondent sur « le souci pour les règles générales de conduite » et sur « le sens du devoir », tandis que « les autres principes de notre nature » comprennent naturellement également l'amour-propre (ou égoïsme). Dôme commente cette phrase en disant :

> Smith pense que l'intérêt propre et l'amour-propre sont d'ordinaire réglés par le sens du devoir. Cela est essentiel pour comprendre pourquoi Smith admet les activités économiques fondées sur l'intérêt propre. On ne pourra jamais trouver, dans la philosophie de Smith, l'idée que l'on doit laisser aller l'intérêt propre sans aucune entrave. (Dôme 2008, 59, notre traduction).

Dôme parvient à expliquer la place que l'amour-propre prend adéquatement chez Smith, en décrivant ce sentiment dans sa relation avec le sens du devoir et en expliquant aussi de la sorte la nature de l'ambition humaine en relation à la sympathie. Nous, agents humains, sympathisons très aisément avec les joies éprouvées par autrui ; c'est un phénomène qui provoque notre propre plaisir. À l'inverse, la sympathie pour les souffrances d'autrui conduit à faire naître nos propres douleurs. En d'autres termes, la richesse ou la joie sont également une source de plaisir *pour nous* ; la pauvreté et la tristesse sont également une source de douleur *pour nous*. Cette sympathie établit un « point nodal de mesure » qui nous permet d'apprécier ces facteurs. Quand nous intériorisons ce point de mesure et que nous commençons à le prendre effectivement pour référence, l'ambition d'acquérir à notre tour de la richesse et des honneurs naît alors en nous. Cette ambition trouve donc à s'agencer au sein des sentiments moraux. Avec cette explication, Dôme réussit cependant également à relativiser cette ambition, louée sans réserve par certains adeptes du libéralisme qui ne tiennent aucun compte de la hiérarchie des sentiments moraux dans l'œuvre de Smith.

En bref, Dôme éclaire la *hiérarchie* des sentiments moraux en montrant qu'elle accorde sa juste place à chaque sentiment moral, comme la sympathie, le sens du devoir et l'amour-propre, . L'ouvrage de Dôme a constitué à ce titre une contribution importante à la compréhension de la philosophie de Smith, contre ceux, nombreux, qui invoquent le nom de Smith pour légitimer des points de vue pris sans tenir compte du système en son entier, comme lorsqu'il s'agit de justifier toute concurrence « libre et sans entrave » au nom de Smith. Mais, grâce au travail de Dôme, de tels recours arbitraires à Smith ne sont plus possibles au Japon, et c'est le plus grand mérite de son travail que de rendre impossible cet usage « idéologique » de Smith.

Quelle est cependant l'originalité des arguments que cet auteur présente ? Car si son approche rend justice à Smith, ses arguments n'ont rien d'original *a priori*. Bien avant Dôme, dans une tradition que nous disions riche, d'autres spécialistes avaient mis en exergue la hiérarchie qui existe au sein des sentiments moraux dans l'œuvre de Smith[2]. En fait, outre le mérite qu'a eu Dôme de faire voir de manière générale cette hiérarchie à un public non-initié, l'intérêt de l'ouvrage qu'il a donné et qui est à l'origine même de son succès, fut de répondre en fait à l'attente de ce public japonais qui, lassé du « néolibéralisme », était en quête d'une théorie économique plus éthique, d'une économie qui fût pour lui un soutien moral. C'est ce que Dôme a apporté, sous ce nom de « Smith » déjà révéré au rang d'une idole parmi tous les penseurs importés au Japon.

4. DIFFICULTÉS QUE LA « RENAISSANCE-SMITH » PEUT SOULEVER

Il est possible que la renaissance évoquée jusqu'ici, si louable à tant d'égards, pose elle-même quelque nouvelle(s) difficulté(s) et, d'abord, elle aussi un souci de simplification excessive. Ce serait une moralisation excessive de la pensée de Smith, venant succéder à une simplification outrancière qui avait fait de celui-ci le héraut d'un égoïsme pur et dur. Est-ce l'on pourrait soutenir la visée, qui apparaîtrait comme un nouveau simplisme, de promouvoir Smith comme un moralisateur, par opposition au précédent « Smith partisan de l'égoïsme » ?

Il peut sembler que les auteurs qui contribuent à cette renaissance au Japon, comme Dôme (et nous limitons sciemment notre propos à eux), raisonnent selon le syllogisme simplificateur suivant :

1) Bien entendu, Smith n'est pas en vraiment un idéologue du (néo) libéralisme. C'est d'abord un philosophe de la morale ; il circonscrit l'action de l'économie libérale dans la morale qu'il a développée dans sa *Théorie* de 1759.

2. De toute évidence, les travaux produits dans le monde occidental sur le sujet existaient également déjà (l'ouvrage sur les « passions et les intérêts » d'Albert O. Hirschman, qui date de 1977 et fut traduit en français en 1980, ou ceux de Jean-Pierre Dupuy et de Jean Mathiot en français, parus en 1992, voir notamment le commentaire de Gilles Campagnolo, 2011). Notre essai portant uniquement sur le Japon, nous n'y renvoyons pas ici et, quant à la tradition spécialisée japonaise, elle est à l'arrière-plan de cet essai, mais non son objet principal qui est d'enquêter sur les présupposés philosophiques de l'interprétation de Smith diffusée au Japon.

2) Or, Adam Smith a toujours raison – et ce qu'il dit est toujours juste.

3) Donc, son argumentation à l'encontre la formule absolutisée du libéralisme est tout aussi juste.

Ce syllogisme est semblable à celui avec lequel l'on avait voulu légitimer l'image d'un « Smith libéral à tout crin ». Il peut donc exister aussi un risque majeur de simplisme, visant cette fois à justifier la présence de la morale dans les activités économiques – *encore* au nom de Smith.

On peut repérer ce risque même dans l'excellent ouvrage de Dôme, qui parle de la « *négligence du naturalisme* » chez Smith, notion que l'on développera plus loin. La philosophie de la morale ne consiste pas chez Smith en simples recommandations de morale ; elle nous présente une hiérarchie, voire même mieux, une *généalogie* des sentiments moraux à partir de la sympathie. C'est un attrait important de cette philosophie. Or il semble que Dôme, lui aussi, néglige parfois ce point. Pour illustrer notre propos, revenons au passage cité plus haut ; au sujet du « sens de justice » chez Smith, Dôme indique que « *Smith pense que l'intérêt propre et l'amour-propre sont d'ordinaire réglés par le sens du devoir et doivent être réglés par lui* » (Dôme 2008, 59, notre traduction ; nous soulignons).

Il est essentiel de remarquer que Dôme ajoute que l'intérêt propre (*self interest*) et l'amour-propre (*self love*) *doivent* être réglés par le sens du devoir : Dôme procède là au changement qui fait passer d'une description factuelle à un commandement moral. Or, ce que Smith remarque en vérité, c'est un fait qu'il trouve dans la vie quotidienne, à savoir que l'amour-propre est régulé par le sens du devoir, mais Smith ne recommande pas cette régulation pour elle-même, car il décrit simplement un fait humain. Pourtant, Dôme conclut à une *obligation*, à partir de cette description d'un fait, et c'est un faux pas. On peut volontiers admettre que Smith nous recommande de vivre en êtres moraux, et très sincèrement encore. Mais ce n'est pas la question. Si l'on veut rester fidèle à l'idée centrale de Smith, on doit alors étudier ses textes, sans tirer de recommandation morale hors contexte. On pourrait sinon risquer d'affaiblir la force argumentative du texte de Smith. Ces textes sont d'autant plus convaincants qu'ils se limitent sciemment à décrire des faits.

Pour approfondir la question, citons un autre exemple bien connu, à savoir le « franc-jeu ». À ce sujet, Dôme forme son raisonnement de la manière suivante : il cite d'abord une phrase très connue de la *Théorie des sentiments moraux* qui porte sur les règles du franc-jeu. La voici :

> *Dans la course aux richesses, aux honneurs et aux faveurs, il [chacun] peut courir aussi vite qu'il lui est possible, et tendre chaque muscle et chaque nerf pour dépasser tous ses concurrents. Mais s'il devait bousculer ou jeter à terre quelqu'un d'entre eux [tous], l'indulgence des spectateurs prendrait immédiatement fin. C'est une violation du franc-jeu qu'ils ne peuvent admettre.* (Smith 2014, 136 ; nous soulignons)

En s'appuyant sur cette idée, Dôme avance, à partir de là, ce qui suit :

> On doit donc conclure que ce que Smith admet, c'est la seule ambition maîtrisée (tempérée) par le sens de la justice. Ce qu'il recommande, c'est d'obéir aux règles du franc-jeu, de refuser de participer aux situations de concurrence que le spectateur impartial n'admettrait pas, et de poursuivre en même temps le « chemin de la vertu » et « la route de la fortune » (Dôme 2008, 101, notre traduction).

Dôme écrit que Smith nous conseille de respecter les règles des activités économiques. Mais, en vérité, Smith décrit *comment* parvenir à observer les règles du franc-jeu. Il n'explique pas *pourquoi* on devrait avoir du respect pour ces règles. C'est une différence très subtile. Mais elle est essentielle pour comprendre la vision de Smith. Changer cela entraîne des suites néfastes graves parce que c'est transformer l'excellente description que donne Smith en une recommandation tout bonnement moralisatrice.

Il faut soulever une autre question : dans la même phrase, Dôme met l'accent sur la coïncidence entre « course à la vertu » et « course aux richesses ». Mais, dans le texte de Smith, si cette coïncidence s'observe, c'est seulement au sein des conditions moyennes et inférieures :

> *Dans les conditions moyennes et inférieures, le chemin de la vertu et la route de la fortune, du moins vers cette fortune que les hommes de ces conditions peuvent raisonnablement espérer acquérir, sont heureusement dans la plupart des cas presque les mêmes.* (Smith 2014, 105 ; nous soulignons)

Il s'agit seulement là d'une remarque factuelle, celle d'une coïncidence heureuse qui peut s'observer dans les conditions moyennes et inférieures de la société, sans qu'il s'agisse en rien de prodiguer quelque conseil. Or Dôme tire pourtant un conseil moral de cette description factuelle.

Revenons à l'exemple des règles du franc-jeu. Il semble que Dôme veuille dire qu'observer les règles est en soi « vertueux ». Si l'on voulait, l'on pourrait appeler « vertu » ce fait d'observer des règles. Cependant, ces mêmes règles naissent *spontanément* de l'échange permis par la sympathie entre les hommes. Si l'on vit selon l'ordre naturel des choses, on ne peut pas *choisir* d'adopter ces règles, on ne peut pas ne pas faire ce choix parce que l'on veut que son action reçoive la sympathie des autres. En d'autres termes, c'est spontanément que l'on adopte ces règles. Si on se méprenait sur ce point, on négligerait l'essentiel de la philosophie de Smith, ce que nous voudrions appeler ici, après d'autres, son « naturalisme ».

Pour apporter un éclairage sur ce naturalisme de Smith, proposons de comparer sa philosophie morale de Smith avec la généalogie de la morale chez Nietzsche.

Comme on l'a remarqué précédemment, Smith ne prône pas l'idée qu'il faille observer des règles, il explique en revanche *comment* ces règles se sont formées, et comment nous les trouvons toutes faites. Il reconnaît l'importance de la morale dans les actions et, probablement, soulignons le mot qui suit, il nous la *recommande* fondamentalement, certes. Mais, au moins dans sa *Théorie*, Smith entend seulement décrire la généalogie de la morale au sein des actions humaines, sans doute comme Nietzsche décrit la généalogie de la morale à sa propre manière. Chez les deux philosophes, la morale naît *spontanément* d'une part instinctive dans la nature humaine. La morale chez Smith est fondée sur la sympathie comme, de manière similaire, elle découle du ressentiment chez Nietzsche. Bien entendu, il existe nombre de différences entre les deux penseurs. Et il va de soi que la sympathie, par exemple, diffère très sensiblement du ressentiment.

Toutefois, il existe un point commun essentiel à ne jamais négliger : les deux penseurs entendent décrire la formation de la morale entre les hommes, mais ni justifier, ni non plus d'ailleurs prôner quelque morale que ce soit. Sur ce point, on évitera assez naturellement sans doute de prendre jamais la description de la généalogie de la morale chez Nietzsche pour une recommandation moralisante. Mais l'on se méprendrait sur la théorie de la morale chez Smith en la confondant avec une recommandation de ce genre. Bien entendu, derechef, Smith reconnaissait tout à fait l'importance que revêt la morale. Mais ce qu'il en écrit dans sa *Théorie*, c'est la manière de on parvenir à respecter des règles de morale, et non *pourquoi* on devrait les respecter.

Dôme néglige par trop le naturalisme de Smith et ceux qui le suivraient l'auteur japonais feraient sans doute de même. Or, si l'on perd de vue ce naturalisme, si l'on pense que Smith voulait simplement borner l'action économique par le moyen de la morale présente dans sa *Théorie*, l'on se méprendrait sur le sens véritable de la philosophie de Smith car, dans ce cas, l'on opposerait simplement les préceptes de la morale aux lois de l'économie, sans comprendre jamais les circonstances dans lesquelles l'homme devient un être moral.

En réalité, Smith met en évidence les circonstances qui font que les actions économiques sont socialement reconnues par les autres, c'est-à-dire ce qui les rend morales. Et ce que Smith enseigne, c'est à analyser minutieusement ces circonstances. Insistons sur ce point : son analyse pousse à réfléchir sur les circonstances qui rendent nos actions morales ; si nous voulons donc que nos actions soient déjà morales, ce qui est nécessaire, c'est d'intégrer cette analyse fondée sur le naturalisme smithien, pas de suivre une quelconque recommandation de morale. En résumé, les règles morales que l'on pourrait trouver dans la philosophie de Smith ne sont jamais de la nature d'une catégorie impérative, mais ce sont des propositions conditionnelles, à suivre si nous voulons être des agents moraux, jusques et y compris au sein de la vie économique.

5. LA CONFUSION SPÉCIFIQUEMENT JAPONAISE ENTRE LES NOTIONS DE SYMPATHIE ET DE COMPASSION

Outre une certaine négligence quant au naturalisme de Smith, un autre malentendu règne encore au Japon concernant sa philosophie. Il porte sur ce qui pousse à prêcher une certaine forme d'altruisme au nom des idées de Smith. Ce malentendu se retrouve surtout chez le public moins éduqué que le monde universitaire, mais il vaut la peine de le mentionner parmi les errances dans la réception japonaise de l'œuvre de Smith.

Chez les hommes d'affaires japonais, surtout ceux partis à la retraite, il existe une tradition longue consistant à exhorter tout un chacun à « moraliser les affaires ». C'est un peu, si l'on veut, une tradition locale, comme en France celle de manifester, et l'on trouvera très facilement, dans les grandes librairies du Japon, des myriades de livres écrit par ces « évangélistes » de la morale des affaires. L'on trouvera des titres comme ceux-ci, volontairement pris au hasard, pour illustrer ce courant : il y a, par exemple, des *Morale du management*, des *Guide de survie pour une philosophie des affaires* ou des *Morale de l'entreprise pour ses clients*, et ainsi de suite. D'ordinaire, un livre de ce genre comporte une autobiographie de l'auteur, c'est-à-dire un homme d'affaires en retraite, généralement au nom notoirement connu, avec les leçons qu'il a tirées de son expérience.

En général, ces auteurs adorent tresser les louanges d'une espèce de communautarisme fondé sur l'altruisme, ce qu'ils donnent comme la leçon de morale la plus grande dans les affaires. Ils conseillent à tous leurs lecteurs de sacrifier à ce communautarisme afin que, curieusement, ces lecteurs réussissent à gagner... plus d'argent. Les mêmes affirment qu'en vue du succès même de l'entreprise, il faut intégrer ce communautarisme au titre d'une dimension inhérente à l'esprit des affaires, et puis, aussi, donner toujours la priorité à sa clientèle.

En général encore, les auteurs en question ne se contentent pas de leur propre expérience pour convaincre leurs lecteurs. Afin de mieux légitimer leurs arguments, ils invoquent volontiers les noms de grands philosophes : Kant, Confucius, etc. Quoiqu'ayant passé du temps pour amasser des fortunes considérables, ils discourent comme s'ils avaient cultivé avant tout un pur idéal humaniste. On devine aisément : Smith est leur auteur favori, puisqu'il est l'« économiste des économistes », l'« idole » que nous avons évoquée au début de cet essai. C'est aussi pour cela que nous avons insisté ; selon ces auteurs-là, il s'agit donc d'être tous communautaristes par devoir, de donner la priorité en tout au bénéfice de la clientèle car notre propre profit en résultera nécessairement e naturellement. En d'autres termes, ils veulent faire de nous tous des contributeurs communautaristes pour le bien de la société, puisque la prospérité de celle-ci est cela même qui rend les affaires possibles. Et puis, on le devine encore aisément : Smith, fondateur de l'économie politique, ne prônait-il d'ailleurs pas ce communautarisme en soulignant le rôle majeur de la sympathie ?

Si quelque ironie est ici permise, c'est que l'exploitation de l'image du Smith communautariste succède chez ces gens-là à l'accumulation du profit réalisé en exploitant une autre image, celle du Smith idéologue du libéralisme concurrentiel. Peut-être serait-ce à peine là exagérer ou caricaturer l'attitude qui a été adoptée envers Smith au Japon, mais il est certain que l'on verra facilement que ce malentendu y persiste effectivement durablement. Au final, ces deux figures de Smith sont bien entendu des simplifications outrancières, chacune soulignant un seul aspect de sa philosophie au détriment de son système. Si les malentendus ont lieu, il n'y a là rien que de naturel.

Pour autant, l'affaire n'est pas réglée, car la simplification communautariste dans la philosophie de Smith ne s'est pas produite sans raison. Que ce soit de négliger le naturalisme de Smith ou de simplifier dans une visée moralisatrice, on est coupable de cacher ce qui pourrait bien être le désir de trouver des préceptes de morale jusque dans le texte du grand penseur. À propos de Smith et en contexte japonais, cette tendance se trouverait peut-être fortifiée par ce que dit le mot *Kyokan* (共感), qui a été choisi pour traduire le terme « sympathie » chez Smith. Par son étymologie, ce terme signifie que l'on « partage les sentiments d'autrui ». On pourrait suggérer comme possibilité que les nuances de ce mot conduisent alors les Japonais à se méprendre sur le sens véritable du concept de sympathie chez Smith.

Pour clarifier ce point, il est utile de faire retour à l'époque de la première introduction de Smith au Japon. Les penseurs Enryô Inoue (1858-1919) et Yujiro Miyake (1860-1945) ont contribué à introduire la philosophie occidentale, en particulier celle des Lumières écossaises ; il écrivait ce qui suit au sujet de la philosophie de Smith :

> C'est Smith qui a exposé la théorie de la compassion en synthétisant l'utilitarisme de David Hume et la théorie de la conscience selon Francis Hutcheson. On peut dire que Smith a foncièrement amélioré l'utilitarisme humien. Ceux qui évoqueront l'utilitarisme devront en général insister sur la sympathie et sur la compassion. Quant à ce point, Smith est beaucoup plus explicite que Hume. (Inoue 1890 (?), 53 ; nous traduisons).

Dans cette citation, on perçoit bien ce qui existe de confusion entre la sympathie, qui est neutre chez Smith, et la compassion, qui est propre à l'altruisme. Inoue interpole la sympathie avec la compassion, qui est depuis longtemps considérée comme une vertu importante dans le cadre culturel japonais, car elle y joue un rôle très important, notamment et surtout dans le bouddhisme.

Pourquoi cette confusion ? Elle peut provenir des nuances présentes dans ce *Kyokan* (共感). D'une part, le mot désigne non seulement la sympathie, mais encore la compassion, et étymologiquement, redisons-le, il signifie que l'on partage le sentiment des autres, ce qui est une bonne chose, et chez les Japonais, selon la définition donnée ici, en particulier lorsque l'accent est surtout mis sur les sentiments « négatifs » (tristesse, douleur, affliction). Ainsi préconiser la compassion pour autrui signifie préconiser d'aider ceux qui souffrent, de partager leur douleur. Cette définition tirerait au moins partiellement son origine d'un désir de considérer la morale comme naturelle et instinctive, comme innée ou inhérente à la nature humaine.

Quoi qu'il en soit, *Kyokan* (共感) joue un rôle si essentiel qu'on l'utilise très souvent dans les discussions pédagogiques, par exemple. C'est un mot-clé de l'instruction donnée à l'école primaire, où l'on préconise que les élèves développent et acquièrent ce fameux *Kyokan* (共感). Le but de l'instruction que l'on donne aux enfants japonais consiste avant tout à construire une communauté de sentiment où tous sont en harmonie les uns avec les autres. Quand l'on y parle de *Kyokan* (共感), l'accent est toujours mis sur la communauté (celle du sentiment, en premier lieu).

D'autre part, bien entendu, cette confusion nuit à une compréhension exacte de la philosophie de Smith. Pourquoi est-elle néfaste ? Simplement parce que ce serait une grave erreur de vouloir comprendre la philosophie smithienne à travers le mot *Kyokan* (共感). On perdrait alors d'emblée de vue le processus de la compréhension en se méprenant totalement sur la philosophie smithienne, qui se conçoit dans un autre cadre intellectuel, et l'on s'écarterait ainsi immédiatement du sens véritable de la sympathie smithienne, voire même du sens de toue la modernisation qu'elle revient à prôner (nous voulons dire, en permettant le cadre théorique de l'édification de la société civile).

Car ce que Smith explique, c'est comment l'on devient individualiste par l'effet de la sympathie. Mais, au Japon, la sympathie, interprétée comme une forme de compassion, constitue précisément la préconisation pour édifier une communauté fondée sur le sentiment commun. C'est donc une erreur lourde que de lire cette théorie smithienne à travers le mot japonais *Kyokan* (共感). Ce qui importe dans la philosophie de Smith, ce n'est pas tant d'« éprouver de la sympathie » pour autrui que le fait de tempérer son égoïsme pour être socialement reconnu dans son action, ou encore, en d'autres termes, pour que nos actions reçoivent à leur tour la sympathie des autres. Cette démarche est nécessaire pour s'engager sur la voie même de l'individualisme. Ce que nous devons impérieusement retenir de la philosophie de Smith, c'est que ce processus d'individualisation est rendu possible par l'analyse précise que Smith donne des circonstances dans lesquelles il a lieu. La sympathie même n'est *pas* une vertu à préconiser, elle est une *condition* de la société civile.

7. EN GUISE DE CONCLUSION

Au début de cet essai, nous avons mentionné la brillante tradition érudite dans la réception japonaise de la pensée de Smith. Elle est connue des spécialistes. Et, dans le fond, il en va de même au Japon que dans le reste du monde : Smith n'y est pas considéré par ces spécialistes comme le fondateur du (néo)libéralisme à la mode actuelle ou, au moins, récente. Car les errances sont nombreuses et ce sont elles que nous avons voulu présenter, car les causes de ces errances propres à l'univers conceptuel japonais sont méconnues à l'étranger. Une phrase très suggestive du grand spécialiste Hiroshi Mizuta semble ici appropriée – elle vient conclure son article sur les « concepts de société civile et de *bürgerliche Gesellschaft* selon Marx au Japon ». Mizuta y insiste sur la *neutralité* de la sympathie smithienne et il reconnaît son importance dans l'édification d'une société civile composée d'agents individuels. Il ajoute en conclusion le point suivant :

> Les Européens qui auront lu cet article pourraient se demander pourquoi nous y avons si vigoureusement insisté sur les conditions fondamentales de la société civile que l'on peut tirer de la théorie de Smith. Ils peuvent nous rétorquer que le problème le plus urgent n'est ni de jouir de la liberté ou de l'indépendance individuelle, mais bien de cultiver l'amour et la solidarité, pour lutter contre l'isolement et la solitude. C'est qu'au Japon, il existe encore beaucoup de résidus du féodalisme. (Mizuta 2009, 414, nous traduisons)

Pour Mizuta, les Japonais n'ont réussi ni à comprendre ni à réceptionner correctement les idées majeures portées par Smith, avant tout l'idée d'une société civile composée d'individus dont l'amour-propre et l'égoïsme sont bien « tempérés » parce qu'ils sont « socialisés » par la sympathie. La preuve, cette remarque la fournit car dire qu'il existe encore des résidus du féodalisme dans la société japonaise aujourd'hui, c'est dire l'inclination des Japonais envers une communauté de type sentimental. Le double échec à bien comprendre et à bien réceptionner les idées de Smith s'ancre, et se manifeste, tout à la fois, dans les malentendus que nous avons indiqués dans ces pages.

Au Japon, l'on a présenté Smith comme un idéologue du libéralisme et aussi, surtout pendant la période de pleine croissance du pays, comme l'inspirateur d'un néo-libéralisme, alors que l'on sait partout (et certains spécialistes japonais aussi) que ce n'est pas le cas. De nos jours, ce qu'on peut appeler la « renaissance » de l'intérêt pour la pensée de Smith rend évidemment impossible cette interprétation simpliste. Mais l'on continue à simplifier l'image de Smith, en cherchant cette fois à l'opposer au libéralisme (qui n'est après tout qu'un choix politique, qu'il est loisible de faire ou pas) ; dans ce but, on forge un Smith prompt à préconiser des règles moralisatrices, et le risque demeure de perpétuer des malentendus profonds et regrettables à l'égard de cette pensée fondatrice.

Car au Japon, comme ailleurs peut-être, le succès des thèses que nous avons dénoncées dans les pages qui précèdent, laisse planer un autre mystère (qu'il y aurait lieu d'aborder dans un autre texte) : pourquoi ces thèses supportent l'ignorance en histoire de la pensée (philosophique ou économique) comme en philosophie économique, voire l'hostilité à l'égard de ces dernières.

RÉFÉRENCES

Campagnolo, G. 2011. "Adam Smith lu par Jean Mathiot : du 'spectateur impartial' au 'travailleur impartial'." *Dialogue* 50 : 469-509

Dôme, Takuo. 2008. 「アダム・スミス：『道徳感情論』と『国富論』の世界」 *Adam Smith : Dôtoku Kanjôron to Kokufuron* no *Sekai* [*Adam Smith et son monde. De la* Théorie des sentiments moraux *aux* Recherches sur la nature et les causes de la richesse des nations]. Tokyo : Chuôkoron.

Dupuy, J.-P. 1992. *Le sacrifice et l'envie. Le libéralisme aux prises avec la justice sociale.* Paris : Calmann-Lévy.

HIRSCHMAN, A. O. 1977. *The Passions and the Interests. Political Arguments for Capitalism Before Its Triumph.* Princeton : Princeton University Press. Trad. fr : *Les passions et les intérêts*, 1980. Paris : P.U.F.

INOUE, Enryô. 1890 (?). 近世哲学史宗教哲学 *Kinsei Tetsugakushi*□ *Shûkyô Tetsugaku* [*Histoire de la philosophie moderne et de la religion modernes* - cours par]. Sans lieu.

MATHIOT, J. 1992. *Adam Smith, économiste et philosophe.* Paris : P.U.F.

MIYAKE, Yujiro. 1900 (?) 近世哲学史 *Kinsei Tetsugakushi* [*Histoire de la philosophie moderne* : cours donnés par]. Tokyo : Tetsugaku-kan Daigaku.

MIZUTA, Hiroshi. 1967. *Adam Smith's Library. A Supplement to Bonar's Catalogue with a Checklist of the Whole Library.* Cambridge : Cambridge University Press.

– 2000. *Adam Smith's Library. A Catalogue*, Oxford : Oxford University Press/ Clarendon Press.

– 2009. アダム・スミス論集 ： 国際的研究状況のなかで *Adam Smith Ronshû : Kokusaiteki Kenkyû Jôkyô no Nakade* [*Recueil de mes articles sur Adam Smith publiés à l'international*]. Kyoto : Minverva Shobo.

ONCKEN, G. (1898) "Das Adam Smith Problem." *Zeitschrift für Sozialwissenschaft* vol. 1 : 25-33.

SMITH, A. 2014 [1759]. *Théorie des sentiments moraux*, trad. fr., introduction et notes de M. Biziou, Cl. Gautier et J.-Fr. Pradeau. Paris, P.U.F.

– 1995. *Enquête sur la nature et les causes de la richesse des nations*, trad. fr. P. Taieb *et al.*. Paris, P.U.F.

QUEST FOR THE CONSCIOUSNESS OF HISTORICITY BY KIYOSHI MIKI – HERMENEUTICAL ANTHROPOLOGY AND PHILOSOPHY OF HISTORY

KIICHIRÔ YAGI*

Abstract
Kiyoshi Miki was a prominent philosopher in the early Shōwa era of Japan. Beginning from the application of phenomenological hermeneutics to the texts of Pascal and Marx, he came forth with a philosophy of history, the core of which is occupied by the present consciousness of historicity. Agreeing with the view that modern individuals were trapped in feelings of anxiety, Miki presented a new type of man who was equipped with both *pathos* and *logos*. His engagement in both the proletarian culture movement of the 1920s and the philosophical grounding of the New Order Movement of the 1930s failed. His unfinished pursuit of a genuinely Japanese philosophy of history and philosophical anthropology reflected the difficulty of philosophical investigation during that time in Japan.
Keywords : Anthropology (hermenutical), consciousness (of historicity), fundamental experience, Kitarō Nishid, Marxism (in Japan), philosophy of history.

Résumé
Kiyoshi Miki (1897-1945) fut le philosophe dominant des débuts de l'ère Showa (à partir de 1925) au Japon. Il entama sa réflexion en appliquant l'herméneutique phénoménologique aux pensées de Pascal et de Marx puis il se mit en quête d'une philosophie de l'histoire où la conscience présente de l'historicité est centrale. Il allait reconnaître un type d'humanité dotée à la fois de *pathos* et du *logos* qu'il réinteprétait. Son engagement dans le

* yagi@econ.setsunan.ac.jp Setsunan University, Neyagawa City, Osaka-fu, Japan
Kiichiro Yagi was Professor of Economics at Kyoto University for decades until he retired. He is internationally famous for his work in Economics and in the History of Economic Thought in particular. He has especially studied German and Austrian Economics. He is presently the Chairman of Setsunan University (Osaka).

movement de la culture prolétarienne et dans les fondements philosophques du Mouvement de l'Ordre Nouveau fut un double échec. Dans sa poursuite d'une philosophie de l'histoire, qui donne sa place aux considerations économiques, en même temps que d'une anthropologie philosophique, Miki a reflété la difficulté de mener une réflexion philosophique sereine durant cette période au Japon.

Mots clefs : Anthropologie herméneutique, conscience de l'historicité, expérience fondamentale, marxisme au Japon, Nishida (Kitarô), philosophie de l'histoire.

JEL Codes : B24, B31

1. FROM TAISHO TO SHOWA: THE YEARS IN WHICH KIYOSHI MIKI LIVED [1]

Kiyoshi Miki (1897-1945) was probably one of the most widely-read Japanese philosophers in the late Taisho [2] and early Showa Eras. His series of pedantic articles published by high-brow journals such as *Shisō (Thought)* and books published by the prestigious publishers Iwanami Shoten were the favorite readings of snobs in those years. His philosophical essays for youth, such as *Jinseiron Nōto (Notes on Life)*,[3] are still being printed today. After Miki's unfortunate death in 1945, his works were collected into a 16-volume set titled *Selected Works of Miki Kiyoshi* (1946-1951). A renewed version was published as the *Complete Works* in a 19-volume set between 1966-1968 [hereafter referred as *CW*], while one supplementary volume was added in 1986.[4]

Miki began his career as a scholar during the period in which Japan joined the great powers after World War I. While superficial

1. This text summarizes a chapter of an unpublished manuscript, which the author wrote nearly half a century ago. Though the author (re)read Karaki (1947), Miyagawa (1958), and Akamatsu(1994) on this occasion, he must apologize for not referring the readers to the vast literature that has appeared in Japan since Miki's death. All the quotes from Miki in this paper have been translated by the author of the paper. However, in making this English version, the author points out to the readers' attention Susan Townsend for her *Miki Kiyoshi 1897-1945 : Japan's Itinerant Philosopher* (2009), which is recommendable to both Japanese and non-Japanese researchers.

2. The Taishō era spanned from 1912 to 1926, while the Shōwa existed from 1926 to 1989.

3. This (Miki 1939-41) was published posthumously by compiling Miki's essay series in a journal for literature (*Bungakukai*) published from June 1939 to 1941.

4. Note that Miyamoto's essay "Haibokusha no Bungaku" and Kobayashi's "Samazamanaru Ishō" were published in the same issue of *Kaizō*, September 1929.

prosperity and a mass cultural boom flourished, emerging labor disputes and conflicts between tenant farmers and landowners broke the peaceful order in both urban and rural areas. The intellectual tide in Japan shifted from culture-oriented idealism to socially oriented modernism. In the Meiji era, absolutist cliques had dominated political life. In this new era, members of political parties were elected to the Japanese Parliament after political campaigns ending with significant voting. Majority members would form the Cabinet. The demands of democracy prevailed and the universal right to vote was obtained (although still excluding women) in 1925. Newly founded socialist parties ran in elections, while the Japanese Communist Party (JCP) was formed underground and extended its influence through social movements and by addressing university and high-school students. However, a law prohibiting associations and activities aiming to alter Kokutai (i.e., national unification under Tennō, the emperor) or to eradicate private property was promulgated during the same year in which general suffrage was introduced. This law exerted its oppressive effects on intellectual activities for two decades. Miki was one of its numerous victims.

Around this time, Japan, which had endeavored to catch up with the advanced nations of the West, entered a new stage in history. It was that the nation had to find its own way in a changing world. One of the most talented novelists, Ryūnosuke Akutagawa (1892-1927), committed suicide at a young age in 1927, leaving the enigmatic phrase "vague anxiety for the future." Many intellectuals felt likewise bewildered and confused for both themselves and Japan. Kenji Miyamoto (1908-2007) won an essay prize from the popular journal *Kaizō* based on a contribution that regarded Akutagawa's work as the "literature for the losers of our times." He thus recommended a new breakthrough to serve the emerging proletarian class.[5] Interestingly enough, the second best prize was given to Hideo Kobayashi (1902-1983) for his essay that interpreted various trends of thought in a detached way as "changeable clothes". These two essays represented a split in the intellectual world between the emerging proletarian culture and modern highbrow cynicism.

5. Miyamoto joined the illegal JCP in 1931 and after release from long imprisonment 1933-1945 became one of its leaders after 1945. Kobayashi was praised generally as the most prestigious critic in Japanese literature up to his death in 1983.

Miki's quest for a genuinely Japanese philosophy of history reflected both this feeling of general anxiety and the split in the intellectual world of those years. When he used the words "historicity" or "philosophy of history," they did not connote historical continuity from the past, but the "consciousness" to direct the nation from its present situation into the future. Miki would transform "historicism," which he considered the dominant tone of the 19th century, into the philosophy of present "engagement" in the historical process.

2. PHENOMENOLOGICAL HERMENEUTICS

Miki's starting point was his encounter with Kitarō Nishida's (1870-1945) *Zen no Kenkyū (An Inquiry into the Good).*[6] Grounded in his practice of Zen meditation, Nishida set "pure experience" below the level of rational recognition, in which no distinction between subject and object or truth and untruth was valid. He argued that logics and ethics must both start from this fundamental unity in such a deep-level experience. At this level, the split between the ego and world also vanishes. Young Miki found approval for his sentimental quest for individuality in this pantheistic vision attributed to Nishida's "pure experience."

After studying under Nishida in Kyoto, Miki had the opportunity to study abroad from May 1922 to October 1925 with financial support from the publisher Iwanami. He first attended Heinrich Rickert's seminar in Heidelberg to study the logic of historical science. This choice was in accord with the general view of academic philosophy in Japan, where German philosophy (particularly the Neo-Kantians) was prevalent. However, Miki had to conclude that Rickert's formalistic conception of history lacked the "consciousness of historicity," which he sough. In this respect, Miki learned more from the young Japanese scholars he met in Heidelberg, including the economist Hyōe Ōuchi (1888-1980) and historian Gorō Hani (1901-1983), both of whom tended to agree with Marxism. Miki further learned the Marxian theory of ideology from Karl Mannheim. He then he moved to Marburg to join Martin Heidegger's seminar. Though Heidegger's

6. This inquiry published in 1911 is generally regarded as the monumental work that the Japanese style of thought illustrated by Nishida produced by integrating ideas from the West and from the East. See Nishitani 1991.

Being and Time (*Sein und Zeit*) was not yet published, Miki developed an existential stance in order to confront the ontological structure of *Dasein* by way of phenomenological hermeneutics. Karl Löwith, then Heidegger's assistant, was a good guide for Miki in this respect. Heidegger suggested that Miki study the hermeneutics of Wilhelm Dilthey, from which his own hermeneutic ontology had emerged. From this study Miki acquired the intrinsic approach needed to "interpret life from life itself" as well as a recognition of the thorough historicity of life. This approach would guide his research up to the end of his life.

After leaving Marburg, Miki remained alone in Paris for several months beginning in August 1924. Blaise Pascal's *Pensées* caught his attention during this time. Miki found the most appropriate material for applying the hermeneutical approach he had learned in Germany from this work. Anxiety and contradictions of life were the essential features of human existence. They were not solved by knowledge, but one had to live through and deal with them via one's own *praxis*. Miki named the image of the human being that he found in the passages in the *Pensées* as Pascal's "anthropology." Upon his return to Japan Miki's reading of the *Pensées* was published as *Pasukaru ni okeru ningen no kenkyū (A Study of Man in Pascal)* (June 1926). This debut publication impressed the public and marked the emergence of a bright new star in academic philosophy.

Miki wrote several philosophical articles just after his return to Japan. In those, he surmised that his phenomenological hermeneutics approach consisted of "fundamental experience" and the "public sphere" or "contemporary consciousness." While Husserl's phenomenology demanded *epokhē* (suspension of ontological judgment) of every sort of value and preconception contained in a naturalistic recognition of the world, hermeneutics interpreted the nature of human existence (*Dasein*) from the preconceptions and fundamental direction of the mind (*Sorge*). They formed a "fundamental experience" in which human beings (*Dasein*) lived. Hermeneutics interprets this "fundamental experience" through its demand for necessity, originality, and comprehensibility. This fundamental experience (*Sorge*) remains unstable and transient as long as it does not enter the "public sphere," which is grounded in rationality (*logos*). Once rationality has penetrated consciousness, such original feelings that were experienced before now fall into oblivion. Thus, the approach to human existence is possible only by excavating forgotten directions (*Sorge*) and their interpretations under the consciousness of contemporaries.

3. MIKI'S ENGAGEMENT WITH MARXISM

Soon after his debut work on Pascal, Miki successively surprised the Japanese public by publishing his interpretation of Marx's materialistic conception of the history and through his engagement with the leftist cultural movement. Together with his close friend Hani, Miki started the journal *Shinkō-kagaku no Hata no motoni (Under the Banner of Emerging Science)*[7] in October 1928. He reorganized it in the next year as *Puroletaria Kagaku (Proletarian Science)*, which was published by the newly founded *Puroletaria Kagaku Kenkyūsho* (Institute of Proletarian Science). Behind this engagement lay his will to participate in the public sphere and the contemporary socio-political life of his times through his view on the consciousness of historicity.

Miki conceived of a three-level interpretative structure to understand Marx's materialistic conception of history (Figure 1). He placed the "proletarian fundamental experience" at the basis. Here, the real praxis of "labor" occupied the core. Miki interpreted Marx's materialism in relation to this "fundamental experience" as follows:

> The art of beings is defined according to the way man relates to them. Besides, man, as well, grasps his essence directly from his relation to them. Therefore man that has relation to human beings who work, i.e. sensual and material praxis, is obliged to understand the art of his existence as both sensual and materialistic. The 'material' in Marxian materialism is thus at first the conception of the self-interpretation of man. In other words, it is a sort of hermeneutical concept and it does not indicate the pure material as itself. The origin from which the true concrete materialism constitutes is labor. (Miki 1928, 40)

Ideology is the self-understanding of man through a rationality (*logos*) that is valid in the "public sphere." The first expression that is directly determined by the orientation of the "fundamental experience" is the "anthropology" as a self-interpretation of proletarian life. This is a bridge between "fundamental experience" and "ideology."

7. The title easily reminds us of the theoretical journal that the German Communist Party published (*Unter dem Banner des Marxismus*) from 1925 to 1936.

Miki later added his own "model of being" (the ontological model) to the genetic core of the ideology. "Fundamental experience" creates a model of being due to its pecularity in the process of abstraction. In his words, "the human being makes theory abstract first by bringing its own self into abstraction." Miki argued that as based on a "romantic fundamental experience," Hegelian philosophy was inevitably contemplative and pantheistic, while Marx's (and Miki's) philosophy was grounded on the "proletarian fundamental experience" and thus was oriented toward *praxis* in the objective conditions of the world.

Before Miki, Kazuo Fukumoto (1894-1983) had renovated the traditional Japanese understanding of Marxism through his own system called Fukumotoism, which integrated the ideas of Vladimir Lenin, Georg Lukács, and Karl Korsch. The core of Fukumotoism was formed by the idea that intellectuals could become revolutionary by acquiring ideal "proletarian class-consciousness."[8] While Fukumoto logically founded his system on "ideology," it could be said that Miki phenomenologically grounded Marxism in the "proletarian fundamental experience." It is plausible that Miki's interpretation of Marx's anthropology was publicly received as a philosophical version of contemporary Marxism.

However, Miki's engagement with Marxism and the revolutionary cultural movement ended in misfortune. He was arrested in May 1930 for allegedly aiding the illegal Communist Party and thereby lost his stable job-position in academia. Further, his interpretation of Marxism was criticized by dogmatic Marxists who advocated for a fundamental distinction between materialism and idealism.[9] Although Miki was a leading founder, he was also expelled from the Institute. It is true that Miki re-interpreted Marx on the basis of his own conceptual framework rather than upon Marx's views. However, most of his critics followed a simplified dogma from the Lenin-type Marxism that had recently been introduced by revolutionary Russia to Japan.

8. Fukumoto stayed in Europe at nearly the same time as Miki and absorbed the new Marxism of Lukács and Korsch, see Yagi 2011.

9. The June 1930 issue of *Puroletaria Kagaku* that was published during Miki's detention carried open criticism against Miki. Miki was discharged from his position as Chief-Editor.

4. FROM PHILOSOPHY OF HISTORY TO PHILOSOPHICAL ANTHROPOLOGY

Miki was released from prison in November 1930, at which time he discontinued his public support of Marxism. However, he rejected the contemporary disdain of "conversion." He devoted himself to writing the *Philosophy of History* (April 1932), which he did not believe was contradictory to his interpretation of Marx before the imprisonment. Miki regarded the conception of history by Heinrich Rickert and Ernst Troeltsch as lacking present consciousness, thus having fallen into relativism. He instead believed that the philosophy of history should be built on the subjective elements of the consciousness of historicity that enabled active participation in *praxis*.

Miki first distinguished the objective history of what happened and is happening (i.e., "history as being") from history as knowledge or narrative, which was ordered by rationality (*logos*). On the one hand, Miki then conceived of "history as fact" as existing at the basis of both. The concept of "fact" (*Tatsache*) in the basis of the philosophy of history is easily recognizable as corresponding to the "fundamental experience" in Miki's anthropological hermeneutics. The "consciousness of history," which is the expression of "fact" in the "consciousness," intervenes between "fact" and "history" (see Figure 2 below). This is analogical to the relationship between "fundamental experience" and "anthropology" in Miki's scheme (see Figure 1 below). The subjectivity of "fact" expresses itself in the "consciousness of history" and performs its effect on the meanings of history. On the other hand, objective "history of being" molds the rationality (*logos*) of the history as its reflected reality. However, as Kenzō Honda (1898–1938) remarked critically, this objective factor in history coalesces in Miki's concept of the "consciousness of historicity".[10]

Miki made a second engagement in actual political movements in 1938 and 1939. He assumed the chief position in the philosophical section of the Shōwa Kenkyūkai (Shōwa Research Association),[11]

10. Honda 1929. Honda taught logics and philosophy at Tokyo University of Commerce (now Hitotsubashi University). He was one of the rare Marxists who was well-versed in phenomenology.

11. On this Research Association see W. M. Fletcher Jr. 1982.

which was a policy think tank originally founded in 1933 by a close friend of Prince Fumimaro Konoe (1891-1945) that later developed into a large-scale multi-sectored research organization designed to serve Prince Konoe's New Order Movement. The sudden continental war in China affected Miki's consciousness to the point that he engaged himself in supporting the forceful domination by Japan over the East Asian nations, which was regarded as a "policy of cooperation". It was his position (at least in his own understanding) that one had to act and respond to the historicity of the present "fact." The result of this engagement was two 1939 pamphlets (*Shin-Nihon no Shisō Genri* [*Principles of Thought for a New Japan*] and *Kyōdōshugi no Tetsugakuteki Kiso* [*Philosophical Grounds for Cooperativism*]). It is now clear that Miki's efforts as an ideologue of the New Order Movement functioned only as a mask for Japanese militaristic expansion through a pseudo-synthesis combining the Western principle of association (*Gesellschaft*) with the Oriental principle of community (*Gemeinschaft*) by drawing on the philosophy of cooperation (*Genossenschaft*). From the beginning, Shōwa Kenkyūkai was under attack by ultra-nationalists who wished to expel any leftist influence from the New Order Movement. It was dissolved by Konoe himself in 1939. There is still debate on whether the intellectuals gathered at this Kenkyūkai were anything more than opportunistic crowds (as W. M. Fletcher Jr.[12] and others saw them).

5. PHILOSOPHICAL ANTHROPOLOGY – UNCOMPLETED WORK

After the *Philosophy of History*, Miki conceived of a new workplan through the concept of *Tetsugakuteki Ningengaku (Philosophical Anthropology)*. He began developing this idea in 1933 and, after some interruption, wrote several chapters in 1936, but did not complete it before his death. Another project was a series under the title *Kōsōryoku no Ronri (Logic of Imagination)*, which Miki continued in the famous review *Shisō* for several years. He died before completing this, too. While the first should be considered as a *magnum opus* in which Miki's originality was condensed, the latter deals with the idea of necessity

12. On the participation of economists in Shōwa Kenkyūkai, see Yagi 1997.

and approaches the idea of *praxis* through historical consciousness, together with a perspective of future developments.

During these years Miki began to use the term 'neo-humanism'. Neo-humanism differs from traditional humanism in its accentuation of the historicity of human beings. From Miki's terminology of 'man-as-type' as the 'unity of pathos and logos', we can recognize the continuity of Miki's thinking, from his interpretation of Marx to the subsequent reflection in the 1930s.

> The "type of man" given to us is the man of anxiety trapped in the thought of anxiety (*Angst*). To overcome such thought philosophy must describe the new type of man as correctly, clearly and concretely as possible. [...] This task must be performed on a new philosophical ground under new historical and social conditions. The reason that Marxism once caught the mind of many young people was that it promised to provide them with a new type of man under the name of "proletariat" while man as a type was lost in other streams of philosophy. However, the elements it provided were not yet fully synthesized into a clear and concrete type of humanity. We cannot keep just generally saying that humans are social beings, or that it is actual lafe that determines consciousness. We have to give new philosophical qualification to e.g. sense and thinking, sentiment and will, body and society, and thus redefine and reshape the social existence of human beings in the new light of philosophy. (Miki 1933a)

The early chapters of Miki's *Philosophical Anthropology* consist of "The Idea of Anthropology" (chap. 1), "The Historicity of Man" (chap. 2), "The Situation of Man" (chap. 3), "The Expression of Man" (chap. 4), and "The Social Nature of Man" (chap. 5). Thus, the historical anthropology Miki described in his former book are enriched by the consideration of the situatedness of the human condition, of the possibility of expressions, and of the social relations. Within these reflections Miki conceived the basic relations of human beings in terms of the I and You (*Ich-Du*) relation, that is categorically different from the I and It (*Ich-Es*) relation. Since the nature of human beings is essentially expressive, all action is thus performed within an "I and You" setting. 'Action' that is pushed by the expressive nature of human being transforms itself from mere 'experience' into an 'event' under the relation of two expressive human beings. This is the condition of the emergence of historicity in which the action as an event is regarded as the historical action.

However, what disturbs me is Miki's strange conception of the 'society' and the 'world'. He argued that because both I and You are subjective and objective beings with equal right of expression, the relation of I and You can emerge only by the existence of the third term, namely the society that envelopes both I and You. On this ground Miki maintains that his anthropology is never the self-consciousness of the individual but self-consciousness of the society. Then, what is Society?

> In a sense, Society is neither I nor You but He. [...] Of course, Society is not He as an individual. Rather what transforms I, You, and He into We is Society. So far as He does not enter We, the true Society is not conceivable. The I and You relation cannot make He enter We. Thus, we must consider Society as the basis of I, You, and He. (Miki 1968, 371, 373)

Thus, the kind of "Society" that is grasped by Miki is a transcendental subject that contains every individual. However, if we view society from the angle of its expression, in other words if we regard it as "the World", then it turns out to be what is called Mu (無, Nothingness) as such.

> In order for an accord between I and You to exist, there must be something general. However, as it cannot be conceived as an objective being, it cannot be a general Being (*Sein*) but must be a general Non-Being (*Nichts*). The World is conceivable as such general being. This World is not the same as the world or the society that we talk about in daily life. They are rather limited as expressions of this World. Individuals are limited in the society but demand their independence despite this limitation. It is because Society has the significance of dialectical generality in its ultimate ground. The society in its common usage, too, contains the original structure of the dialectical generality as a self-limitation of World. (Miki 1968, 329)

Here we envisage Miki's return to Kitarō Nishida's philosophy. Starting with the 'pure experience" in *An Inquiry into the Good*, Nishida developed his logic to deduce the society and the world as the self-limitation of the generality or in other words the self-consciousness of the nothingness. As the nothingness has no peculiarity, it functions to produce the individual subjects as well as the *topos* (場所 *Basho*) by self-awareness and self-limitation. The Society and the World emerge as the self-limitation of nothingness.

A return to Nishida's dialectics of nothingness was probably not Miki's intention. What he would provide in his *Philosophic Anthropology* was a new 'type' of social and historical man that integrates *pathos* and *logos*. When Miki heard that Heidegger has joined the NSDAP in 1933, he condemned Heidegger on the charge of sacrificing reason (*logos*) under the influence of the Nietzschean notion of passion (*pathos*) and appealed to recover the *raison d'être* of rationality (*logos*).[13] However, we notice that Miki himself was very close to Heidegger's devotion to *pathos*, when Miki wrote that "human being will die in society as one is born in society" or admitted society as "Nothingness as subject".

What Miki sought was the type of social and historical human being that integrates *pathos* and *logos*. Utilizing the concept of *pathos*, Miki would mold the series of concepts, 'body', 'social body', 'historical body or historical material'. "Body is *pathos* in nature. *Pathos* is the nature in the inner subjectivity." "While we are limited to be individuals by our body, we can return to the unity of society, the root of our existence, by the intervention of our body" (Miki 1968, 152-3). However, at a higher stage of development, the body as such has to become disciplined through reason awakened by self-awareness. Individuals become self-aware subjects by observing themselves objectively and use their body rationally as a tool. Society that integrates individuals by nullifying their reason under the enthusiasm of *pathos* must restore the rationality of self-awareness of *logos* to affirm the rational interest of individuals. This was what Miki would say in his criticism of his mentor's commitment to the Dionysian folly of NSDAP.

This argument on pathos and logos in respect to series of the body of individuals and of society is integrated into the type of social and historical human being.

> Thus, it is known that the existence of human being with pathos and logos is social and historical. Anthropology that intends to deal with total human being must deal with such human being.
>
> The true historical human being is typical in nature. He represents the whole era with his individuality. (Miki 1968, 160,186)

Miki's quest for a historical type of human being remained no more than the re-assessment of the postulates he had originally wished for, set out and figured. In the context of the early Shôwa era, and

13. Miki 1933b, p. 310-20.

particularly in the war years, one may simply translate Miki's use of the term "Society" as the Japanese *Kokutai* (国体, that is national unity under the Emperor, *Tennô*, 天皇). Then, Miki's acrobatic reasoning becomes more transparent. After the passionate unification of the people to the Kokutai had occurred, could he contribute to restore reason (*logos*) even a bit? Loyal to his philosophical recommendation for the cooperative community of East Asian nations, Miki collaborated with the Army to develop the so-called "harmonization plan" in the Philippines in 1942. After his return from Manila he pursued his contributions to the series published by the review *Shisō* and published *The Logic of Imagination.*

Miki was arrested again in March 28, 1945. An old acquaintance of his, the communist writer Teru Takakura (1891-1986), visited Miki to help him escape but Takakura was captured with a shirt that had Miki's name embroidered. Miki was detained at Toyotama Detention Center and died on September 26, 1945 from an infectious disease he caught in detention. The death of the famous philosopher made the continued detention of political prisoners as late as one month after the unconditional surrender of military Japan known to the public. GHQ of the Allied Forces pressed Japanese government to release all of them.[14]

REFERENCES

AKAMATSU, Tsunehiro. 1994. 「三木清 ： 哲学的思索の軌跡」 *Miki Kiyoshi - Tetsugakuteki Shisaku no Kiseki* [*Miki Kiyoshi. The Locus of Philosophical Meditations*]. Kyoto : Minerva Shobo.

FLETSCHER, W. M. Jr. 1982. *The Search for a New Order : Intellectuals and Fascism in Prewar Japan.* Chapel Hill : North Carolina University Press.

HONDA, Kenzo. 1929. "Miki Kiyoshi shi no kingyō futatsu" ["Two recent pieces of Mr. Kiyoshi Miki"]. *Shisō* April 1929, 112-8.

–. 1970. 「現象学と弁証法」 *Gensho-gaku to Bensho-ho* [*Phenomenology and Dialectics*]. Tokyo : San-ichi Shobo.

KARAKI, Junzo. 1947. 「三木清」 *Miki Kiyoshi.* Tokyo : Chikuma Shobo.

MIKI, Kiyoshi. 1966-1968. 『三木清著作集』 *Miki Kiyoshi Zenshū* [*The complete works of Kiyoshi Miki (CW)*], Edited by Hyōe Ōuchi *et al*<.i>. 19 volumes. Tōkyō : Iwanami Shoten.

14. See Townsend 2009, 240-51.

Listed by chronological date with reference to *Miki Complete Works CW*

–. 1926「パスカルにおける人間の研究」 *Pascal ni okeru Ningen no Kenkyu* [*Anthropology with respect to Pascal*] June 1926. In *CW* I, 1-192.

–. 1928. 唯物史観と現代の意識」 *Yuibutsu-shikan to Gendai no Ishiki* [*The Consciousness of the Present and the Materialistic View of History*]. May 1928. In *CW* III, 1-156.

–. 1932. 「歴史哲学・社会科学概論」 *Rekishi Tetsugaku* [*The Philosophy of History*]. April 1932. In *CW* VI, 1-298.

–. 1932. ・社会科学概論 *Shakai Kagaku Gairon* [*A Concise of the Science of Society and the Philosophy of History*]. April 1932. In *CW* VI, 299-454.

–. 1933a. 不安の思想　とその彫刻 *Fuan no shisō to sono chōkoku* [*The thought of Angst and How to Overcome it*]. June 1933. In *CW* X, 285-309.

–. 1933b. ハイデッガー　と　哲学の運命　*Haidegga to tetsugaku no unmei* [*Heidegger and the fate of philosophy*]. Nov. 1933. In *CW* X, 310-20.

–. 1968. 「哲学的人間学」 *Tetsugaku-teki Ningen-gaku* [*Philosophical Anthropology*]. Written from 1933 to 1936, left incomplete, edited 1968. In *CW* XVIII, 125-420.

–. 1939-1941. 「人生論ノート」 *Jinsei-ron Note* [*A Note on the Discourse of Life*]. Osaka : Sogen sha. June 1939 to October 1941. In *CW* I, 193-362.

–. 1937 and 1939-1943. 構想緑の論理 *Kōsōryoku no Ronri* [*The logic of imagination*]. In *CW* VIII, 1-510.

Miyagawa, Toru. 1958. 『三木清』 *Miki Kiyoshi*. Tokyo : Daigaku Shuppankai.

Nishida, Kitaro. 1911. 「善の研究 *Zen no Kenkyu* [*An Inquiry into the Good*] Tokyo : Kodokan.

Nishitani, Keiji. 1991. *Nishida Kitarō*. Berkeley Los Angeles : University of California Press.

Townsend, S. C. 2009. *Miki Kiyoshi 1897-1945 : Japan's Itinerant Philosopher*. Leiden and Boston : Brill.

Yagi, Kiichirô. 1997. "Economic Reform plan in the Japanese Wartime Economy." In *Economic Development in Twentieth Century East Asia : the international context*, Aiko Ikeo (ed.), 100-15. London and New York : Routledge.

–. 2011. "Was Sozialforschung an Aesopian Term? Marxism as a link between Japan and the West." In *The Dissemination of Economic Ideas*, H. D. Kurz, T. Nishizawa and K. Tribe (eds.), 315-36. Cheltenham : Edward Elgar.

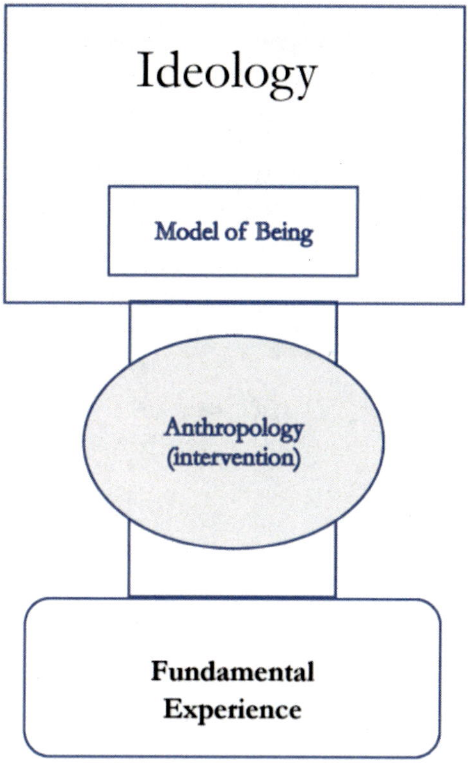

Figure 1. Miki's Conceptual Structure

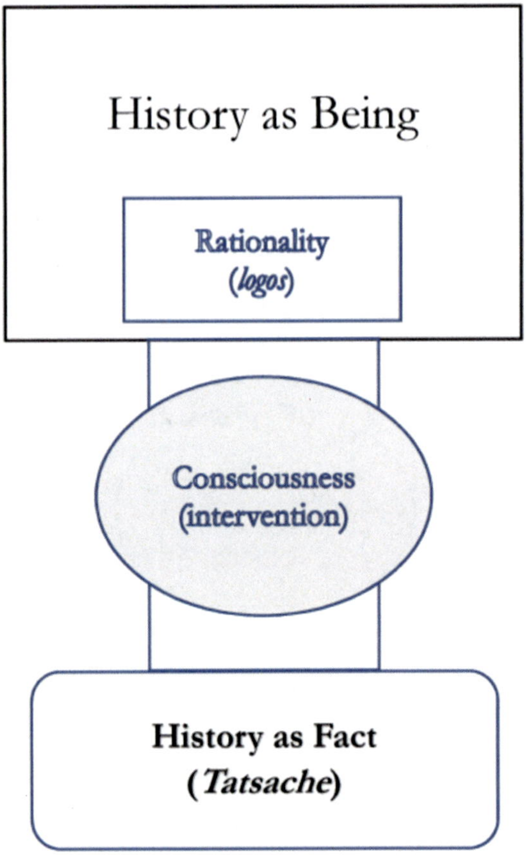

Figure 2. Miki's Philosophy of History

YÛICHI SHIONOYA, REPRÉSENTANT CONTEMPORAIN MAJEUR DE LA PHILOSOPHIE ÉCONOMIQUE AU JAPON

GILLES CAMPAGNOLO

1. PROPOS LIMINAIRE À LA SECTION DOCUMENTAIRE

Décédé le 25 août 2015, Yûichi Shionoya avait acquis une stature internationale en développant en particulier le champ de la philosophie économique. Nous consacrons une partie documentaire à cet économiste soucieux de la réflexivité au sein de sa discipline dans le présent numéro spécial « Philosophie économique au Japon ». Cet hommage est l'occasion de présenter au public de la *Revue de philosophie économique*/ *Review of Economic Philosophy* deux de ses textes inédits en toute autre langue que le japonais. Afin de mieux les situer, nous proposons cette courte présentation en français accompagnée d'une nécrologie en anglais. Nous remercions le professeur émérite Bertram Schefold, qui avait présidé une « table-ronde » d'hommage à Shionoya tenue en 2016 ; son texte constitue également un précieux témoignage de l'interaction entre chercheurs européens et japonais dans notre discipline et de l'influence forte exercée, en l'occurrence dans le cas de Shionoya, par la pensée de langue allemande[1].

1. Un exemple parmi tant d'autres de cette coopération est notamment la conférence tenue à Berlin en 2008 sur cette influence (« Der Einfluss deutschsprachigen Wirtschaftswissenschaftlichen Denkens In Japan »). Elle a donné lieu au volume 115/XXVII dans la collection « Schriften des Vereins für Socialpolitik Gesellschaft für Wirtschafts- und Sozialwissenschaften – Studien zur Entwicklung der Ökonomischen Theorie ». La conférence fut l'occasion de présenter la liste des archives en langue allemande des bibliothèques universitaires au Japon que nous avions dressée (Campagnolo 2012).

Les textes de Shionoya présentés en traduction française dans le présent numéro thématique sont tirés de son ouvrage *Économie et éthique : philosophie de l'État-providence*[2]. Le premier texte constitue l'introduction du volume original, le second son appendice de nature historique et philosophique à la fois. Dans ce texte qui sert à la fois de conclusion au volume, la dernière phrase exprime tout l'esprit de la quête de Shionoya, dans ses propres termes : « dans ce livre, nous avons tenté de remplir consciencieusement et méthodiquement notre devoir consistant à rapporter la dimension des idées à celle des systèmes ». C'était l'esprit de la tâche qu'il avait poursuivie à travers la philosophie économique et c'en était, en somme, à ses yeux, la définition. Il l'indique également dans le premier texte, « L'économie, d'une rive à l'autre », où il file la métaphore de ses vues : « ce livre poursuit le but de faire réfléchir au système de l'État-Providence dans le cadre académique large des rapports entre économie et éthique ». Il était impossible de traduire l'ouvrage en entier, mais la présentation du plan, donnée à la fin du premier texte, fournira au lecteur une idée générale assez indicative de l'entreprise en son entier.

À propos de ces deux textes, jusqu'ici inédits en toute autre langue que leur original japonais, disons encore que, dans « L'économie, d'une rive à l'autre », la métaphore du fleuve permet à Shionoya de lier ses visions de l'essence et du rôle de la philosophie économique. L'occasion du propos est la mesure des enjeux et des difficultés de l'État-providence japonais. Ces réflexions, émises en 2002, nous semblent sans doute encore plus d'actualité à l'heure de cette publication, alors que la politique économique du Premier ministre Shinzô Abe, connue sous le nom d'*« Abenomics »* suscite le débat quant aux résultats qu'elle a donnés comme aux limites qu'elle a atteintes.

Le second texte a été sélectionné, d'une part, pour sa valeur documentaire quant à l'histoire de la philosophie économique au Japon, dont il évoque le moment fondateur puisque Shionoya y retrace le parcours et les idées des deux fondateurs de la philosophie économique au Japon : Kiichirô Sôda et Kôzô Sugimura, et, d'autre part, pour ses dimensions d'épistémologie et de théorie de la connaissance, où se manifestent très significativement l'importance de la philosophie de langue allemande dans le développement de la

2. Tokyo, Presses universitaires de Tokyo, 2002, traduction par Kaori Kasaï (docteure en lettres modernes de l'université Diderot-Paris VII), avec l'aimable autorisation des éditions de l'université de Tokyo et de la fille de Yûichi Shionoya, que nous remercions ici vivement.

philosophie économique au Japon, *Erkenntnislehre* et néo-kantisme en particulier. C'est toute une époque que Shionoya fait revivre dans ce texte[3] ; mais c'est aussi une orientation quant aux exigences pour un renouveau de la philosophie économique au Japon. Celui-ci pourrait s'opérer dans la perspective de ce que Shionoya appelle un « idéalisme » en mesure de répondre aux exigences du présent, alors que les théories économiques contemporaines expriment elles-mêmes le besoin de se revivifier dans la convergence des idées et des systèmes que Shionoya évoque. Il écrit : « De nos jours, la philosophie économique doit synthétiser (ou globaliser) les théories du "bien", de la "justice" et de la "vertu" ; cela signifie que nous sommes parvenus à la jonction entre les deux courants principaux de l'histoire des méthodes en économie ».

Un dossier documentaire pour un auteur décédé est une innovation dans la *Revue de philosophie économique* que la personnalité et le rôle de Yûichi Shionoya comme représentant contemporain majeur de la philosophie économique au Japon justifie amplement pour nos lecteurs. Les pages qui suivent retracent, en guise d'introduction, sa vie et son œuvre.

2. PRÉSENTATION DE LA VIE ET DE L'ŒUVRE DE YÛICHI SHIONOYA

Né en 1932 dans la préfecture de Kôchi (île de Shikoku, Ouest du Japon), Yûichi Shionoya était d'une famille de lettrés. Son père, Tsukumo, est connu pour avoir traduit en japonais dès 1939

3. Donnons ici un seul un exemple de ces événements des années 1920 auxquels Shionoya fait allusion dans son texte et qu'il est impossible de retracer tous. Sugimura écrivit sa thèse de doctorat sur les *Recherches sur la théorie de la valeur dans la société et en économie :* elle fut rejetée, provoquant un scandale connu sous le nom du « vote blanc » (il avait obtenu seulement 13 votes sur 21, alors qu'il fallait ¾ du corps électif choisi selon les règles prévalant alors). Sugimura enseignait déjà à l'université Hitotsubashi. De rage, il voulut abandonner, malgré les objurgations du président de l'université, qui annula la décision du jury et avalisa sa thèse. Mais Sugimura refusa. La polémique s'enflamma et divisa l'université, suscitant des démissions en chaîne, dont celles du président et de Sugimura lui-même. Sur le conseil du successeur à la présidence de l'université, Sugimura préféra publier son texte chez un éditeur indépendant, en apportant quelques modifications. En 1938, alors qu'il travaillait à la Chambre de commerce de Shanghaï (occupée par le Japon), il fut finalement reçu docteur pour une autre thèse : *Structure de l'éthique économique.* Après-guerre, il redevint enseignant à Hitotsubashi. Il mourut en 1948. L'on dit parfois que nombre de ses idées inspirèrent le Premier ministre japonais Oohira (en charge de 1978 à 1980).

la *Théorie générale* de Keynes. Le jeune Yûichi, formé en sciences économiques[4] à l'université de Nagoya (l'une des sept anciennes universités « impériales »), devint en 1972 professeur titulaire de l'université Hitotsubashi. Il devait assumer plus tard la présidence de cette université (1988-1992), ainsi que la vice-présidence (1991-1992) de l'association regroupant les universités d'État, dans un pays où les universités publiques d'État rivalisent avec celles dépendant des municipalités et les universités privées (dont certaines ont les principales facultés de sciences économiques japonaises, comme l'université Keio). La concurrence qui règne impose à ces universités de briller dans la recherche afin d'attirer les meilleurs étudiants, et ce travail difficile de chercheur trouva un exemple frappant de réussite internationale avec Shionoya, qui contribua à la renommée mondiale de l'université Hitotsubashi[5].

Ces recherches portaient en particulier sur la philosophie économique, comprise comme l'étude des valeurs et des questions fondamentales dans l'agencement de la logique économique et des questions morales et sociales. Elles requéraient un matériau que l'histoire de la pensée économique pouvait fournir. Shionoya contribua à éclairer ainsi, d'une part, l'histoire du développement des sciences économiques au Japon même, et d'autre part, les sources d'influence majeures qui avaient contribué à cet essor au Japon, tout particulièrement les sources allemandes : Shionoya devint un spécialiste reconnu de l'École historique du XIXe siècle, ainsi que de Max Weber et de Josef Schumpeter. Il publia à leur sujet et collabora éminemment au sein de la profession au plan international[6].

4. En japonais 経済学 *(keizaïgaku)* désigne la science économique d'origine occidentale au sens le plus strict, selon le terme formé lors de l'introduction de la discipline au Japon : voir l'introduction générale de ce numéro.

5. L'université Hitotsubashi s'appela d'abord « École supérieure de commerce de Tokyo », puis « université du commerce de Tokyo » avant de prendre le nom sous lequel elle est aujourd'hui connue, lors de son déménagement vers la grande banlieue ouest de la capitale, dans la ville de Kunitachi. Le sens de son nom, qui signifie « un seul pont », rappelle le pont qui reliait directement son ancien emplacement au palais impérial au centre de Tokyo. Cette université fut également celle de Sôda et de Sugimura dont Shionoya narre le rôle fondateur pour la philosophie économique japonaise.

6. Un exemple de coopération internationale significatif est qu'en 1986 Shionoya fut l'un des co-fondateurs de la société savante « International Joseph A. Schumpeter Society », qu'il présida de 1990 à 1992. Il organisa notamment en 1992 à Kyôto un colloque qui fit date sur l'auteur.

Ces centres d'intérêt impliquaient et expliquaient la grande attention qu'il manifestait envers les doctrines institutionnalistes et *welfariste :* la théorie du bien-être touchait aux enjeux de l'État-providence, qui le faisaient intervenir dans les débats académique international et politique national, touchant le cas spécifique du Japon. Sa reconnaissance à ces deux niveaux lui valut d'occuper un certain nombre de positions d'expertise nationale comme, de 1995 à 2000, la direction de l'Institut national des enquêtes démographiques et de la protection sociale.

Shionoya publia beaucoup et notamment en anglais. Citons parmi ses titres les plus connus à l'étranger : *Schumpeter and the Idea of Social Science : A Metatheoretical Study* (Cambridge University Press, 1997, réédité en 2007), *The Soul of the German Historical School. Methodological Essays on Schmoller, Weber, and Schumpeter* (Springer, 2005), *Economy and Morality. The Philosophy of the Welfare State* (Edward Elgar, 2005)[7]. Les ouvrages parus en anglais sur Schumpeter, donc, et sur l'école historique allemande en général, lui ont valu la reconnaissance internationale, notamment dans la communauté des économistes allemands.

Mais il convient de souligner pour le public ne parlant pas japonais que sa production dans cette langue, évidemment trop longue pour la rappeler en entier ici, avait un rôle d'orientation dans les débats académique et politique nippons. En particulier, en ce qui concerne la « philosophie économique au Japon », deux de ses ouvrages japonais – à savoir *Philosophie économique : une approche herméneutique* (2009) et celui choisi pour les deux textes du présent numéro : *Économie et éthique : philosophie de l'État-providence* (2002) – ont-ils contribué au renouveau de ce champ disciplinaire surgi dès les années 1920 dans les travaux de Sôda et de Sugimura.

De nature plus théorique, un autre ouvrage, dont le titre se traduirait par *Current Prices Problems* ou *Le coût de la vie dans le monde contemporain* (Shionoya 1973) fait figure de classique dans sa langue originale sur le sujet de la monnaie. En outre, Shionoya accordait une grande importance aux archives présentes à l'université Hitotsubashi où il organisa un « Fonds Schumpeter » et où le « Centre pour l'histoire de

7. Références de la liste complète des ouvrages de Shionoya en langue anglaise en fin de présentation. Il n'existe de publication en langue française à notre connaissance que les textes fournis dans le présent numéro. Les références aux publications en japonais sont données autant que de besoin en notes de bas de page des deux textes traduits.

la littérature des sciences sociales occidentales » abrite de nombreuses collections, dont celle du fondateur de l'école autrichienne d'économie, Carl Menger (Campagnolo 2001).

On l'aura compris, Shionoya fut un personnage très honoré. En 1991, il reçut le *Prix de l'Académie du Japon.*[8] Ce prix lui fut attribué pour son œuvre et, expressément, pour ses travaux en philosophie économique, en particulier sur les systèmes conceptuels touchant la notion de valeur (Ishikawa 1986). Shionoya y met en contraste les principes respectifs de plusieurs doctrines quant aux conceptions de la justice et de la protection sociales et il passe en revue les effets institutionnels de leur mise en application. Il s'inspire notamment d'une lecture interprétative personnelle de *A Theory of Justice* de John Rawls. En 2002, Shionoya reçut également le prix de la « personne de mérite culturel »[9].

Le dernier ouvrage publié par Shionoya (*La pensée économique du romantisme dans les arts, en éthique et dans l'histoire*, 2012, en japonais) témoigne de son intérêt pour cette autre tradition, la britannique, de laquelle son enquête sur les rapports entre keynésianisme et institutionnalisme moderne l'avait rapproché. Ses derniers articles concernaient ainsi la pensée de John Ruskin. Il y argumentait que la perspective de l'école dite « d'Oxford » représentait, pour la pensée anglaise, un équivalent des vues de *Sozialpolitik* présentes dans l'école historique allemande, notamment en raison de l'orientation dite « éthique » au sein de cette dernière (Shionoya 2014).

À la fin de sa vie, Shionoya s'intéressa ainsi à Thomas Hill Green, l'héritier anglais du hégélianisme, à Ruskin et à Hobson dans le volume collectif *No Wealth but Life ; Welfare economics and the welfare state in Britain* (Shionoya 2010). Le dernier texte (posthume) de Shionoya consiste en un article resté inachevé qui trouve son origine dans la communication qu'il avait donnée devant la « Keynes Society in Japan » (Shionoya 2018).

8. Le prix 学士院 (*Gakushiinshô*) est le plus prestigieux prix du monde académique japonais. Il est délivré annuellement par l'Académie du Japon, l'équivalent de l'Académie des sciences morales et politiques en France.

9. Le prix 文化功労者 (*Bunka Kôrosha*) consiste en pratique dans le second prix culturel le plus important au Japon, celui que peuvent recevoir des écrivains de fiction ou des acteurs du théâtre traditionnel, voire des sportifs de grand renom. Le lecteur français en mesurera l'importance au fait que c'est le prix que reçut, en son temps, Junichiro Tanizaki, le seul écrivain japonais à figurer à ce jour dans la « collection de la Pléiade ».

Si l'on voulait résumer l'éthique que Shionoya proposait au final comme sa propre contribution au renouveau de la « philosophie économique » qu'il appelait, il serait sans doute juste d'agencer les trois éléments suivants en un système (que nous ne tenterons cependant pas de formuler, ce qui exigerait une toute autre ampleur que le cadre d'une simple présentation) :

Premièrement, Shionoya pense une théorie morale fondée sur l'utilité, une théorie du bien touchant l'action individuelle et les activités privées (chez des auteurs utilitaristes comme Bentham ou John Stuart Mill et chez les subjectivistes comme Menger) ;

Deuxièmement, il propose une théorie morale fondée sur les droits afin d'établir des critères et des règles de justice (sur le modèle des philosophies de Kant et des auteurs néo-kantiens, d'une part, de Rawls et des théories contemporaines, d'autre part) ;

Troisièmement, il veut voir advenir une théorie de la vertu définie en rapport aux capacités (voire aux capabilités, si l'on reprend le terme anglais d'un autre auteur non-occidental de par son origine, Amartya Sen – Shionoya le reprend toutefois très peu) ; il considère les existences individuelles avant tout (et renvoie amplement à l'usage que les penseurs allemands firent d'Aristote, comme aux idées d'un néo-hégélien anglais comme Green). Ces trois dimensions fournissent le repère des positions que Shionoya conjuguait.

La coordination de ces systèmes éthiques potentiels dans une philosophie « à trois branches » que ses recherches tendent à unifier exigerait en soi une analyse des objets que Shionoya a sélectionnés pour en donner l'évaluation morale. Shionoya a choisi sa terminologie des valeurs fondamentales, en étant lui-même, comme Sôda et Sugimura, profondément inspiré par les écoles allemandes, et il fut conscient de l'importance de souligner leur caractère opérationnel car une action efficace en vue du « bien » requiert un droit fondé sur des règles de justice. Dit autrement, la justice fondée sur des règles institutionnelles de droit exige une conduite visant l'excellence en suivant la vertu de l'être, compris comme agent économique[10].

Mais, une fois le vocabulaire posé (selon des sources d'inspiration qui sont rarement celles des économistes contemporains, reconnaissons-le), quel ordre de priorité adopter entre ces trois dimensions ? Dans

10. Le texte de Bertram Schefold qui suit peut se lire comme une tentative d'articuler ces dimensions dans la pensée de Shionoya, au regard de l'influence exercée par les pensées des auteurs de langue allemande.

sa quête admirable d'une théorie compréhensive[11] de la vie, comprise « pleinement » comme nature humaine « intégrale », Shionoya explora différentes possibilités dans ses œuvres au long de sa carrière. Cette caractérisation doit rappeler deux points essentiels qui peuvent servir de guides que le lecteur pourra, disons-le pour conclure, garder présents à l'esprit. Ce sont les suivants.

D'une part, Shionoya avait forgé ses vues, sur le romantisme comme sur les Lumières, dans un long apprentissage et une pratique approfondie des thématiques germaniques, allemandes (Rickert, Weber) et autrichiennes (Menger, Schumpeter). Il était au Japon l'un des meilleurs connaisseurs de ces auteurs, au moins quant à la facette économique de leurs œuvres[12]. Les textes présentés en traduction dans ce numéro illustrent au plus haut point cette riche connaissance de la philosophie et de l'analyse éthico-historique allemandes, mise au service d'une conceptualisation des tâches de la philosophie économique non seulement au Japon, mais encore à titre général.

Cela nous mène au second point, car d'autre part, Shionoya tirait de cette inspiration par les écoles allemandes les éléments d'une critique méthodologique précise des positions de l'économie dite « néoclassique » bornée par son attention exclusive à l'utilitarisme sous ses formes diverses. Shionoya était un penseur indéniablement critique, tout en jouant un rôle éminent au sein des institutions. Se tenant au courant de l'apport de l'économétrie modélisatrice, il jugeait qu'une « *good society* » devait se pourvoir également, tout particulièrement dans le contexte nippon, d'une éthique de la vertu adaptée au monde contemporain pour servir de fondement solide à une économie conservant le sens du droit (de la justice) et améliorer la qualité de vie en pratique, dans une société dont l'économie post-industrielle connaît les difficultés d'une population vieillissante, voire déclinante. La conservation matérielle est le souci pragmatique des Japonais, y compris des « philosophes économiques » japonais.

11. Au sens de *verstehende*, en allemand là encore, c'est-à-dire en conjuguant l'entendement et le souci systématique d'englober unitairement les disciplines au sein de la connaissance dans les sciences sociales

12. Citons également à cet égard Kiichirô Yagi, qui fait l'honneur de donner un article dans le présent numéro, et dont la renommée internationale n'avait rien à envier à celle de Shionoya, en particulier concernant la connaissance des textes et des archives de Menger (notamment, mais pas seulement, celles conservées au Japon).

Dans cette perspective, laissons le dernier mot à Shionoya Il avait choisi la citation suivante de son auteur de prédilection, Schumpeter (tirée d'un article du *Harvard Crimson* d'avril 1944), pour son propre dernier article, et ce choix dit la philosophie qui inspirait à son tour Shionoya : « une philosophie inhabituelle de la vie [...] une idée de la vie abondante et englobante qui comprend l'économie, la philosophie, la politique, la science, l'art et l'amour » Shionoya commentait cette citation en disant que Schumpeter exprimait ce qui guidait son programme de recherche, que l'on pouvait qualifier (dans une veine wébérienne) de « sociologie compréhensive (allemande) »[13].

C'est un programme sur tant de points similaire qui inspirait le représentant majeur de la philosophie économique japonaise que fut excellemment Yûichi Shionoya.

3. RÉFÉRENCES DES MONOGRAPHIES ET DES OUVRAGES DIRIGÉS PAR SHIONOYA EN LANGUE ANGLAISE

NB : Cette liste n'est pas une bibliographie exhaustive ; elle n'inclut ni les chapitres d'ouvrages, ni les nombreux articles publiés par Shionoya. Il n'existe à notre connaissance aucun ouvrage de Shionoya traduit en langue française à cette heure.

Par ailleurs, les deux textes traduits dans le présent volume sont des inédits en toute langue autre que le japonais. La *Revue de philosophie économique/Review of Economic Philosophy* remercie la maison d'édition et les ayant-droits de Y. Shionoya.

1. 1993 (avec Peter Koslowski) (eds.), *The Good and the Economical : Ethical Choices in Economics and Management*, Berlin et New York : Springer.

2. 1994 (avec Mark Perlman) (eds.) *Schumpeter in the History of Ideas* (en japonais et en anglais), éd. par International Schumpeter Society pour la version anglaise. Ann Harbor : University of Michigan Press.

13. Texte original : « an unusual philosophy of life [...] an idea of rich and full life to include economics, politics, science, art, and love » J. A. Schumpeter, *Harvard Crimson*, 11/4/1944, cité par Shionoya 2010, 267.

3. 1994 (avec Mark Perlman) (eds.) *Innovation in Technology, Industries, and Institutions : Studies in Schumpeterian Perspectives*. Ann Harbor : University of Michigan Press.
4. 1997. *Schumpeter and the Idea of Social Science : A Metatheoretical Study*, Cambridge : Cambridge University Press; (rééd. 2007).
5. 2000. *The German Historical School : The Historical and Ethical Approach to Economics*, Abingdon et New York : Routledge.
6. 2000 (avec Kiichirô Yagi). *Competition, Trust, and Cooperation : A Comparative Study (Ethical Economy)*, New York : Springer.
7. 2005. *The Soul of the German Historical School : Methodological Essays on Schmoller, Weber and Schumpeter*, New York : Springer.
8. 2005. *Economy and Morality : The Philosophy of The Welfare State*, Cheltenham : Edward Elgar Publishing.
9. 2008 (avec Tamotsu Nishizawa) (eds.) *Marshall and Schumpeter on Evolution : Economic Sociology of Capitalist Development*, Cheltenham : Edward Elgar Publishing.

RÉFÉRENCE

Campagnolo, G. 2001. “Un exemple de réception de l’économie occidentale au Japon : le Fonds Carl Menger de l’Université de Hitotsubashi.” In *Japon Pluriel 4 (Actes du colloque de la Société Française des Études Japonaises)*, Lucas N. et Sakai C. (dir.), 211-21. Paris : Philippe Picquier. Trad. japonaise par K. Yamazaki. 2002. メンガー文庫・ある経済思想の原資料 *Mengâ-bunko: aru keizaishisô no genshiryô*, *Bulletin of the Center for Historical Social Science Literature* 22 : 23-39.

–. 2012. “Deutsche Archive in Japan und das Beispiel: Carl Menger und sein Verständnis der Nikomachischen Ethik des Aristoteles – mit der Liste deutscher und öterreichischer Archive von Sozialwissenschaftlern in universitären Sondersammlungen in Japan.” In *Der Einfluss deutschsprachigen Wirtschaftswissenschaftlichen Denkens in Japan’. Schriften des Vereins für Socialpolitik Gesellschaft für Wirtschafts- und Sozialwissenschaften*, H. Kurz (ed.), 131-77. Berlin : Duncker & Humblot.

Ishikawa, T. 1986. “Recension de 「価値理念の構造: 効用対権利」 *Kachoku Rinen no Kôzô - KôyôTaï Kenri* [*La structure des valeurs: de l’utilité contre les droits*] de Yûichi Shionoya.” *Keizaï Kenkyû* [*Études économiques*] 37 : 276-78.

Shionoya, Y. 1973. 「現代の物価」 *Gendai no Bukka* [*Current Prices Problems*]. Tokyo : Nihon Keizai Shinbunsha.

–. 2010. “The Oxford approach to the philosophical foundations of the welfare state.” In *No Wealth but Life: Welfare Economics and the Welfare State in Britain (1880-1945)*, R.E. Backhouse and T. Nishizawa (eds.), 91-113. Cambridge : Cambridge University Press. Version japonaise *Keizaï Kenkyû* [*Études économiques*] 65 : 113-25.

–. 2014. « Ruskin’s romantic triangle: neither wealth nor beauty but life », History of Economic Ideas, 2014/1: 15-50.

–. 2018. 「ケインズにおける哲学・芸術・経済学〜啓蒙主義対ロマン主義の構図に照らして」 *Keynes ni okeru Tetsugaku. Geijutsu. Keizaïgaku: Keimôshugi Taï Romanshugi no Kôzu ni terashite* [*Philosophie, art et économie chez Keynes : un éclairage sur la composition de l'opposition entre Lumières et romantisme*]. In 「ケンブリッジ知の探訪: 経済学・哲学・文芸 / 西沢保, 平井俊顕編著」 (*Kembridgi-chi no Tanpô: Keizaïgaku. Tetsugaku. Bungei* [*Une présentation du savoir cambridgien en économie, philosophie et littérature*], T. Hirai and T. Nishizawa (eds.), 261-80. Kyôto : Minerva Shobo.

AN OBITUARY TO YÛICHI SHIONOYA

BERTRAM SCHEFOLD*

1. INTRODUCTION[1]

Professor Yûichi Shionoya, Honorary Member of ESHET, passed away on August 25, 2015. He died at the age of 83 years. He had been President of Hitotsubashi University from 1989-1992, and he served as Director of the National Institute of Population and Social Security Research from 1995-2000. The following laudation was posted on the site of Honorary Members of ESHET in 2007:

"Shionoya, born in 1932, is Emeritus Professor of Economics and former President of Hitotsubashi University, Tokyo, Japan. In 1986 he was one of the founders of the International Joseph A. Schumpeter Society. He served as the President of the Schumpeter Society from 1990-92 and organized the famous conference in Kyoto in 1992.

Shionoya has emphasized in his works that Schumpeter understood the essence of the German Historical School (GHS) as comprising a belief in the unity of social life and the inseparable relationship among its components and a concern for development. From these evolutionary and comparative perspectives follow other

1. This obituary was presented at the Roundtable *in memoriam* of Yûichi Shionoya, held in May 2016 of the same year, at the Conference in Paris of the European Society for the History of Economic Thought. Bertram Schefold convened and chaired the Roundtable. The text was only very slightly revised for this publication by Gilles Campagnolo, in charge of this special issue, and the author.

* Bertram Schefold is Senior Professor of Economics, Goethe University, Frankfurt am Main, former President of the European Society for the History of Economic Thought and Editor of the series Klassiker der Nationalökonomie. His introductions to the reprint volumes have been released in English translation recently in two volumes : *Great Economic Thinkers from Antiquity to the Historical School* and *Great Economic Thinkers from the Classicals to the Moderns*, London, Routledge, 2016 and 2017.

crucial concepts such as history, ethics, and institutions. Shionoya's contributions focus on Max Weber and Schumpeter as the creative successors of the GHS who developed economic sociology or *Sozialoekonomik* as a characteristic methodology designed to overcome the controversy on method between Gustav Schmoller and Carl Menger in a synthesis of theory and "reasoned" history.

Shionoya has also emphasized philosophical aspects of economics which may come out best in his book *Economy and Morality. The Philosophy of the Welfare State* (Edward Elgar 2005). His important works include *Schumpeter and the Idea of Social Science: A Metatheoretical Study* (Cambridge University Press 1997), and *The Soul of the German Historical School. Methodological Essays on Schmoller, Weber, and Schumpeter* (Springer 2005). His most recent publication is *Marshall and Schumpeter on Evolution. Economic Sociology of Capitalist Development*, co-edited with Tamotsu Nishizawa (Edward Elgar 2008). Yûichi Shionoya has always integrated economics with other social sciences and aimed for a synthesis of theory with the history of economic thought in an erudite and innovative way."

Shionoya was awarded the Japanese Academy Prize for his economic and philosophical works, in particular for *Structure of Values: Utility vs. Right* (1984, in Japanese), and he published a last book, *Economic Thought of Romanticism: Arts, Ethics and History* (2012, in Japanese), a part of which came out as "Ruskin's Romantic Triangle: Neither Wealth Nor Beauty But Life" in the journal *History of Economic Ideas*, 2014.[2]

I primarily came into contact with Yûichi Shionoya through my work as general editor of the series "Klassiker der Nationalökonomie". He contributed to the commentary volumes associated with the editions of Pigou, Schmoller, Schumpeter and Weber. He collaborated with the German historians of the history of economic thought in the "Dogmenhistorischer Ausschuss of the Verein für Socialpolitik". I met him on various occasions in Japan, I reviewed one of his books, and we had an exchange on Max Weber at the meeting of ESHET

2. Further details on Shionoya's life and achievements were added by participants of this Roundtable, namely (in alphabetical order) : Richard Arena ("Yûichi Shionoya on Joseph Schumpeter's distinction between statics, dynamics and evolution"), Cristina Marcuzzo ("Shionoya's appraisal of Keynes"), Kiichirô Yagi ("Shionoya's concept of comprehensive social science : from Schumpeter to economic ontology"), Naoshi Yamazaki ("Reflections on the Legacy of Yûichi Shionoya's Economic Thought").

in Prague. I learnt about his background from the informative book about Hitotsubashi University: *Hitotsubashi University 1875-2000.* (Ikema, Inonoue, Nishizawa and Yamanouchi, 2000).

In this book, we read on page 173: "After Schumpeter's death, half of his collection was donated to Hitotsubashi University Library by Mrs Schumpeter." And indeed, in Shionoya's work, at least as I know it, Schumpeter's conception of economics plays the dominating role, not so much through archival work – although Shionoya contributed to our factual knowledge about Schumpeter, in particular his family background –, but primarily through the conceptual framework which Shionoya reconstructed from Schumpeter's writings. Shionoya presented us with a systematic account of Schumpeter's conception of economics and economic sociology, ordering the sub-disciplines of the economic and social sciences according to scope and method. He would regard Schumpeter not only as a Walrasian theorist (despite Böhm-Bawerk), with a theory of knowledge influenced by Ernst Mach and a dynamic view of the economy taken over from Marx, but also as a defender of historism and the historical school. According to Shionoya's scheme, Schumpeter used four methods: theory, statistics, history and economic sociology, in order to investigate three aspects of social life: statics, dynamics and social and cultural development. And he would then use the Schumpeterian scheme as a measuring rod to evaluate the achievements of Schumpeter's predecessors and contemporaries, such as Schmoller and Max Weber.

2. YÛICHI SHIONOYA ON MAX WEBER AND THE YOUNGEST GENERATION OF THE GERMAN HISTORICAL SCHOOL

Shionoya attempted to show that his own scheme could be derived from the seventh chapter of Schumpeter's early work on *Capitalist Development*, a chapter which was omitted in the English translation, but not, as some thought, because Schumpeter had changed his mind, but because it was controversial. Shionoya went to great lengths to prove that, despite the criticism levelled against Schumpeter's attempt to embed the economy in cultural sociology, the author of *Capitalism, Socialism and Democracy* and of *History of Economic Analysis* had retained this framework.

This is explained in Shionoya's book: *Schumpeter and the Idea of Social Science* (Cambridge University Press 1997). Schumpeter's cultural sociology thus is to be seen in relation to the contemporary sociological work by authors such as Dilthey, Troeltsch, Scheler and the brothers Weber (Shionoya 1997, 52). I am here interested in Shionoya's application of the framework derived from Schumpeter to the interpretation of Schmoller, the historical school and Max Weber. Schmoller's involvement in the so-called *Methodenstreit* (Dispute Over Methods) with Menger and the *Werturteilsstreit* (Dispute Over Value-Judgments) with Weber largely seemed to him based on misunderstandings.

With Schumpeter, Shionoya sees the opponents in the *Methodenstreit* concerned with different objects. The values advocated by Schmoller can well be separated from his objective analysis of the relationships between the values factually upheld and transformed in and by social formations. Schmoller is seen as an empiricist, but one who hopes for realistic hypotheses which might lead to deductive theory. He is a nominalist whose nominalism is not so far removed from Schumpeter's instrumentalism. Schmoller's ethics are part of an organicist interpretation of social formations. A society, with the values it maintains, strives to realize a project of communal life, with goals that are perhaps never reached, but which nevertheless provide a teleological interpretation of actions undertaken. Shionoya interprets this teleology as a rational justification of Schmoller's organicist analogies and as a heuristic useful for the observer. The ethics underlying the setting of goals derive from an overlapping consensus as in Rawls.

The theoretical structure in Schmoller's *Grundriss* (Schmoller 1923) merges with an evolutionary perspective for the family (based on sympathy), for associations such as commune and state (which rely on neighbourhood, personal cohesion and national feeling), and finally for the enterprise (which is based on contract). Shionoya judges that the *Grundriss* is boring in its many details, but he defends the analytical achievement. While I agree that there is more theory in Schmoller than meets the eye, I confess to be quite impressed with the historical exposition in some chapters like Schmoller's discussion of how England owes its ascendency in a large measure to protectionist policies under mercantilism, before free trade becomes profitable. The details not only do matter: they can make fascinating reading.

The above reconstruction of Schmoller's theory – of which we could, of course, only provide a few elements – is taken from Shionoya's contribution to the series "Klassiker der Nationalökonomie". He wrote a great deal more about the German historical school. I here turn to the book he edited on this subject, based on contributions by Japanese readers. His concern still is to reconstruct "within a historical and rational context" (*The German Historical School*, edited by Yûichi Shionoya, 2001). Reconstruction can be historical, aiming at a representation of the contexts and at understanding their meaning. The rational reconstruction is based on the texts; it extracts what is of universal significance (p. 8). The key idea again is to take the nominalism of the historical school as a step towards instrumentalism and the justification of certain ideologies in historical applications as a teleology. He then turns to the institutionalism inherent in the historical school. The analysis of institutions permits typologies in order to structure the complexity of history, but institutions are also means to catch up in development.

Shionoya then introduces what he calls the "two-structure approach to mind and society", which becomes relevant in historical sociology. It can emphasize the unity of social life in a horizontal perspective or its transformation vertically. With Schumpeter he advocates a reasoned history and avoids monocausal explanations. The theme is varied in the comparison of various authors, such as Marx and Max Weber.

Shionoya's contribution on Weber to the series "Klassiker der Nationalökonomie" discusses what he calls Weber's instrumentalism. It is rooted in Weber's ideal types, used to analyse social formations by means of standardised characterisations. They often take the form of negative demarcations like: The capitalism of antiquity is not modern in that slavery inhibits the rational allocation of labour, later made possible through the modern wage system. Weber relied on Austrian economic theory in order to define modern rationality. He was not only concerned with the allocation of consumption and production, but also with the explanation of social dispositions for exchange. Thus, Coase's problem was, according to Shionoya, already addressed by Max Weber. However, I think that Weber primarily had the approach of the *Rechtsschule* in mind. This was a branch of the German economics with the neokantian philosopher of law Rudolf Stammler (1856-1938) as its leading exponent. They analysed different economic systems according to legal rights and institutions and thought that the difference between capitalist and socialist arrangements had primarily to be sought in constitutional regulations, whereas Weber emphasized the relationships of power and the factual capacities to dispose over goods and services.

Weber's last work, his *Wirtschaftliche Geschichte* (*Economic History*), based on the last lecture course he gave in Munich prior to his death, was soon edited posthumously from Weber's own lecture notes and notes taken by students. Weber had been reluctant to give this course, because he was more interested in teaching his sociological categories which he had developed in *Wirtschaft und Gesellschaft* (that is in his large undertaking known as such, *Economy and Society*). To turn to economic history as in the historical school meant for Weber to be confronted with individual developments rather than with general structures, it meant to add description to analysis and to account for the dynamics of capitalist accumulation, while his conceptual apparatus as an economist was mainly that of the static analysis of the Austrians. The imposition of this historical turn meant that Weber was pushed to the limits of his conceptual framework.

3. YÛICHI SHIONOYA'S FRAMEWORK AND THE NATURE OF HIS LATE INTEREST IN THE ROMANTICISM OF RUSKIN

I shall mention here three examples of conceptual problems, which came up in my discussion with Shionoya at the Prague Conference of ESHET.

1° Instrumentalism: Ideal types are said to be not images of reality, but mental constructions with which reality is confronted. However, the comparison is a test whether the ideal type allows a mapping of reality. It is perhaps more a caricature than a photograph, but it is nevertheless a creative representation of something out there. Hence the formation of ideal types requires art, it evokes vision and requires more than the combination of known concepts by means of definitions.

2° Rationality and neoclassical theory: Weber's *Economic History* culminated in a dramatic description of the distributional conflicts which arose with industrialization and became acute in each crisis, especially after the First World War, at the very moment, when he held his lecture course in his University, beleaguered by revolutionary workers and defended by conservative students, their adversaries. No wonder that Weber had to take resort to rhetoric reminiscent of Marx, although he fought with the vigour for which he was famous for the transition towards a liberal democracy. I used the notes recently published of Weber's early lectures on economics at Freiburg and Heidelberg where he had eclectically combined Austrian, classical and Marxian ideas to explain growth and accumulation. Did the late lectures not reflect those early lectures? Were the economics of the mature Weber really all Austrian and neoclassical?

3° Mind and society: Economic history, ethics and institutions and economic ideas have always been transformed together. When Spiethoff, Müller-Armack and others introduced the notion of economic style, they felt to stand in the tradition of Weber and Schumpeter in the attempt to characterize the economic spirit, material conditions and institutional arrangements as interrelated in a unified description of a social formation, with an own logic of functioning.

I concluded that vision and analysis had to go together. Was Weber in his economic history not moving in this direction? I found it admirable how Shionoya took up these questions of mine. He insisted on Weber's positions as he had worked them out, largely on the basis of his profound understanding of Schumpeter's economics and sociology. He therefore could not but be sceptical of my attempt to stress the Marxian element in Weber and to relate him to the proponents of the economic styles who came half a generation later. But he admitted the hermeneutical task of showing how Weber effectively dealt with my problems and he thus challenged me to move on.

Shionoya was as great as a great teacher as he was great as an analyst, and I remember him in this double capacity. I was therefore moved, when I read his last important paper in English on Ruskin (mentioned above). Here he dealt with Ruskin's endeavour to free economics from utilitarianism by insisting that economic production and wealth should serve Life, assisted by beauty, and that the alienation of labour should be overcome through education mediating aesthetic ideals and virtuous behaviour. "Splendour" and "abundance" should characterize the allocation of public cultural goods. Ruskin's romanticism, which does not deny its origins in romantic poetry and visual arts, shall lead towards a new welfare economics with Aristotelian traits: capabilities to lead a good life must be transmitted. Shionoya endeavoured to place Ruskin in the tradition of a non-neoclassical welfare economics that finds a modern expression in the work of Amartya Sen.

This paper alluded to parallels in German economic philosophy. Indeed, one could find an early expression in Novalis and subsequent syntheses in the generation following upon Weber, like Arthur Spiethoff (1873-1957) and Edgar Salin (1892-1974). Spiethoff is best known internationally as a pioneer of the theory of business cycles and major influence on Schumpeter's explanation of them, but he also was important because of the systematic account he gave of the theory of economic styles. Salin coined the phrase "*anschauliche Theorie*", i.e. intuitive or visual theory, which aims at description in accordance with the logic of evolution, as opposed to "rational" theorizing or the building of formal models (Schefold et Campagnolo 2007). Shionoya's late interest for Ruskin thus was another expression of his lifelong work for an integration of economics into a broader theory of culture and society as in Schumpeter and Max Weber.

REFERENCES

IKEMA, M., Y. Inonoue, T. NISHIZAWA and S. YAMAOUCHI. 2000. *Hitotsubashi University 1875-2000. A Hundred and Twenty-Five-Years of Higher Education in Japan.* London : Macmillan.

SCHEFOLD, B. 2016. *Great Economic Thinkers from Antiquity to the Historical School.* London : Routledge.

–. 2017. *Great Economic Thinkers from the Classicals to the Moderns.* London : Routledge.

SCHEFOLD, B. and G. CAMPAGNOLO. 2007. "Théories de la connaissance en économie : théories rationnelles appliquées à l'économie et théorie intuitive selon Edgar Salin.". *Asterion* 5 : 265-97. Online version http://asterion.revues.org.

SHIONOYA, Y. 1984. 「価値理念の構造: 効用対権利」 *Kachoku Rinen no Kôzô - KôyôTaï Kenri* [*Structure of Values: Utility vs. Right*]. Tokyo : Toyo Keizai Shinpo.

–. 1997. *Schumpeter and the Idea of Social Science: A Metatheoretical Study.* Cambridge : Cambridge University Press.

–. 2001. *The German Historical School. The Historical and Ethical Approach to Economics.* London and New York : Routledge.

–. 2005a. *Economy and Morality. The Philosophy of the Welfare State.* Cheltenham : Edward Elgar Publishing.

–. 2005b . *The Soul of the German Historical School. Methodological Essays on Schmoller, Weber, and Schumpeter.* New York : Springer

–. 2012. 「ロマン主義の経済思想: 芸術・倫理・歴史 *Romanshugi no Keizaïshisô - Geijutsu Ronri Rekishi* [*Economic Thought of Romanticism: Arts, Ethics and History*]. Tokyo : Tokyo University Press.

–. 2014. "Ruskin's romantic triangle: Neither Wealth nor Beauty but Life." *History of Economic Ideas* 22(1) : 15-49.

Shionoya, Y. and T. Nishizawa. 2008. *Marshall and Schumpeter on Evolution. Economic Sociology of Capitalist Development*, Cheltenham : Edward Elgar Publishing.

Schmoller, G. von 1923. *Grundriss der allgemeinen Wirtschaftslehre.* Berlin : Duncker und Humblot.

Weber, M. 1922. *Wirtschaft und Gesellschaft.* Tübingen : J.C.B. Mohr ; English translation : Economy and Society, 3 vol., 1968. New-York : Bedminster Press.

–. 1924. *Wirtschaftsgeschichte (Abriss der universalen Sozial- und Wirtschafts-Geschichte aus den nachgelassenen Vorlesungen)*, ed. by S. Hellmann and M. Palyi. München and Leipzig : Duncker & Humblot.

L'économie, d'une rive à l'autre[1]

Yûichi Shionoya
(traduit par Kaori Kasaï)

La société s'incorpore l'économie. Comment celle-ci se développe au sein de celle-là, c'est ce qui change en fonction de la manière dont se produit cette intégration. Le schème de la philosophie économique, telle que je la conçois, peut alors être présenté à travers la métaphore suivante : imaginons l'économie comme un grand fleuve ; sur la rive proche, des institutions sociales se dressent, alignées comme autant de « fondamentaux de l'économie », tandis que, sur l'autre rive, on trouve divers « produits de la civilisation », qui sont, en d'autres termes, comme les « finalités de l'économie ». Il y a aussi des « idées » pour relier, comme autant de liaisons plus stables, ces mécanismes « institutionnels » à ces fruits, ou produits, de notre « civilisation ». À mon avis, la philosophie économique a pour devoir de réfléchir à la nature de ces trois catégories de l'économie, à savoir les « institutions », la « civilisation » et ces « idées » : la philosophie économique ne peut pas se contenter d'observer seulement les mécanismes selon lesquels une économie fonctionne.

1. LES FONDEMENTS DE L'ÉCONOMIE

Les peuples de l'Antiquité, ceux des bassins du Tigre et de l'Euphrate en Mésopotamie, ceux de l'ancienne Égypte dans la vallée du Nil, ceux de Chine le long du Fleuve jaune, purent profiter d'un sol fertile et rendre leur agriculture plus productive qu'ailleurs, élargir la sphère de leurs échanges commerciaux et, au final, enfanter des

1. [NDT] Ce texte constitue la préface de *l'ouvrage Économie et éthique : philosophie de l'État-providence*, Tokyo, Presses universitaires de Tokyo, avril 2002.

civilisations. Et leur préoccupation constante était donc d'aménager le cours des eaux qui irriguaient leurs terres ou qui leur servaient au transport de toutes choses, car ces fleuves étaient la source qui leur procurait en abondance de quoi élever leur bétail et cultiver leurs terres. Pour maîtriser, utiliser et entretenir le cours de ces fleuves, ces peuples devaient en aménager les deux rives, et c'est ainsi qu'il faut de même contrôler le cours de l'économie, qui est comme le cours de ces fleuves à la fois bienfaisant et dangereux, mais toujours indispensable, sur une rive comme sur l'autre.

Généralement parlant, l'économie ne consiste d'ailleurs guère au fond en autre chose qu'à distribuer les ressources qui visent à produire de quoi fournir les biens et les services. Il n'y a guère de différence à cet égard entre cette vie antique assez primitive et la civilisation contemporaine pleine de technologies : dans toutes les deux, il s'agit de distribuer des ressources en fonction des besoins. Le premier principe de l'économie est bien toujours d'être « efficace ». Mais qu'est-ce donc que cette « efficacité » ? Il s'agit de sélectionner rationnellement les traits directeurs des comportements humains, avec précaution, afin de répondre au maximum à la demande qui s'exprime, et cela sous la contrainte de ressources limitées, de moyens donnés et étant donné que certaines préférences ont été exprimées. Si on substitue à ces termes de l'économie les mots plus traditionnels de la philosophie, il s'agit de la « prudence »[2]. En conséquence, pour qu'une économie soit « efficace » dans les faits, des aménagements s'imposent concernant la situation des institutions, dans le but de favoriser une concurrence équitable dans le cours de la vie économique en société.

Au long de l'histoire de l'humanité, il n'y a guère plus de deux cents ans que les hommes, en se défaisant de multiples contraintes qui pesaient sur leur économie, travaillent à produire et développer de l'« innovation » par une transformation systématique des biens qu'ils utilisent, par leurs technologies et par leurs formes d'organisation. Nous dirons qu'avec le développement économique moderne, tel qu'on le connaît depuis l'avènement de la révolution industrielle, une économie de l'« innovation » a graduellement pris la place d'une économie plus simplement centrée sur l'« efficacité adaptative ». Ce changement devint possible du fait des institutions économiques, ce

2. [NDT] Le terme japonais est ici *shincho* (慎重). À divers égards, on peut le rapprocher de la notion de prudence dans la philosophie grecque, en particulier chez Aristote.

qui eut pour conséquence que l'on accepta de se priver de satisfaire certain désir présent pour susciter la création d'un excédent dont l'accumulation doit alors constituer un capital dont on envisage de faire usage dans l'avenir. Ce que j'entends par là, c'est bien entendu le capitalisme, le mécanisme économique de la production capitaliste en régime de propriété privée des biens fonctionnant selon des mécanismes de marché ; son moteur est en effet la privation d'une satisfaction immédiate de certains désirs matériels, ce qui s'accompagne de la quête d'un profit.

En même temps que les échanges économiques sur les marchés surgit un autre système, à savoir la protection sociale, qui constitue à son tour un mécanisme fondamental caractéristique de l'économie contemporaine. Afin de corriger les inégalités dues à l'économie capitaliste de marché, la protection sociale tend à satisfaire les demandes les plus essentielles, notamment celles qui concernent la santé, la retraite, les soins envers les personnes âgées dépendantes, le bien-être au sens le plus général. C'est le gouvernement, et non le marché, qui procède à la redistribution indispensable à cet effet. Le principe de « justice » constitue sa ligne directrice et il s'oppose en tant que tel à d'autres concepts comme ceux d'« efficacité » et de « croissance ». En outre, le type d'actions qui se donne pour but de réaliser la justice consiste en un principe de solidarité, qui prend la forme d'une participation aux décisions communes publiques obtenues à travers des accords formés en commun dans la société ; ce principe s'oppose au principe de l'échange commercial qui dépend, quant à lui, des seules décisions que les individus prennent à titre personnel. Ainsi se forme-t-il un troisième concept systémique, à son tour fondamental pour l'économie contemporaine, à savoir celui de la « justice solidaire », si on veut l'appeler ainsi. Si le mécanisme du capitalisme consiste à satisfaire les désirs d'une personne en les redistribuant dans le cours du temps – selon des échéances différenciées au cours du temps –, les différents systèmes de protection sociale exercent alors, quant à eux, un effet similaire entre des individus différents. Il s'agit là d'un héritage du principe de communauté, qui existait, quant à lui, déjà avant l'économie de marché.

Les constituants fondamentaux de l'économie sont donc ces divers systèmes qui soutiennent la vie économique au sein de la société. Les principes directeurs de ces systèmes, l'« efficacité adaptative », la « croissance par l'innovation » et la « justice solidaire » portent la vie économique en société par les formes qu'ils y prennent ; s'ils se transforment certes dans le cours des temps, le devoir principal, dans la vie économique au sein de la société de nos jours, ne consiste guère en rien d'autre qu'à interroger la cohérence qui doit régner entre ces trois principes. Plus précisément, le développement des systèmes de protection sociale au sein de l'État-providence jusqu'à nos jours s'est fondé sur le concept de justice indiqué ci-dessus, tandis que la gestion de ces mêmes systèmes vient contrecarrer l'efficacité économique et se transforme en obstacle au développement économique, ce qui fait qu'elle est de plus en plus critiquée. Par ailleurs, dans la situation actuelle où l'activité économique tend à stagner et la population à vieillir, il va de soi que la demande de services sociaux ne cessera pas d'augmenter et qu'il faut faire face aux conséquences de la crise financière[3].

2. L'*ULTIMA RATIO* DE L'ÉCONOMIE

Or la question n'est cependant pas si simple. En effet, qu'est-ce donc que les hommes essaient d'obtenir par le truchement de l'économie, pour ainsi dire ? Quelle est l'« *ultima ratio* » de l'économie qui se trouverait au-delà de celle-ci ? Nos ancêtres sont parvenus à forger des civilisations extraordinaires sur les plans moral et matériel ; ils ont contribué de la sorte à accumuler un vaste patrimoine pour l'humanité, à travers des conditions de vie bien plus dures que les nôtres. Et désormais, une fois cette richesse économique, l'abondance des biens, obtenue, il nous appartient de réfléchir à ce que nous devons d'ores et déjà en faire, à ce que nous devons accomplir.

Il est tout aussi certain que l'humanité fait souvent bredouiller son histoire et qu'elle répète ses folies et ses destructions. Le XXe siècle fut à cet égard une période particulièrement chargée à l'échelle de l'histoire du monde tout entier, notamment au vu de l'essor des technologies de destruction massives. L'économie et le commerce sont, quant à elles, des activités qui visent la paix et qui nécessitent de la prudence ; la tentation politique de l'hégémonie se traduit par des invasions, qu'attise l'esprit du nationalisme. Lorsqu'il fallut surmonter des

3. [NDT] L'auteur a évidemment à l'esprit la situation japonaise, même si les caractéristiques des tâches qu'il mentionne se retrouvent dans les autres pays industrialisés.

restrictions économiques qui nous avaient été imposées [4], tout soudain d'un seul coup, cela produisit l'expression d'une passion dangereuse qui submergea le cadre pacifique de toute prudence politique. La tentative qui en résulta conduisit à opprimer des populations entières, tant à l'intérieur qu'à l'extérieur du pays [5], à détruire leurs libertés et à prendre la voie détestable d'une domination dictée par une idéologie totalitaire. Inversement, la valeur du système démocratique consiste *a minima* à refuser toute idéologie de ce genre, grâce à la participation et à la solidarité des citoyens avec leur gouvernement.

Alors que le terme d'« État-providence [*welfare state*] » – créé pendant la Deuxième guerre mondiale comme pendant au terme d'« économie étatique de guerre [*warfare state*] » – désigne, d'un côté, le système de protection sociale en charge d'amortir les excès d'un capitalisme cruel, il est également devenu, d'un autre côté, le cadre idéologique qui permet de maîtriser les folies de certains hommes politiques ; c'est en exigeant plus de coopération démocratique pour le faire fonctionner que cet État-providence peut garantir une base solide aux systèmes d'aide sociale. Le but de l'État-providence est donc de maîtriser un pouvoir dénué de prudence, que ce soit celui du marché ou celui des politiques ; ce but consiste dans la réalisation d'une société de paix, de prudence, de solidarité et de sécurité collective. Le régime qui existe de nos jours au sein de la société, en économie comme en politique, repose pour cela sur ces trois piliers que sont le « capitalisme », la « démocratie » et la « protection sociale », eux que j'appelle ici les constituants d'ensemble de cet « État-providence ».

Comment cet « État-providence » peut-il contribuer à réaliser sciemment et volontairement ces valeurs humaines en aménageant ses propres systèmes constitutifs ?

Imaginons une société où l'on vit longtemps, où l'on vit riche et sans grands soucis, et imaginons que cette société se trouve réalisée grâce au soutien que fournit un tel État-providence. À quel titre peut-on alors être effectivement fier de vivre dans cette société ? L'« efficacité », la « croissance » et la « justice » – tout cela ne reste-t-il pas vain dès lors qu'on ne les lie pas directement aux idéaux et aux vertus de la vie humaine ? Concentrons donc notre regard sur

4. [NDT] De toute évidence, la référence implicite est la marche à la guerre du Japon dans les années 1930.

5. [NDT] C'est-à-dire du Japon.

l'« être » individuel, lui que l'on a tant méconnu jusqu'ici sous tous les rapports, et réexaminons la relation entre cet individu, pris tel qu'il est, je veux bien dire chaque individu, et les systèmes sociaux en question.

Outre un système de marché « libre » duquel dépend la quête de satisfaction des désirs personnels, ce sont à la fois le système de protection sociale (qui tente de réaliser la « justice » sociale) et le système démocratique (qui garantit l'« égalité » au sein de la société) qui assurent dans les faits l'autonomie de cet « être » individuel ; ils lui fournissent même, à chacun en fait, les occasions d'augmenter ses capacités[6]. Mais, selon la théorie économique[7], la « liberté » visée à travers les activités exercées sur les marchés n'est qu'un moyen en vue d'obtenir une satisfaction maximale dans la limite des choix qui sont proposés. Or une véritable « liberté » individuelle comprend deux autres aspects encore, à savoir

1) la « liberté » de perfectionner ses capacités, et d'accomplir des œuvres excellentes, et de réformer ainsi volontairement et raisonnablement soi-même ses pratiques dans des activités sociales variées ;

2) la « liberté » de participer directement ou indirectement aux réformes qui encadrent les institutions ou les politiques qui sont menées, et de s'engager de la sorte dans les prises de décision publiques, en prenant soin de bien chercher à les comprendre et de débattre des questions qui sont du ressort du domaine public. Le premier aspect concerne ainsi le « domaine de l'individu », et le second le « domaine public ».

Une « liberté » individuelle véritable n'est possible que sous la condition de comporter les trois mécanismes suivants : « liberté » du marché, « justice » sociale et garantie d'« égalité ». La « liberté » individuelle véritable concerne en même temps tout à la fois ce qui se situe au-delà même de ces trois facteurs, et qui lui sera donné en sus. Un individu autonome transforme non seulement le fait même de son existence comme individu, mais aussi la société qui l'entoure. C'est pour cette raison que cette « liberté » relie, comme le fait un

6. [NDT] La référence implicite apparaît clairement au terme utilisé dans la philosophie économique d'Amartya Sen : capacités ou « capabilités » (*capabilities*), comme le montre assez la caractérisation donnée dans la phrase suivante.

7. [NDT] 経済理論 (*keizai riron*) renvoie à la théorie économique importée d'Occident, voir la présentation générale de ce numéro.

pont, cette rive-ci à cette autre rive-là, par-delà le courant que forme l'économie. La « liberté » se fonde sur la solidarité et la participation, tout autant que sur la justice et sur l'égalité, elle se rapporte à la protection sociale et à la démocratie – pas simplement à la seule liberté d'exercer ses choix sur un marché, pas seulement à l'échange et à la concurrence. Elle prend ainsi le sens d'une quête active et volontaire d'une plus grande variété dans la formation des capacités morales, dans le développement de l'esprit civique, dans les efforts destinés à réaliser non seulement ses propres projets, mais encore à déployer des talents créatifs, tout cela dans le respect de la personnalité de chacun. Par là-même s'ouvrent également les chemins de la science, de l'art, de la pensée, de la civilisation, de l'art de vivre et de l'identité personnelle pour tout un chacun, bref toutes les facettes de ce qui permet de laisser sa marque dans l'histoire de l'humanité. Bien entendu, cela nécessite des ressources économiques, mais la valeur produite de cette manière outrepasse à divers égards la seule évaluation de type économique : c'est précisément cela, l'*ultima ratio* de l'économie. Si l'on appelle de telles valeurs l'expression d'une « perfection » ou d'une « excellence », il est alors loisible d'imaginer qu'il existe une quatrième norme conceptuelle, que l'on nommera « perfection, ou excellence, à atteindre par la réalisation véritable de la liberté ».

3. METTRE EN CONFORMITÉ LES IDÉES DES VALEURS ET LE SYSTÈME DE L'ÉTAT-PROVIDENCE

Édifier une société dont l'excellence est le but en tant que tel, voilà ce que souhaite toute société qui réalise l'abondance et la justice. Depuis Aristote, cette recherche de l'« excellence » en philosophie morale a conduit à souligner le rôle de la « vertu » plutôt que le bonheur ou la justice. On ne pourra pas bâtir un État-providence idéal seulement sur des discours techniques ou économiques, tels qu'ils existent au sein du système existant présentement. La triade « capitalisme, démocratie, et protection sociale » n'est jamais elle-même qu'une série de mécanismes dressés sur cette rive-ci du fleuve, pour réaliser une telle société d'« excellence »[8]. En premier lieu, en raison du principe économique de « croissance par l'innovation », le marché

8. [NDT] Sur l'autre rive du fleuve donc, si l'on suit ici l'image choisie par l'auteur.

capitaliste constitue la base économique organique de toute société libre. En deuxième lieu, la protection sociale, système d'ajustement qui vient en complément de l'organisme qu'est le marché, se fonde sur un principe éthique[9]. En troisième lieu, la démocratie permet de maîtriser la sphère politique à travers la participation sociale du peuple fondée sur un principe d'égalité ; elle vise à ce que l'espace public puisse se gouverner de manière autonome, tout en arrivant à maîtriser l'économie par le moyen de la solidarité sociale. Autrement dit, la démocratie n'est rien d'autre qu'un processus politique absolument indispensable à la construction d'un système éthique qui soit juste, au sein de l'économie. Ces trois systèmes constituent l'État-providence dès lors qu'ils sont réunis en vue du principe éthique de réalisation de l'« excellence par la liberté », celui qui doit contribuer à faire parvenir à l'*ultima ratio* de l'économie, telle qu'elle a été mentionnée ci-dessus, elle qui se trouve sur l'autre rive du courant économique.

Les régimes socialistes ou communistes eurent beau attirer l'attention sur l'intérêt du peuple par leurs idéologies qui proclamaient chercher la « justice », lorsqu'ils jugeaient que les hommes pouvaient abandonner toute nature intéressée, égoïste, ils déniaient simplement toute validité au système du marché[10] et échouaient ainsi à faire surgir une organisation économique « efficace » comme à susciter de la « croissance » – alors même que, sans « efficacité » ni « croissance », aucun système économique durable ne peut durer, ni même voir le jour. De plus, parce que ces régimes réprimaient les « libertés », ils proposaient seulement des institutions politiques dictatoriales, qui finirent par s'effondrer. Si l'on ne garde pas bien présent à l'esprit que la performance économique est toujours indispensable, il est alors impossible d'adopter une perspective pertinente relativement à l'*ultima ratio* de l'économie – et c'est le cas là où la « liberté » n'existe pas.

Or ceci n'est point l'affaire du passé. Sur cette question de la domination que le « domaine public » exerce sur le « domaine privé », l'on voit bien les restrictions de nature protectionniste qu'exercent certains gouvernements des pays capitalistes, sur le plan économique comme sur le plan social, faisant ainsi courir des risques assez

9. [NDT] 倫理的主導原理 (*rinriteki shudôgenri*) : il s'agit d'un principe éthique initiateur et directeur.

10. [NDT] 市場制度 (*shijô seido*) désigne littéralement le système fonctionnant sur la base du marché. En d'autres termes, l'auteur reproche à ces systèmes de ne pas avoir compris les mécanismes d'incitation des comportements individuels, en effet la raison généralement retenue par les économistes pour expliquer l'échec des économies planifiées.

similaires à ce qui a existé dans les pays socialistes. Il est par conséquent judicieux que les courants poussant vers la déréglementation et vers la marchandisation[11] à l'échelle mondiale favorisent également la transition qui fait aller les choses « du public vers le privé ». Mais c'est aussi pourquoi la bonne gestion de la protection sociale et le souci de sauvegarder la démocratie, qui servent de barrages régulateurs dans l'organisation des marchés, demeurent requis plus que jamais ; il faut donc absolument que la participation individuelle devienne plus importante dans les décisions publiques. Ce point requiert aussi de développer une « raison publique »[12] qui puisse mieux prendre en considération autrui dans son existence et le vivre-ensemble qui en résulte, afin de donner des directions pour aller inversement, quant à elle, « du privé vers le public ». Il est indispensable de concilier ces deux courants, celui qui va « de la sphère publique vers la sphère privée » et celui qui va « de la sphère privée vers la sphère publique ».

Face aux multiples défis tragiques que l'humanité doit affronter, l'État-providence fait donc aujourd'hui face à un devoir très ardu, à savoir construire un système social et économique qui puisse incarner à la fois, toutes ensemble, les valeurs de « liberté », d'« efficacité » et de « développement », tout en respectant l'idée selon laquelle la « justice » possède par elle-même une valeur intrinsèque. Non seulement l'État-providence affronte déjà rien moins qu'une crise de financement, mais il se trouve encore en crise morale, profondément, concernant l'exercice de la « liberté » dans la vie humaine, au sein d'un système où il faut également répondre automatiquement à la demande sociale et y pourvoir. D'ailleurs, la démocratie même, en tant que structure qui permet la prise des décisions publiques, se trouve assez dévitalisée, tandis que la politique devient le lieu d'une quête éperdue du seul profit personnel, un profit fondé sur la triple entente trempée dans l'acier que forment le « monde politique », le gouvernement et le « monde de la finance »[13]. En effet, c'est là une crise de la démocratie politique. Le devoir le plus fondamental des sciences sociales de

11. [NDT] 市場化 (*shijôka*) correspond à un processus qui pousse à un marché constitué par des marchandises échangées, c'est donc au sens d'un accroissement des échanges marchands que se comprend cette « marchandisation ».

12. [NDT] 公共的理性 (*kôkyôteki risei*) désigne une « raison publique » selon la signification d'un sens commun en société, possiblement proche d'un sens civique partagé.

13. [NDT] La référence historique possible au « pacte d'acier » (Allemagne-Italie-Japon) d'avant-guerre n'est pas absolument évidente ici au regard du texte, si elle n'est pas impossible puisqu'il est question d'une menace contre la démocratie.

nos jours consiste donc à prendre un point de vue global qui nous mette en mesure de coordonner toutes ces valeurs dans un système pouvant très concrètement assurer en même temps le maintien de ces trois éléments que sont « capitalisme », « démocratie » et « protection sociale ». À ce stade, la problématique consiste à mettre en conformité le système de l'État-providence avec cette idée.

Le présent ouvrage poursuit cet objectif de réfléchir au système de l'État-Providence dans un cadre académique large envisageant les rapports entre l'économie et l'éthique. Les deux idées motrices dans les sciences économiques sont l'« efficacité adaptative » et la « croissance par l'innovation », alors que les idées éthiques concernent la « justice solidaire » et l'« excellence à travers la liberté ». L'éthique économique constitue l'ensemble des concepts normatifs de l'économie qui visent à réaliser une telle « vie meilleure ». Ce ne sont pas là de simples vues de l'esprit, ni des idées bornées, mais c'est tout au contraire ce que la loi positive intègre en elle dans la législation même, comme à la fois ce que chaque individu conscient s'incorpore dans les habitudes de comportement qu'il forme. Si l'on considère donc les trois matières que sont la « loi », la « morale » et la « coutume » comme autant de « systèmes » fonctionnant au titre de « normes sociales », alors ces trois autres facteurs que sont « capitalisme », « démocratie », et « protection sociale » doivent à leur tour être considérés comme des « systèmes qui fonctionnent comme un tout dans une société organique ». Aborder la « philosophie de l'État-providence » dans son rapport avec ces « pensées », c'est évoquer la manière de vivre en société et le « système » qui les rend concrètes, et cela consiste donc à interroger le rapport entre ces aspects (organisme social et normes sociales) au sein du « système » proprement dit qu'ils forment à eux deux pris ensemble.

Dans le présent ouvrage, l'on considère que l'État-Providence a de nos jours pour devoir de mettre en conformité l'idée de ces valeurs et leur organisation concrète en un système ; ce devoir questionne les rapports entre l'économie et l'éthique. Si la philosophie est constituée des trois domaines que sont l'ontologie (la métaphysique), la théorie des valeurs (l'éthique axiologique) de la méthodologie (ou l'épistémologie), alors la philosophie de l'État-Providence de laquelle le présent ouvrage traite doit accentuer l'aspect éthique qui est caractéristique de l'État-Providence.

4. PLAN DU PRÉSENT OUVRAGE

La première partie de cet ouvrage porte comme titre « Des idées ». Le premier chapitre pose la question de ce que l'économie et l'éthique sont essentiellement, et il cadre le système conceptuel des débats abordés au long de l'ouvrage. La science économique et l'éthique existent déjà comme genres distincts au sein de la science, mais l'on n'a quasiment jamais tenté d'aborder les univers de l'économie et de l'éthique depuis un point de vue qui leur soit commun et qui les conforme l'un à l'autre. Nous considérons chacun de ces mondes que nous avons évoqués, l'économique et l'éthique, comme un grand mécanisme doté d'une capacité extraordinairement universaliste d'unification de la société, mais c'est le concept du « bien » qui doit ici faire l'interface entre ces deux mondes. Ce terme, « le bien », peut parfois paraître trop peu familier aux économistes, c'est pourtant lui qui englobe effectivement à la fois l'utilité, le bien-être, la protection sociale et le bonheur – d'ailleurs, la manière même par laquelle on cherche à obtenir des « biens » [marchands] ne signifie au fond pas autre chose que pratiquer ce « bien », et c'est alors effectivement là un terme d'économie.

Dans les deuxième et troisième chapitres, l'on traite de la recherche scientifique qui porte sur les valeurs idéelles fondamentales [14] qui lient les univers économique et éthique (à savoir : l'efficacité, la justice, la liberté et l'excellence). Le deuxième chapitre aborde l'« efficacité » et la « justice », notions notoirement contradictoires. Le troisième chapitre développe l'autre opposition, qui existe entre « liberté » et « excellence » et que traite le champ de l'éthique normative [15]. Ces recherches ont connu un grand progrès à partir du début des années 1970, tout d'abord avec la théorie de la justice de John Rawls. Les doctrines du type de l'utilitarisme ou des théories du contrat social, les doctrines de la liberté, comme celle des libertariens [16], ou encore le communautarisme par ailleurs ont tous connu un renouveau et suscité des débats passionnants : ces courants de pensée interrogent la nature

14. [NDT] 基本的価値理念 (*kihonteki kachirinen*) désigne la « rationalité en valeur » au sens fondamental des « valeurs de base » – dans la pensée néo-kantienne, par exemple : voir le texte suivant traduit dans ce numéro thématique.

15. [NDT] 規範倫理学 (*kihan rinrigaku*) désigne la théorie morale des normes.

16. [NDT] 自由至上主義 (*jiyû shijô shugi*) désigne le libéralisme accordant une valeur absolue à la liberté : en contexte, il faut comprendre ici la théorie libertarienne.

des mécanismes systématiques fondamentaux au sein de la société, et la réflexion sur les valeurs au sein de la société actuelle ne peut pas se priver de les discuter. Pourtant, en raison de la division du travail académique comme de la spécialisation, ces réflexions philosophiques n'ont selon nous jamais été traitées de front jusque aujourd'hui au sein même des institutions de recherche de l'univers économique, jusques et y compris les questions concernant les régimes de protection sociale.

La seconde partie de l'ouvrage s'intitule « Le système ». L'accent y est mis sur les mécanismes d'organisation systémiques et la réflexion porte sur la nature du principe moral que chaque type d'organisation incarne. Nous considérons alors successivement « capitalisme », « démocratie » et « protection sociale » comme des mécanismes systémiques de l'État-Providence tel qu'il existe de nos jours. Dans chacun des chapitres 4, 5 et 6, il s'agit d'éclaircir la base éthique respective de ces systèmes.

Le tableau 1 ci-dessous met en rapport la première et la seconde partie : les colonnes désignent ces idées des valeurs que sont l'« efficacité », la « justice », la « liberté », l'« excellence » et les lignes désignent le « capitalisme », la « démocratie » et la « protection sociale », à savoir les types d'organisation systémiques. Chacun de ces trois systèmes concrétise ces valeurs et l'on cherchera à évaluer dans quelle mesure c'est le cas, de même que l'on voudra aussi déterminer les rapports entre chacun de ces systèmes [remplir les « cases vides » dans le tableau ci-dessous].

Système/Idée	**Efficacité**	**Justice**	**Liberté**	**Excellence**
Capitalisme				
Démocratie				
Protection sociale				

Tableau 1. *Les rapports corrélatifs mutuels entre « idée » et « système »*

Il convient d'expliquer ici deux facteurs complexes majeurs :

– Premièrement, du fait qu'il existe diverses écoles et divers courants idéologiques, le contenu à inscrire au sein du tableau diffère selon ces écoles, car chacune accentue telle ou telle idée et chacune élabore son propre système de valeurs à partir de là. De ce fait, chaque école possède son propre programme spécifique dans le but d'agencer les trois systèmes. Nous remplirons donc le tableau en nous y prenant école par école.

– Deuxièmement, comme une approche comparative de l'État-Providence le montre à l'échelle internationale, la gestion et la combinatoire des trois systèmes diffèrent selon les pays ; en conséquence, le contenu caractéristique des cases du tableau doit ausi différer selon les pays.

À la différence de ce qui se passe au sein des écoles de pensée, aucun système d'idées claires ne parvient la plupart du temps à s'établir dans un pays ; aussi c'est selon la nature du pouvoir en place que les idées y divergent. Mais, à l'examen que permet l'observation des résultats pour chacun des trois systèmes, l'on parvient cependant à distinguer certains usages typiques spécifiques. La manière dont s'exprime la forme typique de l'État-Providence, c'est alors à partir de données statistiques d'observation que l'on peut tenter de la connaître en trouvant un motif commun.

Nous entendons proposer un tel repère global, comme celui qui suit, afin d'exprimer ce rapport entre les « idées » et les « systèmes » :

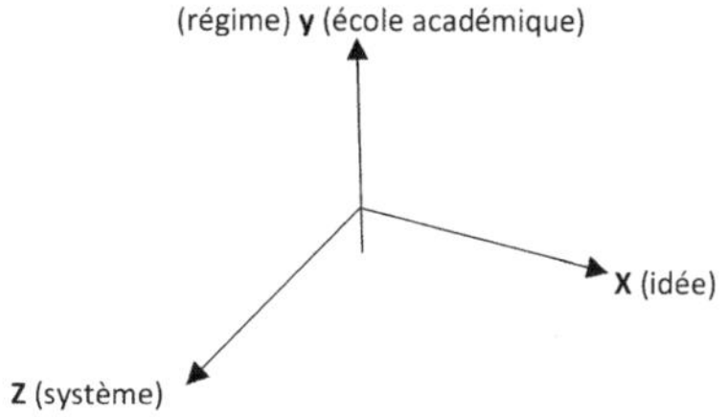

Figure 2. *Les rapports corrélatifs tridimensionnels entre « idées » et « systèmes »*

Le plan formé par l'axe des abscisses *x* (les « idées ») et l'axe des cotes *z* (les « systèmes ») manifeste la relation entre idées et systèmes. Quant à l'axe des ordonnées *y*, il peut désigner soit des « écoles (académiques) », soit des « régimes (politiques) ». Sur le plan formé par l'axe des *x* et par celui des *y*, on montre comment les quatre écoles mentionnées plus haut (utilitarisme, théories du contrat social, libertarisme, communautarisme) interprètent les idées de valeurs (l'« efficacité », la « justice », la « liberté », l'« excellence ») ». Sur le plan formé par l'axe des *y* et par celui des *z*, on verra comment évaluer les systèmes (« capitalisme », « démocratie » et « protection sociale ») selon ces quatre écoles ; dans le cas où le régime de l'État-Providence se calque sur l'axe des *y*, on peut encore dessiner une figure semblable.

Aujourd'hui, une réforme radicale des systèmes de protection sociale à l'échelle mondiale, voilà ce qui doit constituer notre priorité – c'est-à-dire une réforme des systèmes de santé, de retraite, d'aide à la dépendance ainsi que les formules variées du bien-être social en général. Mais, dans des circonstances où les intérêts particuliers s'opposent, quels débats politiques pourront-ils donner des résultats judicieux, alors même qu'ils restent dépendants de mécanismes automatiques systémiques ? Généralement parlant, si le système social doit intégrer des valeurs éthiques et si le système de protection sociale doit dès lors pénétrer la société tout en coordonnant la valeur de justice avec les autres valeurs, chaque mesure de couverture visant la protection sociale doit alors se décider après examen d'une valeur idéale[17]. Dans le chapitre 7, nous abordons les points fondamentaux qui concernent la réforme du système de protection sociale.

Dans l'avant-propos qui précédait[18], j'indiquais que « c'est la philosophie économique reconstituée par l'éthique moderne que j'aborde dans le présent ouvrage ». On a souvent dit que la recherche scientifique en philosophie économique, si on la comprend dans son sens moderne, a pu débuter à l'improviste dans les années 1970. Or je tiens quant à moi à souligner qu'il avait existé auparavant deux économistes japonais, nommément Kiichirô Sôda et Kôzô Sugimura, qui avaient pris la science économique même comme objet de leurs réflexions afin d'établir pour la première fois la philosophie économique au Japon au cours de la première moitié du vingtième siècle. Quant à moi, je considère leur philosophie économique comme tout à fait moderne, même si tout le monde paraît l'ignorer de nos jours ; elle mérite pourtant, bien au contraire, une attention toute particulière. J'ajoute que, dans ma propre perspective scientifique, une bonne partie de mes travaux doit en fait beaucoup aux œuvres de ces deux « philosophes économiques »[19].

17. [NDT] 主導的価値理念 (*shudôteki kachirinen*) : il s'agit de l'idée de valeur directrice pour une entité (pays ou courant de pensée), déterminant ses positions de manière privilégiée.

18. [NDT] Shionoya renvoie au court texte qui précédait cette introduction – texte non traduit dans le présent numéro.

19. [NDT] Notons que le japonais utilise le terme que traduit littéralement « philosophie économique », à savoir *keizai tetsugaku* 経済哲学 : voir l'introduction générale de ce numéro. Le texte concernant les deux économistes cités par Shionoya suit dans le présent numéro.

Les fondateurs de la philosophie économique au Japon : Kiichirô Sôda et Kôzô Sugimura[1]

Yûichi Shionoya
(traduit par Kaori Kasaï)

1. DEUX POINTS DE VUE

Au Japon, ce sont deux universitaires de Hitotsubashi (l'université s'appela d'abord « École supérieure de commerce de Tokyo », puis « université du commerce de Tokyo »[2]), les économistes Kiichirô Sôda (1881-1927) et Kôzô Sugimura (1895-1948), qui fondèrent la philosophie économique et qui l'établirent comme une discipline neuve. Les travaux de Sôda étaient déjà reconnus à l'international et, jusqu'à la fin de la Seconde Guerre mondiale, leurs noms devaient systématiquement être associés dans les articles qui explicitaient ce que les dictionnaires japonais spécialisés nommaient alors déjà « philosophie économique »[3] – cela est resté la source originelle de

1. [NDT] Ce texte constitue l'appendice d'*Économie et éthique : philosophie de l'État-providence* (Tokyo, Presses de l'Université de Tokyo, 2002). La dernière phrase du texte dit le rôle de cet appendice historique et la volonté qui présidait à la rédaction de l'ouvrage en son entier. Sur ce point, voir la présentation de la section consacrée à Yûichi Shionoya dans ce numéro. Les notes accompagnant ce texte ont été rédigées en collaboration par la traductrice et le responsable du numéro ; ces notes sont indiquées par [NDT], les autres notes sont de Shionoya ou des Presses de l'université de Tokyo.

2. [NDT] L'université se trouvait au centre de Tokyo, dans le quartier de Kanda, situé face au palais impérial : voir la présentation de cette section à propos cette université, qui fut également celle de Shionoya.

3. [NDT] 経済哲学 *keizaï tetsugaku* désigne la philosophie de l'économie ayant en vue la science économique d'origine occidentale. Sur ce terme formé lors de l'introduction de la discipline au Japon, voir l'introduction générale de ce numéro.

ce champ même si, depuis lors, le terme a disparu des pages des ouvrages de référence. Or, dans la situation actuelle de la philosophie économique, les travaux de ces deux économistes manifestent une étonnante modernité, notamment sur les points que nous aborderons dans les pages suivantes.

1.1 *Positivisme et idéalisme*

En premier lieu, parmi les courants scientifiques et idéologiques de leur époque, c'est la position prise par ces deux économistes qui mérite notre attention. Au Japon, la philosophie économique a commencé dans les réflexions engendrées par l'introduction de la philosophie allemande, qui y jouit d'un renom certain quoique fluctuant du milieu du XIXe siècle jusqu'au début du XXe siècle. À la même époque, en Allemagne, on avait déjà perdu toute confiance dans l'idéalisme[4] comme dans le positivisme, ce qui laissa place au renouveau de la pensée critique issue de la philosophie de Kant ; celle-ci faisait son retour marqué à la suite des travaux d'Otto Liebmann (*Kant et ses épigones : une approche critique*)[5] et Friedrich A. Lange (*Histoire du matérialisme et critique de sa signification pour le temps présent*)[6]. Ce néokantisme était développé dans les œuvres de Hermann Cohen, de Paul G. Natorp, d'Ernst Cassirer (l'école dite « de Marbourg »), ainsi que chez Wilhelm Windelband, Heinrich J. Rickert et Emil Lask (l'école dite « de Bade », dans le sud-ouest de l'Allemagne). À l'encontre de l'idée positiviste selon laquelle seules les sciences naturelles méritaient d'être prises en considération de manière sérieuse, ceux-ci avaient tenté de rétablir la position d'autres types de sciences sur un plan épistémologique, à savoir celles que la langue allemande nomme les

4. [NDT] Dans ce texte, deux mots japonais au moins traduisent la notion d'« idéalisme » au sens occidental. Ce sont 理念論 (*rinenron*) qui part du principe 理 (*ri*) et a servi à dénommer pendant un temps la philosophie même, comme une « doctrine des principes » (voir l'introduction générale) et 観念論 (*kannenron*) qui désigne un idéal visé (観 *kan*) renvoie à la vue. Cet idéal peut être subjectif au sens de la prise de conscience d'un objet du réel – la notion d'idée ou de sentiment est dans tous les cas présentée avec 念 (*nen*). Il apparaît aussi dans ce texte la dualité 理念主義 *rinenshugi*/ 理想主義 *risôshugi* que nous traduisons aussi tous deux par « idéalisme », le second à comprendre comme opposé au réalisme. Dans la phrase présente, « idéalisme » renvoie clairement au mouvement de Fichte, Schelling, Hegel, qui entendait se substituer à la philosophie critique de Kant, et fut supplanté par le « retour à Kant » de la fin du XIXe siècle.

5. (Liebmann, 1865) : toutes les références données par Shionoya se retrouvent dans la bibliographie finale.

6. (Lange, 1866)

Kulturwissenschaften[7], les sciences historiques et les *Geisteswissenschaften*[8]. Au titre des résultats les plus marquants de cette entreprise, citons les ouvrages de référence que sont l'*Einleitung in den Geisteswissenschaften* (*Introduction aux sciences de l'esprit*) de Wilhelm Dilthey (1883), et *Die Grenzen der Naturwissenschaften* (*Les limites des sciences de la nature*) de H. J. Rickert (paru entre 1896 et 1902).

Dans les circonstances particulières du Japon de l'époque, ce courant allemand fut bien accueilli. Les enseignants de l'université Hitotsubashi, dont le travail portait initialement sur les aspects pratiques du commerce (ils enseignaient la comptabilité et l'usage de l'abaque), se demandaient si le commerce comme tel, ou l'activité économique privée[9] constituaient vraiment des sciences ; ils se mirent à porter leurs recherches vers les aspects interdisciplinaires fondamentaux des sciences humaines et sociales. Dès lors, l'université Hitotsubashi mit sciemment la philosophie, l'histoire et la littérature à la base de l'enseignement des autres disciplines en sciences sociales. Aussi les recherches philosophico-économiques de Sôda et de Sugimura, qui avaient tous deux étudié en Allemagne, conduisirent-elles à assigner sa place à l'économie parmi les sciences sociales. Leur intention originelle consistait cependant à élucider le sens de la vie économique pour tout un chacun. Ainsi Sôda posait-il la question suivante : « Il y a la philosophie des sciences, il y a la morale, et puis la philosophie de la religion, du droit et de la politique – pourquoi n'y aurait-il pas la philosophie économique ? » Cette nouvelle discipline devait finir par dominer son époque et, grâce à ces deux penseurs, l'université Hitotsubashi put jouir d'une reconnaissance exceptionnelle dans le milieu académique nippon.

C'est à l'université de Tübingen que Sôda avait rédigé sa thèse, intitulée *Monnaie et valeur* (1909)[10]. Après neuf ans d'études et de

7. [NDT] Pour désigner les « sciences de la civilisation/ de la culture ». Shionoya utilise l'équivalent japonais littéral du terme allemand que nous restituons.

8. [NDT] Les « sciences de l'esprit » (*idem*).

9. [NDT] 私経済学 (*shikeizaïgaku*). Il s'agit de l'activité économique relative à l'individu particulier, à l'agent économique, et le terme est encore un décalque d'un mot allemand « *Privatwirtschaft* » (économie de l'individu privé) alors en usage.

10. [NDT] Le texte de ce qui était bien une thèse de doctorat (« Inaugural-Dissertation zur Erlangung der Doktorwürde ») est paru en allemand sous le titre *Geld und Wert : eine logische Studie* (Sôda, 1909, rééd. 1924). Un autre ouvrage de Sôda en allemand *Die logische Natur der Wirtschaftsgesetze* (*La nature logique des lois de l'économie*) (Sôda, 1911) parut avec une préface de Carl Johannes Fuchs.

recherches poursuivies à Cambridge, à Fribourg, à Tübingen, à Berlin et à Paris, Sôda enseigna à l'École supérieure de commerce de Tokyo, qui devint l'Université du commerce de Tokyo, tout en prenant le poste de directeur général au sein de la banque familiale Sôda. Il devait décéder à l'âge précoce de quarante-sept ans. Quant à Sugimura, de quatorze ans le cadet de Sôda, il participa au séminaire de celui-ci et il termina ses études à l'École supérieure de commerce de Tokyo, avant de devenir assistant puis d'occuper un poste équivalent à maître de conférences au sein de l'établissement, qui venait alors juste d'obtenir le statut d'université. Entre 1925 et 1927, Sugimura allait poursuivre sa formation à l'université d'Iéna, mais il dut raccourcir son séjour en Allemagne suite au décès de son maître, Sôda. En 1936, alors qu'il était maître de conférences à l'université de commerce de Tokyo, un conflit au sein de l'université allait le chasser du monde académique. Il devait lui aussi mourir assez tôt, à l'âge de cinquante-deux ans. Les disciples de Sôda et de Sugimura, du nom de Kenzô Honda et Toyorô Kawamura, devaient disparaître assez jeunes eux aussi, de sorte que le courant de pensée de la philosophie économique au Japon s'éteignit au bout d'un demi-siècle.

À la tragédie que constituait la perte de ces gens de talent vint s'ajouter le déclin de l'influence de l'idéalisme allemand après la Deuxième guerre mondiale. Le positivisme anglo-américain prit alors sa place comme courant principal (*mainstream*) au sein de la science économique. L'économie comme science empirique, qui n'aurait soi-disant nul besoin de la recherche philosophique, qui ne serait elle-même que spéculation superflue à ses yeux, écarta brutalement toute philosophie ; cette dernière fut également supprimée du cursus des enseignements donnés au sein de la faculté d'économie et les mathématiques prirent cette place qu'avait occupée la philosophie. Durant le demi-siècle qui suivit la fin de la Deuxième guerre mondiale, la science économique au Japon fut dominée par l'économie dite « moderne », d'une part[11], et par l'économie marxiste, d'autre part.

11. [NDT] L'appellation 近代経済学 (*kindai keizaigaku*) désigne sous le terme « modernes » les sciences économiques utilisant principalement l'outil mathématique, ce qui conduit dans ce cas à un pêle-mêle de micro-économie « néoclassique », de macroéconomie « keynésienne » et d'économétrie. Cette appellation très générale s'est formée par contraste avec l'économie politique classique, l'école historique allemande et le marxisme, pour désigner comme marques de « modernité » la mathématisation de la discipline et la formulation de modèles (« micro » ou « macro »).

Si l'on prend en compte le fait que la philosophie néokantienne avait débuté, quant à elle, par une critique simultanée de la pensée scientiste naturaliste imperméable à toute considération axiologique[12] et du matérialisme qui assigne à l'économie le rôle suprême[13], la science économique dépourvue de toute philosophie critique qui s'établit alors favorisait au contraire les succès partagés entre cette économie « moderne », d'une part, et un marxisme d'orientation économiciste, d'autre part.

Les pensées occidentales de la première moitié du XXe siècle avaient eu leur heure de gloire ; elles connurent alors leur décadence. Sôda et Sugimura avaient eu leur place dans la première phase, celle de la critique formulée par un courant préoccupé par les idées. Après cinquante ans pendant lesquels leurs efforts ont été comme mis entre parenthèses, nombreuses sont les tentatives d'ordre philosophique qui semblent de nos jours vouloir à nouveau traiter des idées en économie, de leur sens, de la valeur et des normes économiques suivies au sein de la société, et qui paraissent désireuses de ré-examiner la nature des concepts, des méthodes et du processus de cognition au sein des sciences économiques ; c'est là un renouveau remarquable. Je considère pour ma part que cette tendance, si elle prend la forme d'un *post*-positivisme, doit manifester un élément de renaissance pour une pensée idéaliste.

1.2 *La tradition kantienne*

En second lieu, le contenu érudit de la philosophie économique que Sôda et Sugimura ont formulée mérite aujourd'hui toute notre attention. Leur point de départ se situait dans les philosophies kantienne et néokantienne, qui mettaient notamment l'accent sur les concepts de « valeur » et de « personnalité ». Dans la « révolution copernicienne » opérée par la philosophie critique de Kant, la forme transcendantale

12. [NDT] 没価値性 (*botsukachisei)*) désigne la neutralité axiologique : l'auteur entend vraisemblablement traduire le terme allemand de *Wertfreiheit*, tout en limitant ici la compréhension à l'approche des sciences naturelles ; on rencontrera le terme de nouveau dans ce texte.

13. [NDT] 経済至上主義の唯物論 (*keizaïshijôshugi no yuibutsuron*) dit la primauté accordée aux considérations économiques notamment dans le matérialisme historique marxiste (quoique l'aspect *historique* ne soit pas dit comme tel, il s'agit par exemple du privilège absolu, « économiciste », donné à l'infrastructure sociale sur la « superstructure »).

de la subjectivité vient précéder la conscience de l'existence[14], tandis que, dans la philosophie néokantienne, elle est comprise comme *valeur*. Pour appliquer ce concept kantien fondamental à la science économique, Sôda invoque, d'une part, la monnaie pour étayer une conception de la valeur économique qui fait voir dans l'économie une manifestation de l'activité évaluatrice au sein de la société[15], et il voit, d'autre part, dans cette même économie le lieu de la réalisation de ces valeurs du monde de la culture, de la civilisation.

En outre, d'après l'impératif catégorique[16] de l'éthique kantienne, la personnalité n'est jamais seulement le moyen d'une fin, mais elle doit toujours être considérée comme un but en elle-même. Sôda redéfinit ce concept de personnalité comme l'entité qui possède la capacité de créer des valeurs, tandis que Sugimura devait voir cette personnalité comme la forme que prend la subjectivation de la valeur en société.

À la différence des philosophes Kitarô Nishida ou Tetsurô Watsuji, qui appuyèrent leur orientalisme sur le nationalisme, Sôda et Sugimura utilisèrent différemment pour leur part les idées de l'Occident en philosophie (sans pour autant se limiter à une simple importation), et ils accouchèrent ainsi de travaux dont les résultats obtinrent une reconnaissance internationale. Le néokantisme fut ainsi la première doctrine contemporaine à laquelle le monde philosophique japonais se confronta dans sa période embryonnaire, et cette confrontation active, Sôda la mena autant que Nishida[17].

Depuis les années 1970, la philosophie morale de John Rawls[18] a constitué un grand courant au sein de la philosophie économique contemporaine, en réhabilitant d'une certaine manière la tradition kantienne contre l'empirisme et l'utilitarisme anglo-saxons. Ne dit-on pas de la théorie de Rawls que c'est un « constructivisme kantien »,

14. [NDT] Shionoya utilise les termes 超越論的形式 (*chôetsuronteki keishiki*) pour « forme transcendantale » et 先験的 (*senkenteki*) pour « transcendantal » tandis que 存在の認識 (*sonzaï no ninshiki*) désigne la conscience de l'existence. Ces notions ont leur histoire propre dans le vocabulaire japonais influencé par la pensée allemande. À propos de la « subjectivité », il renvoie sans doute à l'unité originairement synthétique de l'aperception chez le sujet kantien.

15. [NDT] 評価社会 (*hyôkashakai*) signifie littéralement « société de l'évaluation ».

16. [NDT] 定言的命法 (*teigentekimeihô*) exprime le *kategorischer Imperativ* de la philosophie pratique de Kant.

17. [NDT] Voir l'introduction générale de ce numéro. Sôda et Sugimura méritaient autant de reconnaissance que Nishida et ils sont restés trop méconnus en raison d'un manque d'intérêt relatif pour la pensée économique dans les études sur le Japon menées en Occident, d'une part, et à cause de la fascination exercée par un certain « orientalisme », d'autre part.

18. (Rawls, 1971).

du fait qu'elle pose une « valeur » de nature transcendante et qu'elle traite de la « personnalité » morale ? Dans les champs éthique et épistémologique, le contexte de la recherche philosophique qui fut celui de Sôda et de Sugimura était de nature extrêmement moderne et universaliste. Leur tentative rapprochait en effet (et pour la première fois peut-être) la science économique et la pensée kantienne. Quant à la philosophie économique anglo-saxonne de nos jours, elle est dénuée de tout fondement dans quelque idéalisme que ce soit qui lui permettrait d'évaluer la diversité des courants de pensée au sein de l'économie. En outre, en ce qui concerne l'économie du bien-être[19], dominée par la tradition utilitariste anglo-saxonne, l'on n'y traite que de questions d'efficacité sociale et de rationalité en fonction de choix individuels, au lieu de développer de façon consistante les idées des droits, des devoirs et de la quête de l'excellence dans l'activité humaine. Il est de fait que le moteur le plus puissant de la philosophie économique de nos jours reste encore la tradition kantienne.

2. LA VALEUR DANS LE DOMAINE DE LA CULTURE SELON SÔDA

2.1. *Une philosophie économique de la valeur dans le domaine de la culture*

En un mot, les travaux de Sôda[20] établirent la philosophie économique sur l'idée de valeur dans le domaine de la culture[21] ; Sugimura va dans ce sens en examinant les travaux de son maître[22].

19. [NDT] 厚生経済学 (*kôsei keizaïgaku*) traduit le terme "*welfare economics*". Nous proposons de garder le terme français.

20. Les *Œuvres complètes de Kiichirô Sôda* en cinq volumes furent éditées à Tokyo chez la maison Iwanami, en 1931 par les soins de l'« Association pour la commémoration du Dr. Sôda ». [NDT] Toutes les œuvres japonaises sont citées dans la traduction française de leur titre en notes et avec les indications originales dans les références bibliographiques finales.

21. [NDT] 文化価値 (*bunka kachi*) désigne la (ou les) valeur(s) sur laquelle (lesquelles) une civilisation se fonde, le terme de « culture » étant à prendre au sens allemand large de la *Kultur*, par exemple du *Kulturkampf* de l'époque des écoles néo-kantiennes (quoique dans ce cas mâtiné d'une question religieuse ici absente). La valeur domine potentiellement le monde social tandis que le monde naturel ne se fonde pas sur des valeurs, mais sur des propriétés physico-chimiques.

22. Sugimura, Kôzô, chapitre « La philosophie économique » dans l'ouvrage dont le titre signifie « Philosophie économique de la valeur culturelle » (Sugimura 1933, édité sans indication de lieu mais assurément à Tokyo).

Généralement parlant, la philosophie idéaliste allemande comprend la vie comme le fait de « valeur(s) vivante(s) »[23], et les activités humaines comme les processus dont le développement vise à réaliser un (des) idéal(ux). En disciple de Heinrich Rickert, Sôda reprend cette idée de valeur dans le monde de la culture chez l'École dite « de Bade ». Concernant ces valeurs, Windelband et Rickert distinguaient parmi elles la valeur fondamentale, toute intérieure et rationnelle, et la valeur au sein du monde de la culture, la seconde étant la forme qui déploie le sens des activités qui tendent à objectiver la première d'une certaine manière déterminée. La première valeur se présente, par exemple, comme valeur religieuse (le sacré), comme valeur scientifique (la vérité), comme valeur morale (le bien) ou comme valeur esthétique (la beauté), tandis que la seconde doit être à son tour vue comme résultant de la dérivation de l'une ou de l'autre de ces valeurs du premier type. Autrement dit, les activités qui visent à réaliser une valeur de la première espèce constituent le monde de la culture – et c'est de là que l'idée a pu surgir d'une valeur dans le domaine de la culture.

De manière analogue, Sôda prenait en considération les activités et les événements humains au titre d'expressions de la vie des valeurs, à savoir comme des créations de la culture ; ce qui différenciait Sôda de ses maîtres allemands, c'est qu'il juxtaposait alors chacune de ces valeurs dans chacun de ces domaines culturels définis de la sorte sans pour autant vouloir favoriser aucune valeur particulière au titre d'un fondement général[24]. Pour lui, il existe une valeur différente dans chaque domaine, non seulement la religion, la science, l'éthique et l'art, mais aussi la politique, les sphères juridique, économique, technologique, comme dans le langage et dans l'éducation. Pour lui, cela n'a pas de sens de les hiérarchiser. Dans le champ de l'économie, si l'on comprend que c'est à tort que la plupart des gens regardent les activités économiques comme occupant un rang inférieur dans la hiérarchie des valeurs[25], parce qu'ils ne considèrent celles-ci que

23. [NDT] 価値生活 (*kachi seikatsu*) indique le rôle de sujet vital assigné aux valeurs comme telles, la « vie de la valeur ».

24. Voir Sôda, « Le système fondé sur la(les) valeur(s) » (Sôda 1931, vol. 4). [NDT] Le titre original 価値の体系 (*kachi no taïkeï*) ne permet pas de décider pour le singulier ou le pluriel.

25. [NDT] Il faut ici avoir à l'esprit le contexte traditionnel au Japon, les ordres d'une société où les producteurs, avant tout paysans et artisans, mais aussi marchands et commerçants, formaient des castes inférieures : voir l'introduction générale de ce numéro. Les « gens » évoqués sont naturellement les Japonais.

comme des moyens pour les hommes de continuer leur existence, alors la pensée de Sôda a constitué en son temps un « renversement des valeurs »[26], ce qu'a justement remarqué Sugimura – et cela fut un moment très significatif. En d'autres termes, Sôda entendait faire reposer la philosophie économique sur une valeur économico-culturelle dont il établissait la position au même niveau que toutes les autres valeurs. Avant Sôda, l'économie et la philosophie étaient considérées comme des disciplines de nature très différente et les gens ne pouvaient même pas imaginer traiter les questions économiques du point de vue de la philosophie.

Arrivés à ce point, il nous sera utile de fournir une définition de la philosophie économique telle que Sôda et Sugimura la comprenaient. Pour décrire la philosophie économique de manière systématique, Sugimura la divisa en trois sous-domaines, à savoir la « métaphysique économique », la « logique économique » et l'« éthique économique »[27]. La métaphysique économique consiste en une sorte d'ontologie des objets socio-économiques ; elle formule la vision qui doit saisir la signification inhérente aux phénomènes économiques – elle est l'équivalent chez Sugimura de ce que Sôda concevait comme sa doctrine de la valeur dans le domaine de la culture[28]. Les deux autres sous-domaines se fondent sur cette conception. La « logique économique » correspondrait assez, dans nos termes actuels, à la philosophie des sciences ou à l'épistémologie, puisqu'il s'agit d'y rechercher les processus de la démarche méthodologique et de formuler la logique qui est propre à la science économique ; selon Sugimura, il s'agit d'élucider cette logique comme le système épistémique du monde empirique, tout en assurant l'unification du sens immanent des phénomènes. En fait, il s'agit d'une philosophie morale rapportée au système économique. On pourrait considérer que la philosophie des sciences ou la philosophie morale pourraient subsister de manière autonome, mais selon nos deux économistes, elles restent inséparables d'une métaphysique économique. Les travaux de Sôda concernant la

26. [NDT] 価値の転倒 (*kachi no tentô*). Les références à la philosophie allemande sont évidemment ici riches et nombreuses. La question reviendra quand Shionoya évoque Schumpeter commentant Sôda.

27. (Sugimura 1944, 7). [NDT] 経済倫理学 (*keizaï rinrigaku*) désigne l'éthique économique.

28. [NDT] 文化価値主義 ((*bunka kachi shugi*) désigne la doctrine (*shugi* correspond à « -logie », « -isme »).

philosophie économique lui ont permis de développer autant une épistémologie de l'économie qu'une éthique économique sur la base du règne des valeurs dans le domaine de la culture, qui est bien conçu comme un système de métaphysique économique.

En suivant le chemin emprunté par Georg Simmel, Sôda allait placer au premier plan cette métaphysique qui interroge le sens et le but de l'économie en se situant à un niveau plus élevé de la science économique que la science empirique ; ensuite, il allait élaborer une épistémologie qui cherchait à expliciter les conditions de possibilité de la science économique au niveau le plus fondamental de cette science ; enfin, il allait pour terminer dénommer philosophie économique l'ensemble que formaient ces deux matières[29]. Il me semble qu'à ce moment-là, la métaphysique et la logique n'étaient plus vues comme séparées, et la tâche la plus importante que Sôda effectua consistait sans doute ainsi à poser la base épistémologique d'ensemble de la philosophie économique.

Compte tenu de ce que nous venons d'expliquer, nous pouvons maintenant examiner les trois problématiques majeures présentes chez Sôda, à savoir 1) la valeur dans le domaine de la culture comme ce que vise l'épistémologie ; 2) la valeur qui est créée par l'agent[30] comme source et fondement de la valeur dans le domaine de la culture ; 3) la valeur dans le monde de la culture vue comme concept ultime[31].

2.2. *La valeur dans le domaine de la culture comme visée de connaissance*

Il convient d'avoir une méthode scientifique pour ressaisir et comprendre le monde économique mais, comme la philosophie des sciences récente a pu le démontrer, la structure systématique des concepts logiques exige de toute manière de se fonder sur une conception du monde. Selon les termes mêmes de Joseph Schumpeter, l'intuition est la condition préalable à toute théorie, et

29. Voir Sôda, « La nature théorique des systèmes économiques » (Sôda 1931, 3, 33-5).

30. [NDT] 創造者価値 (*sôzôshakachi*) désigne la valeur de l'agent créatif considéré comme une personne.

31. [NDT] 極限概念 (*kyokugen gainen*) désigne l'idée d'un « extrême » au-delà duquel on ne peut aller, un *nec plus ultra*, concept que Sôda crée et que Shionoya explicite, ou une *ultima ratio*, le terme que Shionoya utilise pour son propre compte dans son autre texte traduit dans ce numéro.

cette intuition consiste elle-même dans une conception du monde[32]. Le positivisme et l'idéalisme, qui s'opposent comme cela a été indiqué plus haut, ont des conceptions du monde économique absolument différentes. Pour les positivistes anglo-saxons, peu importe les hypothèses que l'on forge, qu'elles soient arbitraires ou subjectives, car le monde économique qui résulte de la connaissance s'ordonne de toute manière selon des lois objectives ; on s'attend là que le monde s'ordonne selon de telles lois. La question posée y est donc de savoir comment découvrir les mécanismes d'après lesquels fonctionnent les objets de l'économie. En revanche, l'idéalisme allemand considère le monde comme conforme à des valeurs de la culture, à savoir que ce sont des sujets conscients qui conçoivent ces valeurs en connaissance de cause. On y voit l'économie comme l'activité spirituelle consciente qui consiste dans l'effort visant à réaliser de telles valeurs dans le monde de la culture au sein du monde économique. En accord avec cette conception, les sciences sociales en général visent donc moins à éclaircir des mécanismes à l'œuvre, à la différence des sciences de la nature qui traitent, quant à elles, des phénomènes naturels ; dans les sciences sociales, il est plutôt nécessaire de chercher quel rapport à des valeurs tend à réaliser celles-ci comme autant de visées que les activités originelles de la créativité humaine portent, en constituant de la sorte une culture de nature spirituelle ; ces mêmes sciences sociales doivent alors consister dans des enquêtes sur de telles valeurs qui portent ces objectifs. En conséquence, si l'on évoque le monde de l'économie dans l'idéalisme allemand, au lieu d'indiquer des mécanismes économiques que l'on érigerait en universels, l'on doit y exprimer la culture économique portée par un sens qui est, quant à lui, individualisé.

En abordant l'architectonique conceptuelle des sciences économiques depuis le point de vue de l'épistémologie kantienne, Sôda affirmait que ce n'est pas du désordre régnant au sein des disciplines empiriques qu'il convient pour nous d'attendre les indications sur ce qu'il faut sélectionner ou laisser de côté ; c'est, au contraire, une certaine idée innée initiale qui peut nous permettre de formuler une conception systématisée de la réalité. Or, la définition de cette idée initiale, qui doit prévaloir en économie au titre de but de la connaissance, dépendra de

32. [NDT] 世界観 (*sekaikan*) désigne la « vision du monde », la *Weltanschauung* de la pensée allemande.

la valeur (ou des valeurs) dans le domaine de la culture. La valeur dans le domaine de la culture constitue une norme ; la connaissance de la vie économique est rendue possible grâce à la relation entre cette norme et la science économique qui, à son tour, en s'adaptant à cette norme, devient praticable, elle aussi. Sôda choisit la monnaie comme un tel exemple d'idée initiale sélectionnée au sein des sciences économiques, car elle constitue une valeur de ce genre ; il considérait alors que l'on pouvait seulement traiter la valeur dans le domaine de la culture dans le champ économique par la relation qu'elle entretient avec l'idée de monnaie saisie comme sa marque caractéristique, son *Merkmal*[33]. Toutefois, comme Sugimura devait plus tard le signaler, la valeur dans le domaine de la culture restait seulement considérée comme une norme formelle, ce qui interdit d'en régler le contenu, de sorte que la relation entre l'idée de monnaie et la valeur dans le domaine de la culture en économie n'était guère abordée plus avant par Sôda, ce qui constituait incontestablement une lacune.

Ces réflexions conduisirent Sôda à reprendre sa problématique comparative entre sciences de la nature et sciences de la culture sur le modèle de Rickert. Selon la dichotomie que ce dernier avait formulée, les sciences de la nature reconnaissent les faits dans leur généralité et dans leur universalité en adoptant un point de vue axiologiquement neutre, tandis que les sciences de la culture reconnaissent les faits dans leur particularité et dans leur individualité en épousant un point de vue qui prend en considération les valeurs. Sôda allait affirmer, quant à lui, que les sciences économiques pouvaient choisir d'user de la méthode de généralisation tout en maintenant leur but épistémologique consistant à acquérir la connaissance de l'individualité historique comme objet visé par le savoir. Je considère, pour ma part, que le cœur de la réflexion consistait chez Sôda dans une critique de la méthode existentialiste[34], soit un point qui se situe au-delà de la différence qu'il pose entre sciences de la nature et sciences de la culture. Le cœur de son propos consiste à « identifier clairement le contenu inhérent à l'idée directrice

33. Voir Sôda, « La monnaie et la valeur » (Sôda 1931, vol. 2, *passim*). [NDT] En allemand dans le texte. Il s'agit de la reprise de ce terme dans les *Œuvres complètes* de *Geld und Wert* publié en 1909 en Allemagne. Rappelons ici que Shionoya fut un grand spécialiste de l'œuvre de Schumpeter

34. [NDT] Il ne s'agit évidemment pas de l'existentialisme de Kierkegaard ni de Sartre, mais cependant effectivement de questions d'ontologie ainsi que celle de la précédence de l'existence ou de l'essence des objets socio-économiques (Shionoya y revient plus loin).

d'une doctrine économique conceptuellement pure[35], et à constituer en outre, depuis le point de vue des idées (et pas depuis le point de vue réaliste[36] adopté habituellement jusqu'alors), tous les concepts économiques pris dans leur relation à leurs contenus initiaux »[37]. Ici, les termes opposés alors en usage étaient « réalisme » et « idéalisme » ; on les traduirait, dans la philosophie des sciences actuelle, par « réalisme » contre « instrumentalisme » (*realism vs. instrumentalism*)[38]. Bref, Sôda entendait signifier *grosso modo* que l'existence d'un concept n'était pas donnée par avance, mais que celui-ci constitue plutôt seulement un outil ou, mieux, une idée régulatrice à construire de manière idéale en fonction de l'objet que vise la connaissance comme but du savoir[39].

Dans cette perspective, Sôda s'orientait vers une philosophie économique dont la problématique partait du concept principal initiateur pour aller vers l'objet de connaissance visé ; sa motivation était d'éclaircir les fondements théoriques de sciences économiques indépendantes et autonomes. Il avait entamé ses recherches par les questions monétaires, en étudiant notamment la théorie de la monnaie dans le cadre de l'État formulée par Georg Friedrich Knapp[40] ; Sôda avait, quant à lui, recherché le fondement de la monnaie dans la dépendance à l'ordre légal, en d'autres termes dans sa dépendance au pouvoir étatique[41]. La vie économique une fois définie dans son rapport avec la monnaie, l'indépendance de la science économique comme telle n'est donc plus garantie. En outre, dans la théorie économique, où l'on considère en général les désirs de la population comme une prémisse, la fabrication et la distribution des biens qui satisfont ces désirs forment la matière de l'activité économique. Sôda

35. [NDT] 純理経済学 (*junri keizaïgaku*) désigne l'économie « pure », telle qu'on la trouve dans la *reine Wirstchafts-lehre* proposée notamment par le fondateur de l'école autrichienne, Carl Menger, dont le nom apparaît plus loin.

36. [NDT] 実在論 (*jitsuzaïron*) désigne le réalisme par opposition à l'idéalisme (観念論 *kannenron*) : voir note 4.

37. Voir Sôda, « L'épistémologie kantienne et la doctrine économique » (Sôda 1931, vol. 3).

38. [NDT] En anglais dans le texte.

39. [NDT] 認識目的 (*ninshikimokuteki*) indique l'objet dont on a conscience comme objet de connaissance.

40. [NDT] Le titre de l'ouvrage de Knapp est donné par Shionoya en japonais ; il s'agit de *Die staatliche Theorie des Geldes* (Knapp, 1905). Sôda publia l'article intitulé « Die neue Knappsche Geldtheorie und das Wesen des Geldes » [« La nouvelle théorie de l'argent de Knapp et l'essence de l'argent »] (Sôda 1907, 620-55).

41. Voir Sôda, « Monnaie et valeur » (Sôda 1931, vol. 2).

protestait contre la lacune d'échouer à prendre une conscience nette des motifs menant à la constitution de ces concepts, un manque qu'il dénommait la « doctrine psychologiste »[42].

Sôda s'orientait donc vers une philosophie économique qui permettrait de comprendre ce qui doit définir la nature fondamentale de la science économique. Et, comme je vais le montrer plus loin, vers la même époque, c'était Schumpeter qui portait un intérêt à ces sujets semblablement à son collègue japonais, et qui réfléchissait aux fondements des sciences économiques depuis un point de vue méthodologique, dans son premier ouvrage sur la nature essentielle et le contenu de l'économie politique théorique[43].

2.3. *La(les) valeur(s) créée(s) par l'agent comme sources de valeur dans le domaine de la culture*

Jusqu'ici, j'ai évoqué dans un premier temps les rapports entre certains aspects théoriques et l'intuition. Abordons maintenant, dans un second temps, un autre rapport, celui qui prévaut entre l'individu et la société. Sôda cherchait à cerner la(les) valeur(s) dans le domaine de la culture en examinant l'activité des créateurs de génie[44]. Comme nous l'avons vu précédemment, il considérait que la(es) « valeur(s) vivante(s) »[45] se manifestai(en)t à travers les activités humaines, y compris celles de la vie économique ; il voyait le concept de « création dans le domaine de la culture »[46] reposer au centre de cette vie des valeurs. Les activités humaines et les événements historiques prennent du sens et de la valeur en fonction de la création des valeurs tout au long de leur cours. Cette création dans le domaine de la culture revêt deux aspects, à savoir sa visée dans le monde de la culture et sa visée au sein des activités humaines. La première équivaut à « la valeur dans le

42. Voir Sôda, « La nature théorique des lois économiques » (Sôda 1931, vol. 3). [*NDT*] 心理主義 (*shinrishugi*) désigne le psychologisme comme une doctrine non théorique et non économique, donc à critiquer. Sôda retrouvait donc à son tour un débat illustré dès les débuts de la théorie économique autrichienne : voir (Campagnolo 2008). Cette question continue d'intéresser au Japon comme une version japonaise de cet article commandée en 2013 le prouva (Campagnolo et Matsuyama 2013).

43. Voir (Schumpeter 1908) [*NDT*] Références à l'édition japonaise dans le texte original de Shionoya (Schumpeter 1983-1984).

44. Voir Sôda, « Le système fondé sur la(les) valeur(s) » (Sôda 1931, vol. 4).

45. [NDT] Voir note 23.

46. [NDT] 文化創造 (*bunkasôzô*) désigne littéralement la « création de valeur » ; il s'agit naturellement d'un jeu sur le terme « valeurs » rendant inséparables leur(s) sens économique et culturel. La monnaie intervient comme une formation de base réalisatrice.

domaine de la culture » dont il a déjà été question, la seconde désigne « la valeur de l'agent créatif », ou la « valeur créée par l'agent ». Le fondement de la valeur dans le domaine de la culture en tant que but de la connaissance, comme il a été dit plus haut, suit de cette création de valeur par l'agent humain individuel. Selon Sôda, cette relation entre la valeur dans le domaine de la culture et la valeur de l'agent créatif rend alors manifeste la nature du rapport existant entre la société et l'individu. Dans les domaines divers où s'exerce l'activité en société, comme la science, l'art, l'éthique, la religion, l'éducation, la politique, l'économie et la technologie, etc., ce sont les activités créatives, que chaque individu porte en propre, qui ont valeur de création au titre de l'expression libre de la personnalité individuelle. Les résultats de ces créations s'incorporent alors au sein de la société, qui fonctionne grâce à cette coopération mutuelle, et ces résultats ont pour destin de réaliser alors autant de valeurs dans le domaine de la culture. Sôda soulignait le fait que ces deux ordres de valeurs ne concordent pas forcément dans la réalité ; il existe un progrès quasi parallèle entre eux, sans que le point de concordance n'apparaisse, sauf éventuellement à sa pointe ultime extrême[47].

Ce sont sans doute les influences du concept de la personnalité chez Kant et celles du romantisme allemand en général qui ont conduit Sôda à soulever la question du concept de la valeur engendrée par l'agent créatif. Si la personnalité constitue un but, chaque individu prend alors un sens important tout particulier, qu'aucune autre personnalité ne peut venir remplacer. Il serait judicieux de rappeler ici une différence subtile entre l'idée de Sôda et le concept de la personne morale kantienne qui se trouve chez Rawls : le concept de personnalité dans la théorie de la justice de ce dernier concerne une personnalité qui possède déjà un sens de la justice et du bien, tandis que le concept de personnalité chez Sôda (appelons-le « culturel ») est celui d'une personnalité qui tente de réaliser sa valeur dans le monde de la culture comme un but, aboutissement des efforts fournis par l'humanité entière au long de son histoire. La valeur dans le domaine de la culture reprend tout naturellement ces efforts tendus vers la réalisation de la justice et du bien ; dans le cadre d'un concept de personnalité au sein de ce monde la culture, il importe toutefois de parvenir à une

47. [NDT] Voir note 31 *supra :* il s'agit du même terme indiquant un point d'horizon extrême. L'idée est celle d'une concordance à l'horizon le plus éloigné, à l'image d'une convergence asymptotique très éloignée.

forme d'accomplissement, et pas juste de détenir quelque capacité toute simple. Rawls soulignait combien la formation de « la justice » l'emporte sur « le bien » ; pour Sôda, l'important est la formation d'un « bien commun » au genre humain en entier[48], grâce au déploiement de la « vertu ». C'est la manière dont Sôda orientait sa vision vers une problématique de la « création ».

Or tous les êtres humains ont la possibilité de participer à des activités créatives. Mais seule la personnalité vraiment créative défie l'ordre traditionnel pour se rebeller contre la(les) valeur(s) existante(s) au sein de la culture qui prédomine dans une société donnée. Sôda soulignait ce conflit entre la(les) valeurs dans le monde de la culture et la(les) valeur(s) de l'agent créatif ; il y voyait le conflit entre la société et l'individu. Selon lui, la société échoue toujours à apprécier le génie, qui se trouve de ce fait contraint de souffrir un destin tragique en supportant l'amertume d'une vie solitaire.

De manière analogue, Schumpeter, que j'ai déjà mentionné, soulignait le lien de dépendance réciproque entre chaque domaine social considéré en parallèle. Il nommait « dirigeant » le type de l'innovateur créatif dans chaque domaine, et il considérait que l'innovation que celui-ci portait orientait en effet l'activité conduisant à développer chaque domaine social[49]. C'est ainsi que la théorie du développement économique de Schumpeter traite l'innovation au sein de l'économie. En choisissant de regarder les gagnants plutôt que les perdants, Schumpeter disait que les effets créatifs de chaque individu prédominent pour la société dans son entier et qu'ils déterminent la direction que chaque époque va prendre. Il s'agirait là, chez Sôda, des cas où la valeur formée par l'agent créatif finit par l'emporter sur les valeurs déjà existantes dans le monde de la culture. Sôda voyait la relation entre société et individu dans ce rapport entre valeur créée par l'agent et valeur dans le monde de la culture, tandis que Schumpeter y voyait le rapport entre un état statique et une dynamique. Les deux économistes soulignaient chacun à sa manière ces aspects différents du même cadre.

48. [NDT] 共通善 (*kyôtsûzen*) désigne le concept de *bien commun* dans la philosophie classique.

49. Voir (Shionoya, 1995). [NDT] Pour les ouvrages de Shionoya, voir la présentation par G. Campagnolo.

2.4. *La valeur dans le domaine de la culture en tant que concept d'horizon extrême*

Abordons maintenant la problématique que Sôda traitait en employant le terme assez étrange de « concept d'horizon extrême »[50]. Concrètement, il concerne le rapport entre le *Sein* et le *Sollen*, c'est-à-dire entre ce qui est de fait et la valeur[51]. Généralement parlant, fait et valeur sont deux choses bien différentes, et il faut donc les distinguer nettement l'une de l'autre, notamment dans le champ scientifique. Néanmoins, ils ne peuvent pas exister sans avoir rapport l'un à l'autre. D'ailleurs, l'on a souvent tendance à considérer le fait comme quelque chose d'objectif, une base pour la connaissance, alors qu'en réalité, ce n'est point le cas. La vie sociale est l'objet des sciences sociales, pourtant elle n'a d'abord aucune forme qui lui soit spécifique ; il faut un observateur pour faire arbitrairement émerger un formalisme à partir de valeur(s) du monde de la culture afin de rendre connaissable cette vie sociale. C'est ainsi que, dans le champ de la connaissance, la valeur agit sur les faits. Quant à l'action pratique, le fait doit être évalué selon une valeur normative qui permette de juger en quoi il consiste en réalité. Si la première question concerne le rapport entre des valeurs, la seconde concerne les jugements de valeur.

On soutient généralement que les faits ne peuvent pas dériver des valeurs. Aussi sera-t-on tenté de regarder toute tentative d'opérer cette dérivation comme une erreur de type naturaliste. Pourtant, il n'existe de contenu propre, ni à la valeur, ni à la norme, tant qu'une existence posée par une expérience présente bien un contenu concret de cette sorte, qui peut servir de norme. Si l'on garde le *Sollen* à l'écart de toute réalité existante, alors il ne pourra jamais acquérir aucun contenu.

Il y a donc bien dépendance mutuelle entre le *Sein* et le *Sollen* et ils ne doivent être tenus ni dans une trop grande proximité, ni dans un trop grand éloignement. Si on les sépare, en pensant qu'ils existent simplement sans rapport mutuel, on n'aura guère alors besoin de ce « concept d'horizon extrême » compris au sens que lui donne Sôda. Quand le *Sein* persiste dans une direction donnée au sein de

50. Voir Sôda, « La valeur dans le monde de la culture en tant que concept d'horizon extrême » (Sôda 1931, vol. 3) [NDT] Voir n. 31 *supra*.

51. [NDT] Shionoya présente les notions de philosophie allemande d'être et de devoir-être avec les mots transcrits dans le syllabaire japonais *katakana*, réservé aux mots étrangers ; nous choisissons d'utiliser ces termes allemands notoires.

la réalité existante, on ne peut le rapprocher d'aucun but final ni d'aucune norme, car il n'est rien d'autre que ce qui est là, un *Sein*, et par conséquent il demeure définitivement dans cet écart. Pour passer du *Sein* au *Sollen*, il faut une impulsion qui donne un essor qui doit être formidable et, surtout, qui est indispensable. Mais si l'on recherche ce *Sein* sur un horizon infini, alors, à sa pointe extrême, l'on atteindra en fin de compte un *Sollen*. Autrement dit, on atteindra le *Sollen* seulement à l'horizon infini d'un *Sein*. Mais si on ne l'atteint qu'à travers un tel infini, cela signifie bien qu'on ne l'atteindra jamais. C'est pourtant ainsi que, par augmentation graduelle, le contenu de l'expérience que l'on fait de ce qui existe peut fournir un contenu qui préfigure sa forme ultime[52].

Il ne suffit pourtant pas d'accumuler des instances du *Sein*, car il faut au final effectuer un bond qui nous porte depuis ce *Sein* vers le *Sollen*. Le *Sein* n'existe pas non plus sans subir de contrainte. C'est donc qu'il y a plutôt d'abord un *Sollen*, qui conduit par la suite le *Sein* à se rapprocher de lui, du *Sollen*. Je fais ici l'hypothèse que le « concept d'horizon extrême » formulé par Sôda constituait sa propre manière de tenter d'appréhender ce genre de rapport en le neutralisant. La position prise par Sôda opposait de la sorte, d'un côté, les circonstances qui fournissent seulement une norme métaphysique pour des choses qui restent dépourvues de tout contenu et, d'un autre côté, les circonstances qui conduisent à supposer que le *Sein* se présente d'une manière naturaliste et qui disent que la norme se trouve reconduite à partir de là.

Néanmoins, pour exposer sa pensée, Sôda s'appuyait seulement sur des métaphores. Il donnait seulement des exemples du genre dont on jugera par la présentation suivante : [imaginez] un polygone régulier inscrit dans un cercle, à commencer par le triangle ; on peut augmenter le nombre de côtés à 4, 5, 6, ... et ainsi de suite, de sorte que ce polygone finit par devenir un cercle. Ou encore, il calculait les valeurs d'une série géométrique infinie convergente, par exemple une série de taux. Ce n'est qu'à l'aide de ce genre d'exemples que Sôda explicitait son « concept d'horizon extrême ».

Les réflexions philosophiques de Sôda restaient donc incomplètes, mais il se persuadait d'avoir résolu le problème par le seul usage

52. [NDT] les notions d'infini actuel (ou « infini en acte ») et d'infini potentiel (ou « infini en puissance ») ne sont pas présentées comme telles par Shionoya, sans doute car elles ne le sont pas chez Sôda, mais elles sont bien sûr impliquées.

de métaphores de ce type. En outre, de manière très concrète, il appliquait son idée de « concept d'horizon extrême » à l'économie en considérant que la valeur dans le monde de la culture en économie consistait précisément dans ce « concept d'horizon extrême » de la vie économique en tant que telle. Au final, ce que je viens de retracer ici, c'est ce qui constitua la trajectoire intellectuelle suivie par Sôda en traitant le concept de monnaie comme faisant intervenir en pratique la contrainte limitative empirique pesant sur la valeur dans le monde de la culture en économie.

3. LES RECHERCHES DE SUGIMURA EN PHILOSOPHIE ÉCONOMIQUE

En épistémologie de l'économie, Sugimura prêta attention tout particulièrement à la méthodologie des sciences économiques. Il le dit en ces termes lapidaires : « pas de recherche sans méthode »[53]. Il réalisa ses principaux travaux dans les domaines de la métaphysique et de l'éthique économiques. Son propos méthodologique reflétait effectivement sa conception métaphysique du monde. Sugimura refusait la position métaphysique et transcendante de l'école de Bade, qui inspirait Sôda, et il tenta de la compléter de manière empirique et substantielle à la fois. Aussi Sugimura s'intéressa-t-il au détail de ces mécanismes sociaux dont le but consistait à réaliser des valeurs. Il se plaça donc plutôt sous l'influence de l'école dite « de Marbourg », qui participait également du néokantisme. Pour évoquer Sugimura, nous traiterons les trois questions suivantes : 1) sa méthode dans les sciences économiques ; 2) le principe d'économicité, en tant que c'est un concept qui relève du monde des phénomènes[54] ; 3) son idéalisme social[55], une éthique sociale.

53. Voir (Sugimura 1935, 2).

54. [NDT] 経済性原理 (*keizaïsei genri*) peut se traduire par « logique économique », mais il est distinct de ce qui apparaissait chez Sôda. On pensera utilement à Max Weber qui évoque, à propos de l'*homo oeconomicus*, une *absolute Wirtschaftlichkeit* : il isole les motivations strictement *économiques*, il les abstrait comme motivations exclusives de l'agent doté de qualités spécifiques qui laissent percevoir un tout à partir des éléments divers d'une situation économique donnée. Weber recourt aux moyens les mieux appropriés pour atteindre ce but. C'est le sens qu'on peut donner à « principe d'économicité » ; si tel est bien le cas, il n'y a pas d'objection à utiliser ce terme quelque peu jargonnant.

55. [NDT] 社会理想主義 (*shakairisôshugi*). Le terme doit se comprendre dans l'attitude critique que Sugimura tendait à adopter dans la perspective d'une doctrine de l'idéal social – et à titre personnel quasiment rebelle contre les institutions.

3.1. *La méthode des sciences économiques*

Concernant le rapport entre individu et société, un sujet central dans les sciences sociales, Sugimura abordait en particulier l'opposition de deux points de vue majeurs venus en controverse[56], à savoir la construction « des différentielles en mathématiques » issue du newtonianisme, d'une part, et la construction des « développements limités usuels » tirée du leibnizianisme, d'autre part. Seulement en apparence tout d'abord, la première comprend chaque individu comme unité infinitésimale, alors que la seconde semble plutôt vouloir le ressaisir depuis l'intérieur, pour ainsi dire, en considérant chaque être comme étant d'une nature originellement créatrice. Les deux points de vue prônent une méthode atomistique sur le plan épistémologique mais alors que, dans la première construction, tout fait individuel quelqconque prend sens uniquement à l'occasion d'une action (sinon d'une rationalisation), dans la deuxième construction, l'entité considérée mérite un intérêt en soi avant tout, et c'est alors seulement ce qui rend possible de l'unifier organiquement, dans un cadre plus global.

Sugimura considérait que ces deux positions représentaient respectivement les courants de l'objectivisme occidental et du subjectivisme allemand[57], ou l'économie classique en confrontation avec l'école historique allemande, ou encore avec la position de Menger dans l'histoire de la science économique. Sugimura critiquait les ouvrages d'histoire de l'économie qui se contentaient de passer en revue ces doctrines, et il proposait, quant à lui, une histoire des méthodologies économiques qui visait à éclairer les points de vue de ces théories en économie[58]. Dans une autre histoire des doctrines économiques, c'est Schumpeter qui avait tenté de traiter de manière privilégiée l'aspect méthodologique[59] ; Sugimura pensait, quant à lui, que l'histoire des sciences devait s'en tenir à pratiquer la philosophie

56. Voir (Sugimura 1935, 93).

57. [NDT] L'opposition est bien ici entre les termes « occidental » et « allemand », le premier étant sans doute compris plus largement qu'« anglo-saxon », mais le recoupant très largement.

58. Voir (Sugimura 1938a).

59. Schumpeter, Josef Aloysius, *Epochen der Dogmen und Methodengeschichte*, Tübingen, J. C. B. Mohr, 1914. [NDT] Références à l'édition japonaise (Tokyo, Iwanami Shoten, 1980) en note du texte de Shionoya qui évoque aussi Sugimura citant l'histoire des doctrines économiques de Schumpeter (mais sans mentionner le mot « analyse » qui y figure).

des sciences ou encore la méthodologie des sciences – et cette idée-là est bien, elle, vraiment moderne. Au titre de principe constitutif dans l'histoire des doctrines économiques, Sugimura soulignait ce qu'il appelait une conception du monde prise selon la conscience économique[60]. Sugimura ne connaissait que les premiers travaux de Schumpeter concernant l'histoire des doctrines économiques. D'un côté, il les appréciait, mais, d'un autre côté, il allait s'opposer fermement à l'école de Schumpeter comme aux points de vue concernant les conceptions du monde qu'elle devait diffuser[61]. Les arguments que Sugimura avançait à ce propos anticipaient certaines critiques à venir contre la philosophie des sciences née de l'empirisme logique. Toutefois, les recherches ultérieures de Schumpeter portant sur l'histoire des doctrines économiques montrèrent en nombre que son point de vue était plus vaste que ce que Sugimura s'en était figuré, de sorte qu'elles recouvraient aussi largement toutes les problématiques suggérées par Sugimura.

3.2. *Le principe d'économicité comme conception du monde*

Dans sa thèse de doctorat[62], Sugimura avait tenté de fonder la philosophie économique sur la base d'un principe d'économicité dont le but était de manifester une conception du monde permettant d'appréhender l'économie pour la comprendre – bref, une métaphysique économique[63]. À la différence des phénomènes naturels qui ont une régularité inhérente, le principe d'économicité devait expliquer quelle rationalité spirituelle gît au fondement des pratiques humaines. Pour ce faire, le principe d'économicité de Sugimura se conçoit comme une

60. [NDT] 経済学意識における世界観 (*keizaïgaku ishiki ni okeru sekaïkan*) désignerait une *Weltanschauung* considérée selon la conscience que l'on prend de la science économique. Voir note 32.

61. [NDT] Shionoya considère ici comme allant de soi qu'il existe une telle école schumpétérienne qu'il nomme explicitement dans le syllabaire *katakana* (シュンペーターの学派 *Shumpetâ-gakuha*) mais dont il n'explicite pas les « conceptions du monde », comme si, là encore, il allait de soi que le lecteur les reconnaîtrait. On peut penser à la triade « capitalisme, socialisme, démocratie » comme à la notion de « création destructrice » ; on verra plus loin que le rôle de l'entrepreneur innovateur, déjà apparu à propos de Sôda, réapparaît chez Sugimura.

62. [NDT] La thèse de Sugimura, intitulée *Recherches sur la théorie de la valeur dans la société économique* ne fut pas approuvée en tant que thèse, ce qui provoqua un grand scandale qui ébranla l'institution : voir la présentation du dossier.

63. Sugimura, « Le principe d'économicité », *Problèmes fondamentaux de philosophie économique*, *op. cit.* [NDT] Le mémoire évoqué a donné lieu à ce qui constitue un chapitre du livre indiqué.

interprétation du principe de l'utilité marginale de Carl Menger[64]. Cela signifie qu'il appartient, à sa manière, au courant du subjectivisme de langue allemande.

Sugimura n'appréciait en effet guère le classicisme britannique, qui tentait de retenir les apparences d'un ordre économique superficiel depuis un point de vue positiviste ; au contraire, il appréciait énormément Menger et l'école autrichienne, où l'on recherchait le sens même de l'économie pour comprendre véritablement de l'intérieur les pratiques économiques de l'agent comme être humain, dans leur principe même[65]. La théorie de Menger a souvent été prise pour un psychologisme, pour la raison que c'est une doctrine de la valeur subjective[66], mais Sugimura s'opposait à cette vision tendancieuse et il déniait cette interprétation ; en effet, il considérait le principe d'économicité comme devant exprimer en fait un universel historique et philosophique, qui outrepasse la subjectivité individuelle[67]. Si la matérialisation du principe d'économicité se situe bien dans l'économie monétaire[68], c'est que l'évaluation subjective de la valeur y est objectivée par le truchement de la monnaie, manifestant ainsi l'activité d'évaluation qui trouve par là même à s'instancier dans la société. Ainsi l'activité économique se constitue-t-elle selon des ordres rationnels qui rendent les valeurs commensurables[69]. Au sein du mécanisme monétaire, la justice ne réside pas seulement dans ce caractère monétaire de l'économie, mais dans le fait qu'il s'agit de traiter là de l'économie même en tant que telle. De la sorte, Sugimura définissait son principe d'économicité comme un principe objectif qui devait dominer l'ensemble de l'économie. De nos jours, cette

64. [NDT] 限界効用原理 (*genkaï kôyô genri*) désigne littéralement la théorie de l'utilité marginale.

65. [NDT] 人間の内面的な経済的実践の原理 (*ningen no naïmentekina keizaïteki jissen no genri*) désigne les principes des activités économiques pratiques saisies de l'intérieur, *subjectivement*, ce qui donne lieu à une interprétation qui oppose en termes exactement antagoniques l'approche dite « autrichienne » à celle des économistes britanniques.

66. [NDT] 主観価値学説 (*shukan kachi gakusetsu*) désigne littéralement la théorie de la valeur subjective.

67. [NDT] 歴史哲学的普遍性 (*rekishi tetsugakuteki fuhensei*) désigne un universel à la fois philosophique et historique. Voir *supra*, n. 42.

68. [NDT] 貨幣経済 (*kahei keizai*) désigne l'économie monétaire (à partir du sens de la monnaie matérielle) et renvoie chez Sugimura aux termes mêmes du vocabulaire employé par Sôda.

69. [NDT] 価値通約性 (*kachi tsûyakusei*) désigne la mesure commune en termes de valeur, quasi au sens aristotélicien.

interprétation n'est point si étrange qu'il y paraît, et elle nous semble au contraire toute naturelle[70]. En d'autres termes, entre le désir qui tenaille et les ressources pour le satisfaire, l'économie se trouve dominée par la rareté et la distribution efficace des ressources constitue ainsi le principe fondamental de l'économie – c'est bien là tout ce que l'on peut lire aujourd'hui dans nos manuels de sciences économiques, alors qu'il est certain que ce sont à l'origine des concepts issus de l'école autrichienne.

Comme il a été mentionné plus haut, Sugimura critiquait Sôda parce que, selon lui, Sôda avait échoué à lier d'une manière intrinsèque la valeur dans le monde de la culture en économie avec la monnaie. Sugimura considérait que le principe de l'utilité marginale relevait intrinsèquement de la valorisation des biens par des agents multiples, et que son extériorisation apparente passait ainsi par l'évaluation monétaire. C'est ainsi que le concept de la valeur dans le monde de la culture en économie pouvait s'incorporer une théorie conçue à son instar selon un principe d'immanence, à savoir précisément ce principe d'économicité, et c'est ainsi que ce principe se rattachait à son tour spécifiquement à son extériorisation caractéristique, ce qu'il appelait alors son concept de la monnaie[71].

3.3. *L'idéalisme social comme éthique sociale*

Contrairement à la doctrine de la valeur dans le monde de la culture chez Sôda, influencé en cela par Rickert, l'éthique économique[72] de Sugimura mériterait vraiment qu'on l'appelle un « idéalisme social »[73]. Sugimura suivait en cela les idées de Natorp et de l'école de Marbourg. Pour Sugimura, la doctrine de la valeur dans le monde de la culture évoquait encore seulement un idéal de culture[74] car elle ne tenait pas compte des contraintes sociales effectives. En outre, il considérait que

70. [NDT] Ceci, au regard de l'importance que les mécanismes de la sphère financière ont prise, naturellement : Shionoya reprend les termes de Sugimura comme 貨幣機構 (*kahei kikô*) qui désignent la structure et le mécanisme monétaires.

71. [NDT] 貨幣概念 (*kahei gaïnen*) désigne le concept de monnaie dans sa généralité, mais recouvre les aspects précités.

72. [NDT] 経済倫理学 (*keizaï rinrigaku*) désigne l'éthique économique directement empruntée aux considérations néo-kantiennes sur la *Wirtschaftsethik*, en particulier chez Rickert. Voir *supra*, n. 27.

73. [NDT] Voir *supra*, n. 55.

74. [NDT] 文化理想 (*bunka risô*) désigne un idéal dans le cadre des valeurs de la culture envisagée « formellement ».

la valeur dans le monde de la culture, à force d'insister sur le sujet de la personnalité au sens de Kant, ne cherchait plus à savoir au sein de quel contexte ou dans quel mécanisme celle-ci peut se réaliser. Sugimura voulait envisager un mécanisme social capable de réaliser le concept kantien de la personnalité humaine. Au sens où l'on pourrait unifier l'idée régulatrice et la socialisation, on pourrait appeler à juste titre « idéalisme social » cette pensée qui guidait ainsi l'idéal d'une éthique économique chez Sugimura[75].

En conséquence, Sugimura critiquait tout à la fois les tendances poussant à l'abstraction comme celles qui tendaient à un universalisme qui excluait l'orientation personnaliste qui le précédait, sans pour cela établir de rapport ni avec l'économie ni avec les structures institutionnelles. Sugimura introduisait en revanche du lien social dans le but de poser la question suivante : quelle éthique domine la société, si on comprend celle-ci au sens où elle forme une communauté ? En un sens, c'était bien là un point d'aboutissement des réflexions de Sôda puisqu'il avait juxtaposé, quant à lui, les valeurs issues de diverses formes d'activité sociale sur un seul et même plan. Au lieu de parler de valeurs éthiques de façon abstraite, tout en ignorant de ce fait chaque domaine concret au sein de la société, et en prenant soin d'éviter d'appliquer ces valeurs à la vie économique (comme si elle émanait d'un ordre supérieur[76]) ; en les plaçant sur le même plan que chaque domaine concret du social, il était possible de commencer ainsi à questionner pour de bon la personnalité éthique, dans le but de lui demander compte de la manière dont elle se constituerait dans le contexte social, bref en quoi pouvait bien consister une éthique immanente à l'économie elle-même. En d'autres termes, pour Sugimura, il s'agissait d'« adapter l'éthique au lieu-contextuel »[77]. La personnalité se trouve régulée par de tels « lieux sociaux » divers. Il ne suffit donc pas d'évoquer à ce propos tel lieu abstrait seulement, par définition délimité, mais Sugimura allait jusqu'à affirmer que

75. Voir (Sugimura 1938b).

76. [NDT] L'énoncé 天降り的に適用するのでなく (*amakudari ni tekiyô suru denaku*) indique le refus de l'application de tout ordre supérieur (ou quasi-« divin » quoique ce soit ici sans référence au dieu personnel chrétien, mais au « ciel »).

77. [NDT] 場の倫理 (*ba no ronri*) désigne une « doctrine du lieu » où la notion de « *ba* », au sens du « lieu », a une longue histoire comme notion essentielle qui rapproche la pensée japonaise de la phénoménologie, dont on ne saurait ici développer l'analyse : voir notamment (Berque 2000). Sugimura inscrit la philosophie économique dans l'horizon de la philosophie générale (japonaise et mondiale) à une place qu'il entend revendiquer pour elle.

la rationalité économique, ou l'économicité[78], constitue l'éthique économique même – c'est-à-dire qu'il considérait que son principe de l'économicité, dans le sens qu'il acquiert au regard de l'« économie » de l'époque moderne, n'est en somme rien d'autre que l'éthique économique même.

En contraste avec Sôda, Sugimura abonda dans un sens réaliste et il traita de sujets majeurs pour la science économique en tant que telle. Il semble toutefois qu'il manquait à ses réflexions d'établir une correspondance stricte entre sa conception du monde et son éthique sociale. Dans sa conception du monde, le point de vue pris pour l'enquête a le sens d'une économie fondée sur la rareté, ou sur un concept d'efficacité ou de rationalité économique, à son tour appuyé sur l'idée de rareté. Il s'agit bien là de la perspective économique que l'on peut appeler « principe d'économicité » en utilisant les propres termes de Sugimura. Mais lorsque celui-ci pose comme autant de sujets éthiques et sociaux des questions concernant l'éthique du capitalisme dans les temps modernes, ou l'éthique d'un régime qui serait à venir après le régime capitaliste, les idées d'« égalité » ou de « droits de l'homme » paraissent seulement traitées comme des questions d'éthique sociale[79].

En conséquence, Sugimura soulignait que l'éthique économique du capitalisme consiste bien dans l'efficacité dont il témoigne dans certaines de ses phases, mais une tendance vers le socialisme fait son apparition chez lui aussi, au moins à titre de catégorie de pensée : Sugimura finit par affirmer que le socialisme ferait partie de l'éthique sociale. Cette position se rattache à ses recherches sur la théorie de la justice ainsi que sur l'idée d'un État-providence, dont l'on ne peut pourtant pas examiner l'éthique sociale uniquement à travers la conceptualité du « principe d'économicité » – la raison en étant que l'efficacité économique ne conduit pas forcément à l'« égalité », ni à la « justice ». C'est donc en prenant en considération l'intérêt humain spirituel au seul titre de bons sentiments[80] que Sugimura traitait de l'éthique sociale et des questions concernant le socialisme ou l'État-

78. [NDT] Voir *supra*, n. 54.

79. [NDT] Les lacunes dans les réflexions de Sugimura notées par Shionoya apparaissent une seule fois dans ce texte faisant voir que ces notions, pourtant essentielles s'il en est, ne sont pas thématisées (et les termes japonais sont ceux de l'usage le plus général, de sorte qu'on ne peut guère rien en tirer ici sur la manière dont la pensée japonaise les aborde).

80. [NDT] 心情的 (*shinjûteki*) renvoie aux sentiments, au « cœur ».

providence – il lui manquait un concept philosophique fondamental de mise en relation au monde qui aurait pu faire qu'il donnât un développement suffisant à ces sujets à leur tour.

4. L'IDÉALISME ALLEMAND ET SCHUMPETER

Il a déjà été question de Schumpeter à plusieurs reprises dans cet essai. Cet auteur dépasse de loin toutes les dimensions que portent les orientations du *mainstream* des sciences économiques de nos jours – mieux, on pourrait considérer le fait même qu'il a existé comme portant un témoignage critique contre l'économie contemporaine. Sous l'apparence d'un des principaux chefs de file du positivisme, Schumpeter devait en réalité la plus grande partie de ses réflexions à l'idéalisme de langue allemande. Pour évoquer Sôda et Sugimura, nous avons eu intérêt à citer Schumpeter, non seulement en raison des affinités électives entre ces auteurs, mais aussi pour les différences que l'on ne peut pas, quoi qu'il en soit, ignorer. Si de multiples travaux de Schumpeter connaissent un regain d'intérêt de nos jours, il convient alors de faire retour sur les travaux de Sôda et de Sugimura aussi, car ils partageaient la même conscience que Schumpeter des enjeux du sens à donner à l'économie, et d'autant plus même qu'ils étaient différents de lui.

Sôda fut contemporain de Schumpeter (1883-1950), il avait deux ans de plus que lui. Ils vécurent tous les deux leur jeunesse à une époque où le monde scientifique de langue allemande était à son apogée dans les sciences économiques. C'est dans ce cadre qu'ils débutèrent tous deux par réfléchir sur les fondements de l'économie en tant que science et qu'ils initièrent leurs recherches par des travaux en épistémologie de l'économie. Pour Schumpeter, le résultat fut en 1908 son livre *Das Wesen und der Hauptinhalt der theoretischen Nationalökonomie*. On n'a pas la certitude que Sôda ait eu connaissance de cet ouvrage, mais il est assuré en revanche que Schumpeter avait lu *Geld und Wert* (1909) de son contemporain japonais, puisqu'il en donna une recension dans la revue *Zeitschrift für Volkswirtschaft* de l'université de Vienne (pendant quelques années, Schumpeter écrivit pour cette revue une dizaine de recensions d'ouvrages qui venaient de paraître). Cette recension de ce *Monnaie et valeur* de Sôda fut publiée en 1911 ; c'était plutôt une notice assez courte (à peine une vingtaine de lignes) si on la compare aux notices sur les ouvrages d'autres spécialistes mieux connus. *Geld und Wert* était la thèse de doctorat soutenue par Sôda à l'université de Tübingen ; le texte demeura méconnu à l'époque. Il est loisible de citer ici la recension en entier :

> Il est bien rare de voir un travail aussi massif paraître. Cette thèse contient des réflexions très éminentes. Quoique l'auteur se montre un peu unilatéral, il démontre au fil du texte non seulement une conscience économique et philosophique aiguë, mais encore une perspicacité qui vise juste et un don pour la théorie qui méritent la plus grande admiration. Gageons que cet ouvrage deviendra un classique. Il n'a rien à voir avec d'autres de ces livres médiocres sur la théorie monétaire récemment parus en Allemagne. Lui traite pour l'essentiel des phénomènes monétaires, usant pour ce faire sans doute de plus de termes philosophiques qu'il n'est nécessaire, surtout quand il s'appuie sur la théorie de la valeur au sens du psychologisme[81]. Pour autant, dans leurs grandes lignes, ses arguments sont à peu près justes en ce qui concerne la valeur monétaire. L'auteur critique la théorie de l'État chez Knapp, il lui réplique avec justesse. Néanmoins, on remarquera quelques points négatifs sur des questions très controversées : premièrement, il emploie un concept de valeur sociale qui n'a rien à voir avec les faits économiques, et qu'on ne peut pas utiliser en pratique ; deuxièmement, il est entré dans des passages bien spéculatifs pour une introduction de nature sociologique dans son ouvrage[82].

Dans cette recension, il est clair que Schumpeter s'oppose en économiste à toute philosophie spéculative. Au contraire de Sôda et de Sugimura, il soutenait en effet un point de vue positiviste et antimétaphysique. Cependant, Schumpeter ne se contentait certainement pas d'en rester au seul fonds commun du positivisme, puisqu'il traitait lui-même également de problématiques plus larges. C'est sur ce point que l'on trouvera une communauté de pensée entre lui et les économistes japonais évoqués dans cet essai.

On pourrait encore expliquer les idées de Sôda, telles que Schumpeter les voit, comme nous l'allons faire brièvement ici.

81. [NDT] 心理主義的価値論理 (*shinrishûgiteki kachironri*) désigne une interprétation psychologisante de la théorie de l'utilité marginale. Ces interprétations faisaient florès, et le sujet s'inscrivait donc dans un courant majeur de la pensée à l'époque (voir Campagnolo et Matsuyama 2013).

82. Recension publiée par Schumpeter (Schumpeter 1911, 245). [NDT] Traduction de la version japonaise, vérifiée (par G. Campagnolo) sur le texte allemand original.

Premièrement, le « renversement des valeurs »[83] qu'opérait Sôda consistait à juxtaposer diverses valeurs culturelles sur un même plan, sans chercher à établir de hiérarchie entre elles ; Schumpeter, quant à lui, prenait en considération les rapports réciproques entre les domaines sociaux, à savoir l'économie, la politique, le droit, l'art, l'éthique, et les sciences. Sur ce point, Schumpeter refusait toute hiérarchie unilatérale entre le domaine économique et les autres domaines, ce que le matérialisme historique faisait au contraire abondamment de son côté. Mais Schumpeter appelait « développement culturel et social »[84] l'ensemble des processus graduels suivis au sein de ces domaines variés, et il pensait sa propre science sociale de manière globale dans le but d'appréhender ce développement[85].

Deuxièmement, toujours selon Schumpeter, cette division même de la société en plusieurs sphères n'est en fait qu'une opération de transformation qui résulte de l'application arbitraire par des scientifiques des conceptions qu'ils ont fondées sur un formalisme qui leur est inhérent[86]. À ce sujet, les deux économistes adoptaient une philosophie instrumentaliste de la science. Tandis que Sôda voyait la valeur dans le monde de la culture en tant que but de la connaissance, Schumpeter considérait qu'une vision préalable était indispensable pour en fournir quelque théorie que ce fût. La différence entre eux tenait alors au contenu même de la prémisse instrumentaliste. Chez Schumpeter, il s'agissait de l'idée d'un équilibre dans l'ordre économique[87], tandis que chez Sôda, c'était bien la valeur dans le monde de la culture en économie, telle que nous l'avons vue. Sur ce point, l'opposition est assez claire entre le positivisme, d'après lequel l'économie est un mécanisme qu'accompagne l'édification de divers ordres juridiques, et l'idéalisme, qui comprend l'économie comme une

83. [NDT] 価値の転倒 (*kachi no tentô*) : voir *supra*, n. 26.

84. [NDT] C'est ici une référence à la théorie du développement chez Schumpeter (*Theorie der wirtschaftlichen Entwicklung*). La dimension culturelle y est soulignée par Shionoya.

85. Voir (Shionoya 1995, chap. 3).

86. [NDT] 先天的な形式 (*sententekina keishiki*) désigne un formalisme « inné », littéralement « congénital » à l'opération scientifique, ce qui distingue cette dernière du formalisme transcendantal : voir *supra*, n. 14.

87. [NDT] 経済的均衡秩序 (*keizaïteki kinkô chitsujo*) désigne l'ordre qui accompagne un équilibre de type économique, soit, en contexte de théorie marginale, les théories de l'équilibre partiel et général, qui ne sont toutefois pas nommées.

activité spirituelle suscitée par la valeur dominante dans le monde de la culture.

Troisièmement, quant au schéma qui définit comment chaque domaine social se développe, la conception de l'entrepreneur innovant chez Schumpeter[88] et celle du dirigeant créatif chez Sôda finissent toutefois par concorder. L'économiste japonais recherchait le motif de la valeur dans le monde de la culture sous le genre de la créativité individuelle en action, comme dans la réalisation de soi de la personnalité[89]. La conception que Schumpeter a de l'essor et des fluctuations économiques impliqués par l'innovation se retrouvait chez Sôda, même si Schumpeter n'avançait pas, quant à lui, ce concept-là de valeur.

Un quatrième point concerne, pour finir, l'interprétation à donner de la pensée de Menger. On a dit que Sugimura voyait le principe d'économicité chez Menger comme le point le plus avancé dans le développement des contenus essentiels de l'historicisme allemand, qui se dirigeait selon lui vers un universalisme historique et philosophique, et Sugimura faisait en conséquence état des points de convergence entre l'école autrichienne et l'historicisme allemand. Que l'on approuve ou non cette interprétation[90], toujours est-il de fait que Schumpeter, issu de l'école autrichienne, montrait de l'intérêt pour la perspective des auteurs historicistes en particulier – j'attire, quant à moi, l'attention sur le fait que Schumpeter reprenait deux de leurs points de vue, l'un concernant le développement historique, l'autre d'après lequel les domaines de la vie sociale sont inséparablement liés, de sorte qu'ils finissent en fait par s'agencer dans une cohésion globale. Et de fait, unifier ces deux perspectives peut conduire à l'idée de ce « développement culturel et social » évoqué plus haut. L'idéalisme de langue allemande, dont l'historicisme fit partie, s'intéressait forcément à ces aspects du développement global des sociétés, une question que, par principe, ne pouvait pas résoudre l'approche positiviste, puisqu'elle séparait par hypothèse l'étude spécifique de chaque domaine du monde

88. [NDT] 創造的指導者の概念 (*sôzôteki shidôsha no gaïnen*) désigne le concept de l'esprit innovateur et créatif du leader, (du *Leiter* ou du *Führer* en allemand) qui correspond bien à l'entrepreneur selon Schumpeter.

89. [NDT] 人格の自己実現 (*jinkaku no jikoshitsugen*) désigne la « réalisation de soi » (*self-realization*).

90. [NDT] Voir plus haut les passages sur la lecture que Sugimura donne de Menger.

social. Pour traiter la problématique générale immense que soulevait l'idéalisme, Schumpeter tentait, tout en se dotant d'une méthode positiviste, de franchir ces limites inhérentes à ce même positivisme. Ce fut dans le cadre d'une tentative similaire qu'il rencontrait Sôda et Sugimura, les acteurs majeurs de ce type d'idéalisme au Japon.

5. EN GUISE DE CONCLUSION : COMMENTAIRES ET APPRÉCIATIONS

Nous l'avons dit : la philosophie économique se construit pour nous selon trois domaines distincts, à savoir la métaphysique, la méthodologie, et l'éthique économique. Concernant la méthodologie, j'ai moi-même travaillé dans le passé sur l'analogie qui existe entre la méthode de Weber (son « idéal-type »), qui vient tout droit du néokantisme de Rickert, et celle de Schumpeter (son « instrumentalisme »), qui provient de son côté du positivisme présent chez le Mach de la première période[91]. Si nous essayons maintenant d'introduire la valeur dans le monde de la culture telle que le voit Sôda, nous pourrons conclure ce qui suit : tout en appartenant à la lignée de Rickert, Sôda élaborait la notion de valeur dans le monde de la culture en lui appliquant sa théorie de la personnalité, et il s'appuyait pour ce faire sur sa conception du dirigeant créatif, dans la vision très concrète qu'en avait également Schumpeter. Cela veut dire que la méthodologie de Sôda ne se bornait pas à énoncer tout bonnement une méthodologie. Qu'est-ce que je veux dire par là ? Ceci : l'approche que Sôda donna de la valeur dans le monde de la culture était elle-même *a priori* d'une nature métaphysique ; toutefois, il lui fallait bien déterminer le contenu de cette valeur dans le monde de la culture comme un « *a posteriori* » et, pour Sôda, c'est là que se situait en quelque sorte le « point d'Archimède » de ses recherches en sciences sociales. Tout en explicitant, d'un côté, la base épistémique de chacune des sciences sociales, il tentait, d'un autre côté, d'établir une éthique de la création dans le monde de la culture[92], en donnant pour

91. Voir (Shionoya 1995, chap. 8). [NDT] Il s'agit d'une référence à Ernst Mach, père viennois de l'« empirio-criticisme » que Shionoya a étudié, moins sous cette facette de son œuvre que sous celle citée ici, qui la précédait.

92. [NDT] Voir *supra*, n. 46.

ce faire un statut de vérité intrinsèque[93] au concept de personnalité. Bref, les trois domaines de la philosophie économique se trouvaient pour lui très étroitement liés.

On ne devrait donc comprendre l'éthique de Sôda ni comme un contractualisme social[94], ni comme un utilitarisme, mais bien comme une doctrine éthique de la vertu[95]. Le principe initial relatif à cette vertu est un perfectionnisme. De même que Rawls accoucha d'une théorie de la justice qui pouvait s'inscrire dans la lignée de la tradition kantienne, Sôda introduisait sa doctrine de la valeur dans le monde de la culture des auteurs kantiens ou des penseurs néokantiens, en l'interprétant comme un perfectionnisme. Si je puis me permettre un mot supplémentaire, la conception de l'entrepreneur comme agent créateur chez Schumpeter n'explique pas seulement non plus le mouvement de l'économie, mais elle peut encore être comprise comme une téléologie, qui sert alors à justifier la réalisation d'un développement perfectionniste dans les domaines variés où l'humanité déploie ses activités.

En outre, en suivant son principe d'économicité, Sugimura donnait, quant à lui, une interprétation de Menger[96], excellente en comparaison des autres travaux, postérieurs à la Deuxième Guerre mondiale, sur le même sujet. On se borne à interpréter d'habitude la théorie de Menger comme une théorie de la valeur subjective, de laquelle on pourra toujours faire usage pour déterminer les prix, mais Sugimura voyait la chose de la manière suivante : en partant de la théorie transcendantale de Kant, il voyait dans la théorie mengérienne un principe de construction des notions adaptées au monde de la vie économique en général, et il regardait ce principe comme étant à la fois universel, philosophique et historique, et outrepassant en cela toute subjectivité

93. [NDT] 内実 (*naijitsu*) désigne la vérité profonde « intérieure », qui existe en réalité sous les apparences.

94. [NDT] 社会契約主義 (*shakaï keiyakushugi*) désigne une doctrine mettant en avant le contrat en société. La référence aux multiples théories occidentales sur le sujet demeure, sans doute sciemment, passablement vague.

95. [NDT] 徳の倫理学 (*toku no rinrigaku*) désigne une « doctrine de la vertu » dont l'écho kantien est évident (c'est la *Tugendslehre*). De même 卓越主義 (*taku-etsu shugi*) renvoie à une doctrine de la perfection (sans nécessairement intégrer l'idée d'un progrès, mais sans l'exclure d'emblée pour autant).

96. [NDT] Shionoya fait référence avec Menger à (Sugimura 1926). Voir (Campagnolo 2004, 224).

individuelle ; c'est ce qu'il appelait son « principe d'économicité » et c'est ce qu'il donnait comme base à la philosophie économique en son entier. Pour Sugimura, le « principe d'économicité » devait constituer le principe immanent[97] que l'école historique allemande avait dû en quelque sorte posséder au fond de son approche organiciste. Sugimura considérait que Menger avait au fond tenté d'éclaircir le sens inhérent à une question qui était à la fois historique et philosophique et que les idées de l'école historique allemande comportaient. Certes, l'école historique allemande avait échoué en pratique à élucider la question du progrès économique dans ses régularités apparentes, mais Sugimura considérait que, dans le cadre de la « querelle sur les méthodes » qui avait opposé Menger et l'école historique allemande, celui-ci avait en somme mis en demeure celle-là d'effectuer un retour indispensable à son principe fondamental intrinsèque[98].

Pour Sugimura, cette découverte du « principe d'économicité » signifia qu'il parvenait à sa propre doctrine d'une conception du monde économique[99], tandis que, chez Weber, par exemple, dont la vision de la société était pourtant plus large que celle de Sugimura, ce qui devrait correspondre au « principe d'économicité » consistait dans la conception même de la « rationalité »[100]. On voit que se forme là une analogie entre, d'une part, le rapport existant entre « la valeur dans le monde de la culture » chez Sôda et l'idée du « dirigeant créatif » et, d'autre part, la relation à voir entre « le principe d'économicité » chez Sugimura et la « rationalité » selon Weber. Concernant économie et société[101], tous étaient partis en quête de ce principe intrinsèque auquel le subjectivisme de langue allemande tentait de donner une forme à sa manière.

97. [NDT] 内在的原理 (*naïzaïteki genri*) désigne un principe d'existence intrinsèque, une immanence incontournable.

98. [NDT] Shionoya évoque la « querelle sur les méthodes » (*Methodenstreit*) des années 1880 qui opposa Menger tout particulièrement au chef de file de l'école historique allemande, Gustav von Schmoller. La polémique donna lieu à des échanges acerbes et à des écrits essentiels pour la méthodologie économique. Il faut citer ici pour le lecteur de langue française (Menger 1883/2011).

99. [NDT] 世界観学的考察 (*sekaïkan gakuteki kôssatsu*) renvoie au concept de *Weltanschauungslehre*.

100. [NDT] 合理性 (*gorisei*) désigne la rationalité dans le sens général mais également dans celui déjà rencontré de concept d'« efficacité » au sens d'une rationalité économique.

101. [NDT] On relèvera l'allusion au titre de l'ouvrage majeur de Max Weber.

En outre, dans le cadre éthique formulé par Sugimura, le « principe d'économicité » se reliait à la constitution du système social entier, à travers la manière dont la personnalité se formait. L'éthique de la valeur dans le monde de la culture, en quoi Sôda voyait plutôt une activité inhérente à la personnalité, trouvait ici un développement grâce à Sugimura, pour aboutir au final à l'éthique d'un système social. Cette éthique constituait à son tour la condition même rendant possible une activité personnelle de ce genre. Il en résultait que la négociation entre le système et la personnalité passait au cœur de la problématique de l'éthique économique chez Sugimura. Cela fut considéré à son tour comme la problématique d'un socialisme devant venir après le capitalisme. Mais, selon nous, tout se passe comme si l'on développait là un perfectionnisme dans la perspective d'une théorie de la justice.

Remarquons que le constructivisme kantien développé par Rawls fit son apparition aux États-Unis sans entretenir aucun rapport avec la tradition allemande qui avait existé après Kant ; nous considérons donc que les approfondissements que Sôda et Sugimura donnèrent à leurs idées sont des héritages originaux de la philosophie sociale post-kantienne ; c'est ce que nous avons amplement montré dans les pages qui précèdent. Ce qui mérite d'autant plus notre attention dans un cadre éthique, c'est ce perfectionnisme sous la forme d'une théorie du système des valeurs constitutives de la valeur dominante dans le monde de la culture chez Sôda. Relier l'éthique de la « justice » avec celle de la « vertu », d'un point de vue kantien, voilà qui a constitué un projet très important, que l'on peut regarder comme constituant un paradigme. Ainsi, la philosophie économique avait donc déjà pris naissance au Japon suite au contact avec les auteurs néokantiens, et elle n'a certainement pas pris fin comme la fleur qui n'aurait pas apporté de fruit après elle ; bien au contraire, elle a permis de montrer tout le potentiel dans ce schéma de base d'une perspective kantienne qui est encore à développer. C'est pourquoi nous pouvons alors placer les pensées de Sôda et de Sugimura à la source de cette philosophie économique japonaise, dont nous sommes persuadés que le schéma a pour destinée de se développer encore plus avant.

Pour conclure, tentons d'embrasser maintenant, d'un point de vue synoptique, la philosophie économique telle que nous venons d'en traiter. Dans l'histoire des méthodes employées en économie, il y avait deux grands axes de coordonnées que Sugimura a soulignés : d'une part, il y avait l'ensemble constitué par le positivisme, l'empirisme et l'objectivisme, et d'autre part, il y avait cet autre groupe, celui constitué par plusieurs formes d'idéalisme[102] et le subjectivisme ; ces deux groupes se sont très longtemps opposés à travers leurs spécialistes. C'était un utilitarisme, celui de Bentham, qui avait établi la philosophie économique en un immense système ; or sa pensée appartenait donc au premier ensemble. La prémisse fondée sur cet utilitarisme voulait que l'homme fût à jamais en quête de son bonheur ; elle expliquait la conception de l'être humain fondée parallèlement sur un psychologisme et sur un mécanicisme[103] ; on sait que l'utilitarisme contemporain hérite de cette vision. Son éthique concerne une théorie du « bien »[104] qui s'accorde avec une téléologie économique[105]. Or l'idée kantienne du statut de l'être humain développant son autonomie, cherchant à la fois la perfection pour soi-même et le bonheur pour autrui, appartenait au second groupe. Cette situation lançait un véritable défi à l'utilitarisme et elle manifesta l'efficacité du second groupe ; elle aboutit notamment, d'abord, à la « théorie de la justice » de John Rawls et, ensuite, à la théorie de « la personnalité » ou de la « vertu » chez Thomas Hill Green[106]. C'est de manière analogue, en partant de Kant, que les théories de Sôda et de Sugimura constituèrent en leur temps des tentatives pour fonder une théorie de la « vertu »[107].

De nos jours, la philosophie économique doit synthétiser (ou globaliser) les théories du « bien », de la « justice » et de la « vertu » ;

102. [NDT] Voir *supra*, n. 4. Shionoya juxtapose la dualité évoquée entre 理念主義 (*rinenshugi*) et 理想主義 (*risôshugi*) en utilisant les deux termes, ce qui complique la traduction en soulignant la diversité des idéalismes.

103. [NDT] 心理主義的・機械主義的人間観 (*shinrishugiteki kikaishugiteki ningenkan*) indique littéralement (dans un parallèle que le tiret typographique japonais souligne) l'analogie du fonctionnement de la *psyche* et d'une mécanique, ce qui marque une certaine perception de l'être humain.

104. [NDT] 「善」の理論 (*« zen » no riron*). L'auteur désigne la théorie du bien saisi comme principe. L'idéogramme est entre guillemets japonais et il ne s'agit évidemment pas du « zen » au sens religieux.

105. [NDT] 目的論的経済学 (*mokutekironteki keizaïgaku*) désigne l'application littérale stricte d'une téléologie (c'est-à-dire d'une « doctrine des buts ») à la conception scientifique en économie.

106. Voir (Green 1997). [*NDT*] Shionoya s'intéressa, à la fin de sa vie, aux auteurs britanniques comme Green (héritier anglais de la philosophie hégélienne), Ruskin et Hobson : voir la présentation (G. Campagnolo) et le texte d'hommage (B. Schefold) relatifs à Shionoya.

107. [NDT] Les termes anglais, allemand, français et japonais pour « vertu » demanderaient une exégèse impossible dans ce cadre et qui constitue, comme l'auteur le dit, au fond, une source vive d'inspiration de l'œuvre de Shionoya.

cela signifie que nous sommes parvenus à la jonction entre les deux courants principaux de l'histoire des méthodes en économie. La science économique s'intéresse de nos jours de plus en plus aux « systèmes », mais si elle devait ignorer la dimension des « idées »[108], elle se priverait alors de cette tension entre positivisme et idéalisme de nature philosophique sans laquelle il nous serait à jamais impossible d'éclaircir tout ce que ces deux genres de tentatives impliquent.

Dans ce livre, nous avons tenté de remplir consciencieusement et méthodiquement notre devoir consistant à rapporter la dimension des idées à celle des systèmes.

RÉFÉRENCES

Berque, A. (dir.). 2000. *Logique du lieu et dépassement de la modernité.* Bruxelles : Ousia.

Campagnolo, G. 2004. *Critiques de l'économie politique classique.* Paris : P.U.F.

–. 2008. "Was the Austrian School a 'Psychological' School in the realm of Economics in Carl Menger's view?" In *Carl Menger. Discussed on the Basis of New Findings*, G. Campagnolo (ed.), 165-86. Frankfurt/Main & Wien : Peter Lang Verlag..

—. et Naoki Matsuyama. 2013. カール。メンガーにとってオーストリア学派は経済学の〈心理学〉派だったのか？ ["L'école autrichienne d'économie était-elle une école 'psychologisante' d'économie aux yeux de Carl Menger ?"]. 経済学研究 *Keizaigaku Kenkyu* [*Economic Studies. Journal of Economics of Hokkaido University*] vol. 62(3) : 177-206.

Green, T. H. 1997. *Collected Works*, ed. by P. Nicholson, 5 vols. Bristol : Thoemmes Press.

Knapp, G. F. 2012 [1905]. *Die staatliche Theorie des Geldes.* Bremen : Unikum in Europäischer Hochschulverlag.

Lange, F. A. 1866. *Geschichte des Materialismus und Kritik seiner Bedeutung in der Gegenwart*, 2 vol. Iserlohn : J. Baedeker.

Liebmann, O. 1865. *Kant und die Epigonen : Eine kritische Abhandlung.* Berlin : Reuther and Reichard.

Menger, C. 1883. *Untersuchungen über die Methode der Socialwissenschaften und der politischen Ökonomie insbesondere.* Leipzig : Dunckler et Humblot. Trad. fr. *Recherches sur la méthode dans les sciences sociales et en économie politique en particulier* (trad. intégrale, présentation et commentaire par G. Campagnolo). Paris : Éditions de l'EHESS, 2011.

Rawls, J. 1971. *A Theory of Justice.* Cambridge (MA) : Harvard University Press.

Schumpeter, J. A. 1911. "Sôda, *Geld und Wert.*" *Zeitschrift für Volkswirtschaft, Sozialpolitik und Verwaltung*, XX : 245.

108. [NDT]「理念」の次元 (*« rinen » no jigen*) ; il s'agit de la dimension des « idées » de la raison, comme pour *rinen* au début de ce texte, que Shionoya boucle de la sorte.

–. 1980 [1908]. *Das Wesen und der Hauptinhalt der theoretischen Nationalökonomie.* Leipzig : Duncker und Humblot

–. 1983-1984. 『理論経済学の本質と主要内容 (*Riron keizaigaku no honshitsu to shuyo naïyô*) [*L'essence et le contenu principal de l'économie nationale théorique*] Trad. japonaise par Tadao Ôno Yasuma Takui, 2 vols. Tokyo : Iwanami Shoten.

SHIONOYA, Yûichi. 1995. 「シュンペーター的思考－総合的社会科学の構想 (*Shumpeter teki shikô – sôgô teki shakaïkagaku no kôsô*) [*La pensée de Schumpeter, le concept d'une science sociale globale*]. Tokyo : Toyo Keizai Shinpo-sha.

SÔDA, Kiichirô. 1907. "Die neue Knappsche Geldtheorie und das Wesen des Geldes." *Jahrbücher der Nationalökonomie und Statistik* vol. 34, n°. 3 : 620-55.

–. 1909. *Geld und Wert : eine logische Studie.* Tübingen : H. Laupp ; rééd. Tübingen : J. C. B. Mohr, 1924.

–. 1911. *Die logische Natur der Wirtschaftsgesetze.* Stuttgart : F. Enke (préface par C. J. Fuchs).

–. 1931. 左右田喜一郎全集 (*Sôda Kiichirô zenshu*) *Œuvres complètes de Kiichirô Sôda*, 5 volumes, Tokyo, Iwanami, contenant notamment

Vol. 2 : 「貨幣と価値 (*Kaheï to kachi*) [« Monnaie et valeur »] p. 121-426.

Vol. 3 : 経済法則の論理的性質 (*Keïzaï hôsoku no rironteki seïshitsu*) [« La nature logique des systèmes économiques »] p. 3-252.

経済法則の論理的性質 (*Keïzaï hôsoku no rironteki seïshitsu*) [« La nature théorique des lois économiques »] p. 134-49.

カント認識論と純理経済学 (*Kant ninshikiron to junri-keïzaïgaku*) [« L'épistémologie kantienne et la doctrine économique »], p. 253-89.

極限概念としての文化価値 (*Kyokugen gainen to shite no bunka-kachi*) [« La valeur dans le monde de la culture en tant que concept d'horizon extrême »] p. 435-76.

Vol. 4 : 価値の体系 (*kachi no taïkeï*) [« Le système fondé sur la(les) valeur(s) »], p. 45-122

SUGIMURA, Kôzô 1926. カール・メンガー社會科學方法論の研究 *Kâl Mengâ Shakai Kagaku Hôhôron no Kenkyû.* [*Une enquête sur la méthodologie de Menger en sciences sociales*]. Tokyo : Shogakenkyûkan.

–. 1933. 文化価値主義の経済学 *Bunka kachi shugi no keïzaïgaku* [*Philosophie économique de la valeur culturelle*], vol. 9 des *Œuvres d'économie* dirigées par Yasuki Futatsugi et Kôzô Sugimura. (Sans lieu d'édition, probablement Tokyo) : Kaïzo-sha.

–. 1935. 「『経済哲学の基本問題』 *Keïzaï tetsugaku no kihon mondaï* ["Le mécanisme de la valeur de la société économique"]. In 経済社会の価値機構 *Keïzaï shakaï no kachi-kikô*) [*Problèmes fondamentaux de la philosophie économique*], 177-267. Tokyo : Iwanami Shoten.

–. 1938a. 『経済学方法史』 *Keïzaïgaku hôhô shi* [*Histoire de la méthodologie économique*]. Tokyo : Risô-sha.

–. 1938b. 『経済倫理の構造 *Keïzaï rinri no kôzô* [*La structure de l'éthique économique*]. Tokyo : Iwanami Shoten.

–. 1944. 「改訂経済哲学通論」 *Kaïteï keizaï tetsugaku tsûron* [*Introduction à la philosophie économique*]. (Sans lieu d'édition, probablement Tokyo) : Risô-sha.

RECENSION D'OUVRAGE

Anthropologie économique. Cours au Collège de France, 1992-1993
Pierre Bourdieu
Paris, Seuil, 2017

NICOLAS BRISSET*

Je commencerai cette note de recension par un remerciement[1]. Le travail que les éditeurs des cours au Collège de France de Pierre Bourdieu ont entamé en 2012, date de publication du cours intitulé *Sur l'État* (Bourdieu 2012), est non seulement remarquable de précision, mais également des plus profitables pour les générations qui, comme la mienne, n'ont pas eu l'occasion d'entendre le sociologue de son vivant. On pourrait poser la question de la légitimité de cette entreprise, tant il est quelquefois assez déstabilisant de lire un exposé oral dans lequel l'orateur concède dire ce qu'il dit uniquement dans la mesure où la chose est dite et non écrite. Fallait-il brûler retranscriptions et enregistrements ? La réponse s'impose à la lecture des cinq volumes publiés à ce jour : non. Ces ouvrages apportent un éclairage précieux sur la pensée de Bourdieu, mais également sur sa manière de concevoir ses arguments, sa manière d'hésiter, de revenir en arrière, de se positionner en face de ses contemporains. La lecture d'*Anthropologie*

1. Cette note a profité des remarques constructives de Judith Favereau, de Raphaël Fèvre et de Philippe Steiner, que je remercie chaleureusement..

* Université de Nice Côte d'Azur, CNRS, GREDEG. nicolas.brisset@univ-cotedazur.fr

économique marque particulièrement par l'intérêt et la connaissance dont Bourdieu fait montre à l'égard des économistes de son temps, qu'il lit, décortique, et dont il s'inspire[2]. De quoi alimenter le débat relatif à son « économicisme ». Nous y reviendrons.

L'ouvrage est riche et se compose de deux parties principales : la première traite de la question de l'analyse théorique du don, la seconde expose la théorie bourdieusienne de l'économie comme ensemble de champs. Dans cette note, je me concentrerai sur la première de ces deux problématiques, dans la mesure où elle soulève et actualise bon nombre de questionnements relatifs à l'œuvre du sociologue. Mon objectif sera d'abord d'exposer rapidement l'analyse bourdieusienne du don telle qu'elle est présentée dans ce cours, avant de revenir sur les débats auxquels elle avait donné naissance dans les années 1980 et 1990. Enfin, j'esquisserai une contribution à ces débats, en insistant particulièrement sur la thèse historique qui semble sous-tendre l'analyse que Bourdieu fait des sociétés non capitalistes.

1. LA DOUBLE VÉRITÉ DU DON

L'analyse bourdieusienne du don a fait couler beaucoup d'encre[3]. Le cours d'*Anthropologie économique* a ici le grand mérite de l'exposer de manière claire et didactique. Bourdieu, on le sait, inscrit son analyse sociologique dans une double négation, à la fois du subjectivisme phénoménologique et de l'objectivisme structuraliste. En ce qui concerne le premier positionnement, Bourdieu rejette toute analyse réduisant la réalité sociale aux expériences vécues. En affirmant que le don maussien ne peut être strictement ramené à une relation d'altruisme, Bourdieu se fait continuateur de Lévi-Strauss et de sa célèbre analyse (Lévi-Strauss 1989) : il est vain de s'abandonner aux représentations « indigènes » du don comme pur acte de générosité, le risque étant de tomber dans la négation du don conforme à ces représentations *via* le constat de l'impossibilité pure et simple d'un

2. Il est d'ailleurs assez remarquable de constater que Bourdieu est plus prompt à citer les économistes standards que les tenants de la sociologie économique naissante (à l'exception d'Harrison White) ou que les tenants de l'hétérodoxie économique (Steiner 2018).

3. On renverra dernièrement à l'ouvrage de Philippe Steiner (2016), qui inscrit l'œuvre de Bourdieu dans le cadre de l'histoire de l'altruisme.

don vécu comme strictement altruiste, c'est-à-dire sans contre-don (Derrida 1991). Bourdieu invite donc à un changement de perspective :

> L'analyse du don doit opérer un changement d'objet : elle doit passer du don à l'échange, c'est-à-dire à une relation transcendante aux actes d'échange qui, dès qu'on l'explicite, contredit (il n'y a pas de don sans contre-don) la vérité vécue [...]. (Bourdieu 2017, 25)

Bourdieu prend néanmoins également ses distances vis-à-vis du structuralisme de Lévi-Strauss, parangon (selon lui) de l'erreur scolastique consistant à prendre « les choses de la logique pour la logique des choses », citation de Marx que Bourdieu a rendu célèbre. Il s'agit de rompre avec l'illusion du surplomb créé par l'isolement scientiste :

> Il faut une espèce d'intrépidité scientiste pour dire que le savant a raison contre l'expérience indigène. (Bourdieu 2017, 30).

C'est de cette double mise à distance que naît la volonté de prendre le don par les deux bouts : celui de la structure (il n'y a pas de don sans contre-don, et donc pas d'altruisme véritable), et celui de l'expérience vécue (vivre le don comme un altruisme). Telle est la fameuse « double vérité du don », qui représente une pierre importante de la sociologie bourdieusienne (Bourdieu 1980, 193 ; 1997, 276). La manière dont Bourdieu réconcilie ces deux « vérités » est connue : c'est la dénégation sociale du calcul intéressé (au contre-don) qui permet d'occulter l'apparente contradiction entre les deux « vérités » du don :

> Pour que le don marche vraiment, il faut un univers de relations sociales enchantées, comme disait Max Weber, dans lesquelles tout le monde se raconte des histoires et tout le monde accepte d'écouter des histoires. (Bourdieu 2017, 61)

Il s'agit dès lors d'étudier la construction sociale de la dénégation du calcul, et en négatif la construction sociale de l'altruisme vécu. Cette déconstruction passe chez Bourdieu par l'identification de trois éléments nécessaires : le temps qui, se glissant entre le don et le contre-don, est une condition de l'oubli de la nécessaire (car structurelle) réciprocité ; l'approche des individus par leurs dispositions (habitus) à l'oubli ; l'étude de l'économie des biens symboliques comme champ d'expression et de formation des dispositions : le donnant-donnant se déploie (*via* le capital symbolique) dans plusieurs sphères, le don économique pouvant par exemple engendrer un contre-don politique, ce qui engendre le processus de dénégation. C'est donc par le prisme de la dénégation que Bourdieu analyse les sociétés « pré-capitalistes » :

> Ces sociétés, en effet, travaillent de manière désespérée à refuser que les rapports entre les gens soient menés par le cynisme, c'est-à-dire qu'ils soient objectivement conformes à leur vérité objective. (Bourdieu 2017, 67)

On perçoit rapidement l'ambiguïté de l'analyse. La double vérité du don serait en réalité une simple vérité objective gardée sous silence, celle du donnant-donnant, de l'intérêt (économique et symbolique) et du calcul. Comment interpréter autrement l'affirmation selon laquelle « Je crois qu'on peut accepter que la disposition au calcul existe universellement » (Bourdieu 2017, 50) ? C'est notamment à partir de cette brèche que certains sociologues du MAUSS soulignent le paradoxe bourdieusien de l'étude du don (Chanial 2010). On ne peut ici que renvoyer à la magistrale critique d'Alain Caillé, dans un texte encore trop méconnu (Caillé 2014). Dans les premières pages de ce texte, on peut lire :

> Malgré ses évidentes tentatives de sophistication, la sociologie de Bourdieu me semblait ne pas échapper à l'économisme commun à presque tous les marxismes, vulgaires ou non. (Caillé 2014, 56)

En effet, la thèse de la dénégation sociale du calcul, compris comme anthropologie universelle, pousse à se représenter les sociétés capitalistes modernes comme des sociétés qui s'acceptent simplement telles qu'elles sont objectivement. Une objectivité sociale au sein de laquelle tout se réduit *in fine* à l'intérêt matériel, et où la valeur des individus est surdéterminée par leur positionnement au sein du champ économique. Un positionnement économique établi en fonction des capacités (dispositions) de chacun à se démarquer dans le cadre du jeu économique. On touche ici à deux problématiques intimement liées. Premièrement, celle de savoir si Bourdieu étend effectivement à l'ensemble des sphères sociales la logique économique de l'intérêt et de l'accumulation, qui deviendrait un « principe zéro » à la Popper (Caillé 2014, 81) ; secondement, la problématique de la hiérarchie des champs (et, par voie de conséquence, celle de la conversion des types de capitaux). Sur ce dernier point, Caillé défend que pour Bourdieu, le capital économique est bien la racine première de l'analyse, c'est-à-dire ce à quoi peuvent être réduites toutes les formes de capital. Une telle lecture est en partie corroborée par l'affirmation bourdieusienne selon laquelle c'est précisément la dénégation de l'échange économique [4] qui est à l'origine du capital symbolique dans les sociétés féodales.

La publication de ces cours donne l'occasion de réfléchir à nouveau frais à la portée de cette critique [5]. En effet, il est reproché à Bourdieu de ne pas assumer réellement la « double vérité du don » dans la mesure où la vérité subjective serait en fin de compte réductible à la vérité objective de l'intérêt matériel. De sorte que la sociologie bourdieusienne pourrait être réduite à une sociologie du deuil social par la disposition (l'*habitus*), à savoir de l'acceptation des déterminations économiques de nos destinées : les champs extra-économiques ne seraient *in fine* que les instruments de légitimation des positions économiques (Caillé 2014, 138). Cette lecture matérialiste de Bourdieu passe peut-être un peu vite sur le fait que le calcul légitimé n'est pas l'équivalent du calcul refoulé. Autrement dit, la dénégation est un fait social qui a des effets (un fait social épistémiquement objectif, pour reprendre le vocabulaire searlien). Bourdieu aborde par exemple, dans ses textes sur l'Algérie, la question du gaspillage dans les sociétés kabyles en ces termes : « le gaspillage de moyens [est] peut-être la condition de survie de sociétés qui, si elles comptaient, renonceraient » (Bourdieu 1977, 31). Le refoulement du calcul a donc des effets objectifs, notamment sur la dynamique du pouvoir et de la domination. C'est notamment le propre de l'analyse bourdieusienne de l'État comme accumulation de capital symbolique : un état ne pouvant se construire en s'assumant explicitement comme instrument de domination économique, la dénégation est alors un ingrédient essentiel et décisif de sa construction. La sociologie bourdieusienne est une sociologie de la domination et de son maintien. Mais le type de maintien (la forme de la dénégation) compte. Le propre de l'économicisme est, à partir de là, pour Bourdieu, de nier purement et simplement l'objectivité du symbolique, et *in fine* de tomber dans l'anthropocentrisme. Ainsi peut-on lire dans *Le sens pratique :*

> En réduisant cette économie [« archaïque »] à sa vérité « objective », l'économisme en anéantit la spécificité, qui réside précisément

4. Donc de l'économie au sens substantif du terme, et non simplement le principe formelle du calcul économique appliquée aux sphères symboliques.

5. Nous ne faisons ici qu'effleurer la critique de Caillé, qui est beaucoup plus profonde et juste que nous ne pouvons le laisser transparaître dans ces quelques lignes.

> dans le décalage socialement entretenu entre la vérité « objective » et la représentation sociale de la production et de l'échange. (Bourdieu 1980, 193)

2. L'OUBLI DE L'HISTOIRE ?

Bourdieu est clair : les sociétés capitalistes modernes sont structurellement différentes des sociétés pré-capitalistes dans la mesure où on assiste au sein des premières à la disparition de la dénégation dans de larges sphères sociales. Or, cette dénégation avait des effets objectifs sur le déroulement de la vie humaine. La libération de l'esprit de calcul engendre le passage d'une forme personnelle de domination à une forme impersonnelle, passant par le marché et l'accumulation de richesses. Il n'en reste pas moins que le concept de dénégation porte avec lui une image particulière de la transition des sociétés « pré-capitalistes » vers les sociétés capitalistes. Le capitalisme, ici défini comme le déchaînement des forces marchandes et des forces de l'accumulation du capital économique à l'ensemble des sphères sociales (Polanyi 1983), est considéré comme toujours en puissance : il suffirait de lever la dénégation pour qu'émerge le système économique sous-jacent. Bien entendu, cela ne signifie aucunement que l'économie du donnant-donnant laisse à voir l'organisation humaine de l'économie dans sa pureté. Bourdieu a bien assez étudié la construction des dispositions aux calculs économiques pour éviter ce reproche :

> Il a fallu une série d'inventions historiques pour que s'instaure cet univers historique que l'économie économique accepte comme naturel, comme allant de soi. (Bourdieu 2017, 81)

Néanmoins, il n'en reste pas moins que sa définition des sociétés pré-capitalistes (le terme est symptomatique) comme des sociétés de dénégation ouvre une brèche dans l'argument : le marché s'installerait inexorablement (même au prix d'une construction lente et marginalement différenciée) à partir du moment où la place lui est laissée nette. La fin de « l'hypocrisie » sociale, que constitue une économie de don, est-elle nécessairement synonyme d'émergence d'une économie de marché, mettant enfin explicitement au centre le capital économique ? Le fait est que Bourdieu n'a analysé la transition que par le prisme de la colonisation (Bourdieu 1977). On n'a donc pas chez lui de théorie de l'émergence du calcul « assumé » comme fondement du capitalisme. Il semble néanmoins que ce soit cette vision de l'histoire sous-jacente à l'analyse qui pose véritablement problème.

Sur ce dernier point, contrairement à ce qu'affirme Alain Caillé, c'est dans l'historiographie marxiste qu'il est possible de trouver des ressources potentiellement critiques de l'historiographie implicite bourdieusienne. En effet, Bourdieu semble à plusieurs endroits de son œuvre accepter le thèse historique portée par ceux que Robert Brenner a qualifié de « néo-smithiens » (Brenner 1977). Dans son célèbre article de 1976, point de départ du *Brenner's debate*, Robert Brenner s'inscrit en faux contre la thèse d'un capitalisme lattant dont l'émergence pourrait être considérée comme une « libération » de forces déjà là. La preuve en est que le déclin de la féodalité n'a pas débouché partout sur le même type de système politico-économique : la France tombe dans l'absolutisme [6], l'Angleterre dans le capitalisme, qui plus tard s'étendra au continent (Meiksins-Wood 2009 et 2011). Bourdieu semble, au moins tacitement, accepter la thèse néo-smithienne du capitalisme comme libération (comme fin de la dénégation). Il n'est sur ce point pas anodin de constater qu'il fait à de multiples reprises référence à *La Grande Transformation* de Polanyi (1983). Dans son cours sur l'État on peut lire :

> Dans *The Great Transformation*, Polanyi (une de mes grandes inspirations) montre comment le marché ne s'est pas fait tout seul, *motu proprio*, mais a été le produit d'un travail, en particulier de l'État, orienté souvent par des théories mercantilistes. L'État a contribué volontairement à structurer cet espace qui nous apparaît comme une donnée, alors que c'est une institution. La genèse d'un pouvoir fiscal et d'un pouvoir économique à base fiscale va de pair avec l'unification de l'espace économique et avec la création d'un marché national. (Bourdieu 2012, 319)

La référence à Polanyi est intéressante dans la mesure où pour ce dernier, le passage des sociétés non-capitalistes au capitalisme de marché au moment de la Révolution industrielle se fait principalement

6. Un absolutisme qui, selon les marxistes politiques, et contrairement à ce que soutien Perry Anderson (1976), ne préfigure pas la transition économique vers le capitalisme marchand.

sous la pression d'un progrès technique allant pratiquement de soi (Polanyi 1983, 64) et dont l'État n'entame en définitive que le rythme. De sorte que les transformations sociales marquant la transition (fin de la tenure féodale, lois sur les enclosures, abrogation de *Speenhamland*, etc.) sont en définitive réduites à la simple levée d'obstacles à la marche quasi inexorable d'une société de marché (Meiksins-Wood 2011, 33-41). Un processus qui aboutira *in fine* aux crises politiques de la moitié du XXe siècle. Si donc la constitution d'un État moderne va de pair avec l'émergence d'une économie de marché, c'est bien, chez Polanyi, le progrès technique qui engendre la pression marchande, puis les réformes de l'État, et non l'inverse[7]. Une théorie historique conforme aux aspirations bourdieusiennes, c'est-à-dire mettant réellement le symbolique au même niveau que l'économique, nécessiterait au contraire de comprendre l'émergence de rapports sociaux rendant nécessaire le progrès technique et *in fine* l'économie de marché. C'est sur cette voie que se sont engagé les tenants du marxisme politique. Dans ses travaux, Edward Thompson insiste par exemple sur la mutation des types de calcul et d'intérêt au moment de la révolution agricole, creuset de la révolution industrielle. Lorsque Thompson envisage l'émergence du capitalisme moderne, il interroge l'affrontement de systèmes objectivement contradictoires : l'économie morale de la foule (Thompson 1971) est objectivement en contradiction avec les normes de calcul s'imposant aux moments des révolutions agricoles et industrielles. L'analyse de Bourdieu semble toute autre :

> L'échange généreux est-il autre chose que le déploiement dans la succession temporelle des différents moments d'une transaction que le contrat rationnel resserre dans l'instant ? [...] L'échange de don est un échange dans et par lequel on s'efforce de voiler la vérité de l'échange, c'est-à-dire le calcul comme garantie de l'équité de l'échange. Si le « donnant-donnant » est la vérité de l'échange de dons, l'échange de dons est un donnant-donnant qui ne peut s'avouer comme tel. [...] En accentuant systématiquement la signification symbolique des actes ou des rapports de production, on se refuse à poser l'économie en tant que telle, c'est-à-dire en tant que système régi par des lois originales, et à reconnaître explicitement les fins économiques par rapport auxquelles l'action économique est objectivement orientée,

7. Une thèse similaire à celles développées par Karl Marx dans l'*Idéologie Allemande* et dans *Misère de la philosophie*, et qu'il amendera de manière substantielle dans *le Capital* (Brenner 1985).

celles du calcul intéressé, de la concurrence, de la compétition ou de l'exploitation. (Bourdieu 1977, 35-6)

Le concept de dénégation jette donc un voile très différent sur les luttes ayant émaillé la révolution industrielle. En effet, à quoi se réduit l'attitude critique que relève Thompson chez les défenseurs de l'utilisation commune des forêts et des terres (Thompson 2014) si on l'analyse uniquement à la lumière du refus de considérer l'économie pour ce qu'elle est objectivement ? Ne retombe-t-on pas simplement dans la vision en terme d'infrastructure et de superstructure, consistant à considérer le social comme constamment à la traîne de l'économique (Thompson 1976, 137) ? On débouche finalement sur un des reproches les plus importants faits à la sociologie Bourdieusienne : son incapacité à saisir la lutte et la critique (Boltanski 2009). C'est notamment l'un des grands messages de Thompson, lorsque ce dernier refuse de considérer les révoltes comme de pures convulsions (Thompson 2015) : il y a des manières de s'opposer à l'économisme, qui sont l'expression d'autant de représentations du monde. En termes bourdieusien, la forme de la dénégation compte peut-être plus que ce qui est dénié. Au final, on comprend pourquoi Bourdieu est un penseur de la domination, et non de l'émancipation, un penseur du pouvoir et non de la résistance, ce qui le pousse vers une lecture *neo-smithienne* de la transition.

Néanmoins, tout n'est peut-être pas si simple. En effet, dans son cours sur Manet, Bourdieu (2013) analyse par le menu la manière dont des dominés deviennent dominants, à savoir une révolution symbolique par le bas. Une piste précieuse que le sociologue nous laisse, et pour laquelle nous remercions, encore une fois, les éditeurs de ses cours.

REFERENCES

Anderson, P. 1976. *L'état absolutiste I - L'Europe de l'ouest.* Paris : Maspero.

Boltanski, L. 2009. *De la critique. Précis de sociologie de l'émancipation.* Paris : Gallimard.

Bourdieu, P. 1977. *Algérie 60. Structures économiques et structures temporelles.* Paris : Éditions de Minuit.

–. 1980. *Le sens pratique.* Paris : Éditions de Minuit.

–. 1997. *Méditations pascaliennes.* Paris : Seuil.

–. 2012. *Sur L'État.* Paris : Seuil.

–. 2013. *Manet : une révolution symbolique.* Paris : Seuil.

–. 2017. *Anthropologie économique.* Paris : Seuil.

Brenner, R.. 1976. "Agrarian Class Structure and Economic Development in Pre-Industrial Europe." *Past and Present*, 70 (Février) : 30–75.

–. 1977. "The Origins of Capitalist Development : A Critique of Neo-Smithian Marxism." *New Left Review* 104 : 25–92.

–. 1985. "Marx's First Model of the Transition to Capitalism." In *Marx en perspective*, B. Chavance (dir.), 203-30. Paris : Éditions de l'EHESS.

Caillé, A. 2014. *Don, intérêt et désintéressement. Bourdieu, Mauss, Platon et quelques autres.* Paris : Éditions Le bord de l'eau.

Chanial, P. 2010. "Bourdieu, un 'héritier' paradoxal ?" *Revue Du Mauss* 36(2) : 483-92.

Derrida, J. 1991. *Donner le temps. 1. La fausse monnaie.* Paris : Galilée.

Lévi-Strauss, Cl. 1989. "Introduction à l'œuvre de Marcel Mauss." In M. Mauss, *Sociologie et anthropologie*, ix–lii. Paris : P.U.F.

Meiksins Wood, E. 2009. *L'origine du capitalisme : une étude approfondie.* Québec : Lux Éditeur.

–. 2011. *L'empire du capital.* Québec : Lux Éditeur.

Polanyi, K. 1983. *La Grande Transformation.* Paris : Gallimard.

Steiner, Ph. 2016. *Donner... Une histoire de l'altruisme.* Paris : P.U.F.

–. 2018. "Bourdieu (Pierre), Anthropologie économique. Cours au collège de France, 1992-1993". *Revue Française de Sociologie* 59(2) : 164–66.

Thompson, E. 1971. "The Moral Economy of the English Crowd in the Eighteenth Century." *Past and Present* 50 (Feb) : 76-136.

– 1976. "Modes de domination et révolutions en Angleterre". *Actes de La Recherche En Sciences Sociales* 2 (2-3) : 133-51.

–. 2014. *La guerre des forêts. Luttes sociales dans l'Angleterre du* xviii e *siècle.* Paris : La Découverte.

–. 2015. *Les usages de la coutume. Traditions et résistances populaires en Angleterre* xvii e-xix e *siècle.* Paris : Seuil.

RECENSION D'OUVRAGE

Commerce et marché dans les premiers empires : sur la diversité des économies
Karl Polanyi, Conrad M. Arensberg & Harry W. Pearson. Édition de Michele Cangiani, Jérôme Maucourant *et al.*
Paris, Éditions Le Bord de l'Eau, 2017.

PATRICK GILORMINI*

Il s'agit de la seconde édition française d'un ouvrage collectif, *Trade and Market in the Early Empires. Economies in History and Theory* (1957) qui, dix ans après la mort de Polanyi, était parue en français en 1975 chez Larousse dans une traduction de Claude et Anne Rivière sous le titre *Les Systèmes économiques dans l'histoire et la théorie*. Cette nouvelle édition bénéficie d'une introduction inédite par Michele Cangiani et Jérôme Maucourant ainsi que d'une postface par Alain Guery, intitulée *Des marchés au marché, d'une transformation à une autre*. L'avant-propos d'Alain Caillé met en évidence la thèse centrale du livre : « Le marché n'a pas toujours existé, il n'y a que peu de temps qu'il est advenu ».

L'influence que Karl Polanyi exerce depuis les années 1950 sur ce que l'on pourrait appeler un « institutionnalisme des origines des temps historiques » suffit à légitimer la réédition qui permet au public francophone d'entrer désormais plus avant dans le laboratoire où se forgeait sa conception de l'économie comme processus intégratif. Parmi les formes d'intégration, nous retrouvons le rôle de l'administration domestique destinée à assurer la subsistance humaine

*. ESDES, Université Catholique de Lyon.

par la production et le stockage direct pour un groupe familial fermé, une catégorie qu'il ne devait plus retenir pas dans ses ouvrages ultérieurs.

Dans l'édition de 1975, une préface structuraliste marquée par l'anthropologie marxiste de Maurice Godelier introduisait le sujet pour le public français ; elle marquait l'attachement à la valeur-travail comme garantie de scientificité. L'anthropologie économique des années 70, soucieuse de libérer le genre humain des questions relatives aux modes de production (notamment dans le cas de l'esclavage) trouvait là une recherche fondée sur des invariants structurels et un refus de la perspective anthropocentrique occidentale. Les critiques avaient alors souligné la nouveauté du propos qui montrait comment les rapports économiques se sont institutionnalisés dans les sociétés préindustrielles. Alors que les travaux de sociologie économique français étaient encore rares, l'ouvrage soutenait que l'économique ne pouvait s'analyser qu'à travers le social. On appréciait aussi la manière dont le post-keynésianisme donnait à l'économie une teinture de sociologie et de psychologie dans le souci d'une meilleure opérationnalité. L'économie n'est pas la fonction essentielle dans certaines sociétés, comme elle l'est dans les sociétés industrielles, et les concepts de la théorie économique sont donc impuissants à rendre compte du fonctionnement de ces sociétés. La présentation d'une approche économique « substantive »[1] fondée sur l'interaction de l'homme et de l'environnement, en rejetant toute notion d'évolution, pouvait paraître prendre ses distances de l'approche marxiste en vogue à cette époque.

Polanyi s'était exilé en Amérique du Nord, où il vécut de 1947 à sa mort (en avril 1964). Cette période est marquée par d'importantes contributions en histoire et en anthropologie, dont cet ouvrage collectif est le fruit le plus décisif. Polanyi rédige quatre de ses dix-huit chapitres. C'est grâce à une bourse de la fondation Ford que Polanyi avait pu prendre la direction de l'*Interdisciplinary Columbia Project* qui

1. Le choix de « substantive » (au lieu, par exemple, de « substantielle ») est ici volontaire en référence à la source à laquelle Polanyi a nourri son intérêt et le projet de distinguer deux types d'économie, « formalisée », d'une part et « substantive », conformément à l'interprétation qu'il donnait de la version posthume (1923) des *Principes d'économie politique* de Carl Menger. Voir à ce sujet les indications données dans la biographie française de Carl Menger (Campagnolo 2008) et dans (Becchio 2011).

portait sur les aspects institutionnels de la croissance économique (Maucourant 2011).

La nouvelle édition française, qui reprend la traduction de 1975, est précédée d'une « Introduction » par Michele Cangiani et Jérôme Maucourant, d'un avant-propos d'Alain Caillé et elle se conclut avec une postface d'Alain Guery.

Polanyi s'inscrit dans une perspective comparative qui reste discutable, mais l'intérêt de son travail demeure aujourd'hui dans sa critique des fondements de la « science sinistre »[2]. En s'opposant au formalisme en économie, Polanyi propose une approche substantive de celle-ci. Le formalisme économique renvoie chez Polanyi moins à la mathématisation qu'au type de la rationalité utilitariste procédant de l'ajustement individuel des moyens aux fins dans un univers de rareté supposée. Cette conception consiste en une rationalisation *a posteriori* de l'économie de marché. L'économie substantive admet l'existence d'une sphère naturelle et évidente de pratiques matérielles relevant de la satisfaction des besoins et elle renvoie l'économique à un processus universel visant à assurer la « survie » des agents. Pour Polanyi, l'économie de marché ne va pas de soi comme système autorégulateur :

> Aucune société ne saurait naturellement vivre, même pour peu de temps, sans posséder une économie d'une sorte ou d'une autre ; mais avant notre époque aucune économie n'a jamais existé qui fût, même en principe, sous la dépendance des marchés [...] Quoique l'institution du marché ait été tout à fait courante depuis la fin de l'Âge de pierre, son rôle n'avait jamais été que secondaire dans la vie économique (Polanyi 1983, 87).

Polanyi s'appuie sur l'anthropologie et sur l'histoire pour réfuter l'idée que la nature de l'homme est utilitariste et qu'elle le pousserait spontanément à échanger, ou à chercher un gain matériel. Ce qui prime chez Polanyi c'est la question de l'approvisionnement de la société, plutôt que celle du calcul coût/bénéfice de l'*homo œconomicus*. L'économie « substantielle » d'où procède la pensée de Polanyi est un processus institutionnalisé d'interactions entre l'homme et son

2. La *dismal science* est une expression de Thomas Carlyle (1795-1881). Le « modèle » que Carlyle avait à l'esprit, le servage médiéval, de l'époque des Plantagenêt, fondé sur l'obéissance à la hiérarchie s'opposait au moderne « *cash nexus* » (« lien nodal de l'argent ») qui manifeste son règne dans l'échange sur les marchés.

environnement, destiné à fournir à la société ses moyens d'existence, sa « subsistance ».

L'ouvrage réédité aujourd'hui comprend une première partie qui analyse le cas des économies de l'Antiquité mésopotamienne et de l'Asie mineure S'y exprime notamment le spécialiste d'assyriologie qu'était A. Leo Oppenheim (1904-1974). Elle conduit Polanyi à souligner l'absence de marchés créateurs de prix dans la Babylone d'Hammourabi ou dans la Tyr phénicienne. Le commerce sans marché est une figure de l'économie antique. C'est une entreprise discontinue liée aux exigences du politique. Jusqu'au début du VIIe siècle av. J.-C., les empires de Mésopotamie, de Syrie et d'Egypte pratiquaient le commerce à grande échelle, sans avoir recours à la monnaie comme moyen d'échange, ni au marché comme régulateur de l'offre et de la demande. Sur les petits marchés locaux, les contraintes collectives provenant de la coutume et de l'intervention du monarque exerçaient une influence déterminante sur la formation des prix. Pour Polanyi le procès économique « substantif » est anonyme dans la société antique, et les moyens d'existence de l'homme sont insérés dans des institutions dont la nature n'est pas primordialement économique. Cette étude complète celle de Polanyi dans *The Livelihood of Man* (1977) sur *Commerce, marché et monnaie dans la Grèce antique* (Polanyi 2011, 223-400) où se révélait la dette des dix siècles d'histoire économique romaine envers la pratique hellénique des marchés ; celle-ci était apparue dans l'Égypte grecque, sous la tutelle du système bureaucratique de planification centralisée où l'appui des banquiers privés d'Athènes permettait d'accroître l'efficacité d'une économie dirigée par l'État.

La deuxième partie est consacrée à la séparation du commerce et du marché. Elle s'ouvre par une réflexion épistémologique et méthodologique du spécialiste de l'anthropologie appliquée, Conrad Maynadier Arensberg (1910-1993). Il souligne la contribution que l'approche déductive de l'économie centrée sur les interactions et les processus peut fournir en favorisant les explications par une anthropologie centrée sur les faits et les modèles sociaux. Arensberg invite les anthropologues à prendre en compte dans leurs analyses les trois catégories de l'économie substantive (réciprocité, redistribution, échange) qui donnent la primeur à l'action et au processus, tout autant qu'à s'attacher aux valeurs et aux significations communes.

L'ethnologue américaniste Anne C. Chapman (1922-2010) montre, sur le cas des ports de commerce à longue distance des civilisations aztèques et mayas, que les échanges démocratiques sur les marchés locaux n'avaient pas leur place dans le système commercial réservé à une élite et aux besoins de l'État. Souvent le commerce précède le tribut et le négoce l'administration, et les vaincus se les voit imposer au final. Le cas d'Ouidah, qui fut le port esclavagiste du royaume du Dahomey, analysé par Rosemary Arnold, montre comment le commerce et le marché sont administrés par des groupes séparés de fonctionnaires. Le commerce approvisionne le palais, l'armée, et les maisons des grands, en contrepartie d'obtenir les autorisations et les moyens des exportations (les esclaves prisonniers). Cette affaire, liée à la guerre, est une affaire d'hommes. Le marché, lui, pourvoit aux besoins ordinaires de la population. Sur la place du marché, les vendeurs sont des femmes. Elles pourvoient aux besoins quotidiens des villes en produits de la campagne.

Dans le cas des berbères de l'Atlas, étudié par Francisco Benet, le *souk* est une institution légale, sociale, politique et religieuse qui sert des fins économiques. Il ne s'agit en aucun cas d'un marché pour des échanges libres effectués au hasard. Les marchés des montagnes sont des endroits où l'on peut se procurer des vivres frais, comme la viande ou le beurre. Ces terrains neutres n'en demeurent pas moins des barils de poudre. Même si les femmes désireuses de bénéficier de l'approvisionnement y jouent un rôle pacificateur, les marchés intertribaux peuvent être le théâtre d'explosions de violence et devenir le lieu d'affrontements sanglants.

Dans les villages indiens analysés par Walter C. Neale, le système économique relevait de relations de réciprocité quant aux services échangés et de relations de redistribution, quant aux produits agricoles. Il s'agissait d'une économie sans marché, d'une économie « statutaire » plutôt que contractuelle. Le revenu foncier était la part du produit de la terre qui revenait au dirigeant (selon des critères de redistribution et non de marché). Dans le cas de la réciprocité comme dans celui de la redistribution, il n'existe aucune égalité de traitement, ni parts équitables ni paiement en fonction de la valeur. Ce modèle se caractérise par sa centralité ; tous les points de la périphérie sont liés au point central, et le statut de chacun sert de critère pour organiser la communauté villageoise.

La troisième partie est consacrée à l'analyse institutionnelle. Elle prend acte du fait que la présence d'un système de marché ne s'applique ni à toutes les sociétés ni à toutes les époques, mais qu'il s'agit d'un phénomène principalement occidental qui s'est développé à partir du XVIIIe siècle. Pour Polanyi, l'économie ne saurait donc se réduire à l'étude des phénomènes de marché. Les faits économiques étaient à l'origine *encastrés* dans des situations qui n'étaient pas de nature économique. Ce n'est que tardivement que le concept d'économie s'est cristallisé et qu'il a pu être pensé de manière autonome. Les éléments-clefs de l'économie dite « substantive », qui trouve son origine dans la lecture par Polanyi de la version posthume de 1923 des *Principes d'économie politique (Grundsätze der Volkswirtschaftslehre)* de Carl Menger (édition donnée par son fils, Karl Menger), sont précisés en nommant notamment la réciprocité, la redistribution et l'échange comme formes d'intégration qui apportent de la stabilité et de l'efficacité aux processus économiques. Les formes du commerce, les usages de la monnaie et les éléments de marché sont trois éléments au sein du système des échanges (de son autre nom, la « catallaxie ») qui forment un tout indivisible, quand bien même leurs évolutions furent différenciées dans le temps et dans l'espace. L'examen critique de cette triade catallactique devrait permettre de comprendre que, non seulement le marché n'est pas le seul cadre de référence, mais aussi que les sciences sociales, au premier rang desquelles la sociologie, ne devraient pas le prendre comme point de départ l'élaboration des concepts de l'économie comme processus institutionnalisé.

La critique des conceptions sociologiques courantes de l'économie, présentée par Terence K. Hopkins, ainsi que celle des mauvais usages de la théorie économique en anthropologie, énoncée par Daniel B. Fusfeld, offrent selon nous des contrepoints féconds aux thèses de Polanyi. En concentrant l'attention sur les choix individuels, la théorie économique ne permet pas d'appréhender des processus d'institutionnalisation de ses propres objets (le marché, le capital, la firme) qui relèvent de dynamiques sociales plus globales. De même, le postulat de rareté et le concept de surplus sont pour Harry W. Pearson des abstractions inadmissibles par rapport aux conditions sociales réelles dans lesquelles se déroulent les activités quotidiennes à travers lesquelles l'homme vise à assurer sa subsistance. Pour nous, le défi lancé aux sciences économiques dans cet ouvrage consiste à interroger leur capacité d'offrir des grilles d'analyse pour comparer des cultures diversifiées, en s'intéressant aux besoins humains et aux coûts qui en résultent pour les hommes (Perroux 1961). L'enjeu est de penser une économie du genre humain justifiée autant par les mobiles allocentriques des acteurs que par les choix égocentriques d'un *homo œconomicus* abstrait. Il s'agit en somme de « réencastrer » l'économie au sein de la société.

Une autre nouveauté notable, par rapport à l'édition française précédente, est la postface de l'historien Alain Guery, qui témoigne d'une excellente connaissance des fondements épistémologiques de l'économie en développant une critique de la loi « naturelle » du marché, toute implicite. L'étude historique des marchés, depuis le Moyen-Âge jusqu'au XVIIIe siècle, dans la lignée de René Passet (2010), souligne combien l'économie a pu se constituer en une science normative et positive en omettant de prendre en compte les évolutions au long cours. Karl Polanyi semble ici rechercher des racines différentes de celles qu'il avait étudiées dans *La grande transformation*.

Polanyi remonte ainsi à la crise de la civilisation que fut la chute de Rome ainsi qu'à la période ultérieure de la recomposition de l'espace rural entre le Xe et le XIIe siècle. La question de la subsistance de l'homme conduit à voir des marchés (re)naître et des municipalités émerger. Les bastides assurent à la fois un rôle de garnison et de marché rural. Le marchand apparaît dans l'entourage du seigneur. Les marchés ne sont plus à l'extérieur des portes de la ville (sur le *forum*) dès lors que l'enjeu est d'assurer la pérennité des approvisionnements urbains à partir des surplus des récoltes et de faire face aux risques d'émeutes de la faim. Dans toute l'Europe, les marchés sont alimentés par des « greniers d'abondance » (*annone*) où le souverain opère une régulation *par les stocks* en achetant les céréales au moment des récoltes pour les revendre aux marchands des villes. Les seules exceptions à cette organisation de l'approvisionnement en grains (par le « préfet de l'annone », système issu du Bas-Empire romain) étaient la France et l'Angleterre. Une des conséquences de la guerre de Cent ans qui opposa les Plantagenêts aux Valois du XIVe siècle au XVe siècle fut la disparition de l'annone dans ces deux pays, qui devaient désormais pratiquer une régulation *par les flux*, avec l'aide d'une police spécifiquement dédiée à cet effet, la « police des grains ». En France, des mercuriales[3] permettaient

3. C'est-à-dire des listes des prix courants des denrées sur les marchés.

l'achat massif de grains venant de la Baltique. Turgot croyait à l'appel des marchés et il les laissa fonctionner librement jusqu'aux révoltes frumentaires de 1775. Les rumeurs de complots visant à créer la famine se multiplièrent alors. Les paysans qui représentaient près de 90 % de la population française ne faisaient aucune confiance au marché. Leur idéal était l'autosubsistance : produire d'abord pour soi et pour les siens. Ce qui contraint alors la population du pays entier à s'en remettre au mécanisme du marché, c'est l'exigence du paiement en espèces que requiert le seigneur. La multiplication des prélèvements forcés a pu conduire au développement des marchés. Ce fut là l'une des conséquences de la politique de Colbert qui avait consisté à dégager de force des surplus pour approvisionner les marchés urbains.

Toutefois l'autosubsistance continuait de dominer, y compris chez les paysans aisés, dits les « gros laboureurs » car elle reste la garantie d'une sécurité alimentaire pérenne, notamment face aux aléas du climat qui empêchent parfois de « faire la soudure » entre deux revenus. Si les prix sont trop élevés sur les marchés urbains, le risque d'émeute implique de recourir à la police. Les paiements en nature restèrent en conséquence longtemps dominants tandis que venaient s'ajouter à eux les reconnaissances de dettes, qui jouaient le rôle d'une « quasi-monnaie » locale. Nobles et ecclésiastiques s'approvisionnaient en droiture [4] sans passer par les marchés, tandis que les bourgeois faisaient appel à des marchés de pourvoiries [5], et là non plus il n'existait pas vraiment d'appel du marché.

Il paraît important de prendre en compte les textes dans lesquels les raisonnements économiques se trouvent enchâssés. La théologie scolastique fournit de nombreuses études de cas au milieu de considérations théologiques. Ainsi, sur la question de l'usure, les éléments de la pensée économique se trouvent au sein de la pensée des théologiens et dans le droit canon. Le concept de valeur confère une valeur rédemptrice au travail. Le marché *a priori* impensable s'y trouve toutefois théorisé, quoique sous la forme du contrat. Durant tout le XVIII [e] siècle, c'est dans la multiplication de la forme

4. Contrairement à la traite commerciale (comme la « traite des esclaves »), le « circuit en droiture » consiste à effectuer un aller-retour direct entre la métropole et la colonie désignée. C'est une pratique moins rentable, mais moins risquée, que le commerce « triangulaire ».

5. C'étaient des marchés passés devant notaire par lesquels un pourvoyeur, entrepreneur ou agent domestique, s'engageait à fournir un approvisionnement régulier de certaines denrées à des prix convenus d'avance.

du mémoire judiciaire (*factum*) adressé aux autorités que se trouve la pensée économique de l'époque. On y découvre que, longtemps, les marchés ont été pensés seulement en termes de contrôle de l'approvisionnement urbain.

Si l'ouvrage rend compte d'une première transformation de ces pratiques, l'une de ses limites tient à son approche comparative de sociétés *très* éloignées *dans le temps*. Chaque situation apparaît nouvelle alors même que, comme l'a montré Veblen, elle est souvent l'effet d'une dynamique économique évolutionniste qui comprend des « effets de seuil ». Le socle de la continuité dans les pratiques se trouve dans les institutions. Il faut donc rendre raison de la résistance populaire au marché et des tensions qui existent entre l'économie morale coutumière dans la population pauvre, d'une part, et le processus de développement capitaliste, d'autre part. Ceci rejoint notamment l'idée d'approcher l'histoire « par le bas », une idée dont Edward Palmer Thompson (1963) fut le précurseur en affirmant que l'expérience est toujours première par rapport au contexte, et qu'il n'y a pas de structures, mais seulement des processus.

Une lecture contemporaine de Polanyi nous conduirait à rejeter l'idée d'institutions qui ne se définiraient que par l'infrastructure économique, au profit d'une approche qui prendrait également en compte les processus historico-culturels et ceux d'identification sociale. L'ouvrage de Polanyi permet ainsi de « dénaturaliser » les institutions en montrant combien les habitudes ont un rôle important dans leur évolution. Depuis la chute de la Gaule romaine jusqu'au XIIIe siècle, nous assistons au lent mouvement d'augmentation de la population qui exigeait de sécuriser les approvisionnements. Les marchés libres n'apparurent qu'aux frontières et sur les *limes*, ces espaces sécurisés par la noblesse assistée d'une bourgeoisie d'affaires où le marché suscitait de nouvelles contraintes pour les paysans.

La réédition de l'ouvrage auquel avait participé Polanyi participe à la critique de l'utopie libérale pour laquelle la confrontation des intérêts est censée conduire à une « harmonie » que ni la politique ni la morale ne sauraient réaliser. Cette critique mobilise l'anthropologie et elle remonte bien plus en amont dans le temps que n'avait su le faire, il y a bientôt quarante ans, Pierre Rosanvallon. Celui-ci nous avait alors permis de comprendre le marché comme un modèle politique alternatif, dissocié de toute forme d'autorité, en traçant la perspective d'un rétrécissement du politique en vue de l'avènement d'une société civile où le marché se présentait comme « une loi de régulation de l'ordre social sans législateur » (Rosanvallon 1979, 46). L'utopie libérale était donc bien une idée du XVIII e siècle, qui faisait contraste avec les théories du contrat social et ce qu'elles impliquaient de volontarisme social.

Suite la crise financière de 2008 et à la montée du protectionnisme (qui a pu trouver à s'exprimer notamment à travers le *Brexit* britannique ou l'élection aux États-Unis de Donald Trump), une actualité de l'ouvrage réédité ici peut consister à nous faire réfléchir à l'évolution de nos sociétés, alors que l'idéologie du « rôle directeur du marché » montre, selon certains, des signes d'épuisement croissants. Dans cet ouvrage sur des empires bien antérieurs à ceux de nos jours, les contributeurs, et pas seulement Polanyi, avertissent que l'idée d'un marché s'ajustant lui-même est purement utopique, mais ils nous conduisent à considérer les nouvelles formes de circulation des biens et des services que sont, outre le marché, les pratiques de réciprocité dans le don et le contre-don ainsi que la redistribution. Par ailleurs, ce retour historique et anthropologique rappelle combien furent rares les périodes de l'histoire où le marché autorégulé fixait les prix économiques.

La vague actuelle de protectionnisme que l'on peut constater et la guerre commerciale qui s'ensuivrait et que l'on peut redouter sont-elles autant de préludes à un affrontement global qui nous inviterait à repenser également les coûts que les populations subissent sur les plans sociaux, culturels et politiques ? L'apparition d'une société libérale à l'échelle du globe ne serait peut-être pas alors le fruit d'une évolution spontanée et naturelle, mais elle apparaîtrait issue d'un choix politique et idéologique qui s'est imposé à la fin de la guerre froide. L'effacement actuel de ce choix, au profit d'un retour à des rapports sociaux oscillant d'une apologie du convivial à un accaparement (celui des terres, notamment), serait possiblement dans ce cas le signe d'un « ré-encastrement » de l'économie de marché au sein de sociétés que traverserait une culture politique différente qui tendrait à disqualifier en son principe même la vision libérale du monde et de ses empires.

REFERENCES

BECCHIO, G. 2011. "Existe-t-il une doctrine Menger qui soit hétérodoxe ? Sur la lecture et l'interprétation des *Grundsätze der Volkswirtschaftslehre* (seconde version 1923) par Karl Polanyi." In *Existe-t-il une doctrine Menger ? Aux origines de la pensée économique autrichienne*, G. Campagnolo (dir.), 167-86. Aix-en-Provence : Presses Universitaires de Provence.

CAMPAGNOLO, G. 2008. *Carl Menger, entre Aristote et Hayek. Aux origines de l'économie moderne.* Paris : CNRS Éditions.

MAUCOURANT, J. 2011. *Avez-vous lu Polanyi ?* Paris : Flammarion.

PASSET, R. 2010. *Les grandes représentations du monde et de l'économie.* Paris : Les Liens qui libèrent.

PERROUX, Fr. 1961. *L'économie du XXe siècle.* Paris : P.U.F.

POLANYI, K. 1957. *Trade and Market in the Early Empires. Economies in History and Theory.* New York : Free Press.

–. 1977. *The Livelihood of Man.* New-York : Academic Press.

–. 1983. *La Grande Transformation.* Paris : Gallimard.

–. 2011. *La subsistance de l'homme : la place de l'économie dans l'histoire et la société.* Paris : Flammation.

ROSANVALLON, P. 1979. *Le Capitalisme utopique. Histoire de l'idée de marché.* Paris : Seuil.

THOMPSON, E. 1963. *La formation de la classe ouvrière anglaise.* Paris : Seuil.

BULLETIN D'ABONNEMENT / *SUBSCRIPTION FORM*

Revue de Philosophie Économique

Review of Economic Philosophy

Je soussigné(e) / *I would like to put the following order and will sign this order form below*

Nom / *First Name* :..........
Prénom / *Last Name* : .....
Institution / *Institution name* :..
N° TVA / *VAT number (if applicable)* : ....
Adresse / *Address* : ....
....
C.P. / *Zip Code* : .... Ville / *City* :..
State (if applicable) : ....
Pays / *Country* :...

Commande / *Contents of the order* :

.... abonnement(s) annuel(s) à la *Revue de Philosophie Économique* (deux numéros par an), au prix de 50 euros TTC (frais de port inclus) pour la France et de 55 euros TTC (frais de port inclus) pour l'étranger.
Yearly subscription (two issues per year) for 55 € (p&p included)

.... fascicules, au prix de 30 euros TTC (frais de port en sus), selon détail ci-dessous :
Or order by issue, at individual price of 30 € per issue (p&p to be added)
(Notice: unless otherwise specified, all issues contain both English and French essays, each essay displays abstracts in both languages)

.... ex. du numéro / *copie(s) of issue* 1, vol. 17, décembre 2016, *Varia*, 978-2-7116-5215-0

.... ex. du numéro / *copie(s) of issue* 1, vol. 17, juin 2016, *Néolibéralisme(s) et démocratie(s)*, 978-2-7116-5214-3

.... ex. du numéro / *copie(s) of issue* 2, vol. 16, décembre 2015, 978-2-7116-5213-6

.... ex. du numéro / *copie(s) of issue* 1, vol. 16, juin 2015, *Justice et environnement* / Justice and Environment, 978-2-7116-5212-9

.... ex. du numéro / *copie(s) of issue* 2, vol. 15, décembre 2014, *Varia*, 978-2-7116-5211-2

.... ex. du numéro / *copie(s) of issue* 1, vol. 15, juin 2014, *Les figures de l'entrepreneur / The Entrepreneur* : *Facets of Yesterday and Today*, 978-2-7116-5210-5

.... ex. du numéro / *copie(s) of issue* 2, vol. 14, décembre 2013, *Varia*, 978-2-7116-5209-9

.... ex. du numéro / *copie(s) of issue* 1, vol. 14, juillet 2013, *Critical Realism in the Social Science, Agency and the Discusive Self*, 978-2-7116-5208-2

.... ex. du numéro / *copie(s) of issue* 2, vol. 13, décembre 2012, *Varia*, 978-2-7116-5207-5

.... ex. du numéro / *copie(s) of issue* 1, vol. 13, juillet 2012, *Experimental Economics* : *Some Methodological Aspects*, 978-2-7116-5206-8
.... ex. du numéro / *copie(s) of issue* 2, vol. 12, décembre 2011, 978-2-7116-5205-1
.... ex. du numéro / *copie(s) of issue* 1, vol. 12, juillet 2011, 978-2-7116-5204-4
.... ex. du numéro / *copie(s) of issue* 2, vol. 11, décembre 2010, 978-2-7116-5203-7
.... ex. du numéro / *copie(s) of issue* 1, vol. 11, juillet 2010, *Markets, Governance and Human Development*, 978-2-7116-5202-0
.... ex. du numéro / *copie(s) of issue* 2, vol. 10, décembre 2009, 978-2-7116-5201-3
.... ex. du numéro / *copie(s) of issue* 1, vol. 10, juillet 2009, *Enjeux éthiques en économie de la santé (French language only)*, 978-2-7116-5200-6
.... ex. du numéro / *copie(s) of issue* 2, vol. 9, décembre 2008, 978-2-7117-3511-2
.... ex. du numéro / *copie(s) of issue* 1, vol. 9, juillet 2008, *Démocratie d'entreprise (French language only)*, 978-2-7117-3510-5
.... ex. du numéro / *copie(s) of issue* 14, 2006/2, 978-2-7117-3507-5
.... ex. du numéro / *copie(s) of issue* 13, 2006/1, 978-2-7117-3506-8
.... ex. du numéro / *copie(s) of issue* 9, 2004/1, *Le concept d'identité / Identity Concept*, 978-2-7117-3502-0
.... ex. du numéro / *copie(s) of issue* 8, 2003/2, 978-2-7117-3501-3
.... ex. du numéro / *copie(s) of issue* 7, 2003/1, *Autour de John Rawls (French language only)*, 978-2-7117-3500-6

Paiement / *Payment should be sent* :

❑ par chèque bancaire à l'ordre de « Librairie Vrin » (joindre le chèque au bulletin d'abonnement) / by *Bank Order written to "Librairie Vrin"*
❑ par virement sur notre compte / *by wire transfer to our account*
BIC : PSSTFRPPPAR
IBAN : FR28 2004 1000 0100 1963 0T02 028
❑ par règlement administratif (joindre le bon de commande au bulletin d'abonnement)

Date : .... Signature

À renvoyer par courrier postal ou électronique :
Please send via postmail or email the order form completed with date and signature:

Librairie Philosophique J. Vrin
À l'attention de Frédéric Mendès
6 place de la Sorbonne
75005 Paris – France
fmendes@vrin.fr